Race Relations in Britain

Andrew Pilkington

University Tutorial Press

Published by University Tutorial Press Limited
842 Yeovil Road, Slough, SL1 4JQ

ISBN 0 7231 0859 5

Published 1984

Printed in Great Britain at The Pitman Press, Bath

To my parents

Evan and Puck Pilkington

Acknowledgements

The publishers would like to thank the following for use of extracts: extracts from Field et al., *Home Office Research Study No. 68* (HMSO 1981), reproduced with the permission of the Controller of Her Majesty's Stationery Office (pages **86, 87, 88, 115**); extracts from Bottomore and Rubel, *Karl Marx: Selected Writings*, by permission of Pitman Publishing Ltd., London (pages **44, 45, 46**); extracts from David J. Smith, *Racial Disadvantage in Britain* (Pelican Books 1977), reprinted by permission of Penguin Books Ltd. (pages **84, 89, 92, 93, 112, 114**); extract from Little, A., *Performance of Children from Ethnic Minority Backgrounds in Primary Schools*, Oxford Review of Education, Vol. No. 2, 1975 (page **122**); extracts from D. Smith, *The Facts of Racial Disadvantage: a National Survey* (PEP No. 560, 1976) by permission of the Policy Studies Institute (pages **84, 92, 113, 114**); table from D. Milner, *Children and Race* (Penguin 1975) by permission of D. Milner (page **131**); extract from Giner and Salcedo, 'Migrant workers in European Social Structures' in *Contemporary Europe* (RKP, 1978), adapted from Castle and Kosack, *Immigrant Workers and Class Structure in Western Europe* (OUP) by permission of OUP (pages **96–7**).

Despite every effort, the publishers have been unsuccessful in seeking permission to reproduce a table from A. Little, Educational Policies for Multiracial Areas (Goldsmiths College, University of London, 1978) (page **123**). They ask the author or his agent to contact them should this book succeed in coming into their hands.

Preface

This book has been designed with two aims in mind – firstly to show how Sociology can help improve our understanding of race relations in Britain and secondly to use the topic of race relations to exemplify general sociological 'themes and perspectives.' As such the book hopes to fill what is widely recognized to be a gap in existing Sociology textbooks.

Needless to say, the production of this book has required the assistance of a number of people. Thanks are due to my colleagues who expressed a friendly interest in the venture and my students who constituted the original guinea pigs for the book's main ideas. Particular thanks are due to Anne Gilkes who produced the highest quality typescript from my barely decipherable handwriting. Above all, however, I am grateful to Patsy whose constant support and encouragement were invaluable and who, with Jessica and Katherine, had the unenviable task of living with me while the book was being written.

Andrew Pilkington
Nene College

Contents

Chapter 1 The nature of sociology and race relations   1
          The nature of sociology   1
          Defining a race relations situation   11
          Post-war immigration to Britain   12
          Summary   18

Chapter 2 Racial discrimination   21
          Newcomers or Blacks?   21
          The extent of racial discrimination in Britain   23
          Summary   28

Chapter 3 Racial prejudice   30
          The relationship between racial prejudice
          and discrimination   30
          The extent of racial prejudice in Britain   32
          Summary   39

Chapter 4 Perspectives on race   43
          Classical sociology and social inequality   43
          Classical sociology, race and ethnicity   55
          Contemporary sociological approaches to race:
          consensus and conflict   56
          Contemporary sociological approaches to race:
          systems and action   64
          Perspectives on race: functionalism, Marxism
          and conflict theory   68
          Summary   73

Chapter 5 Race and employment   76
          Underclass or working class?   77
          The extent of racial disadvantage in employment
          in Britain   83
          The position of migrant labour in Europe   95
          Summary   98

Contents

Chapter 6   Race and housing   100
             Perspectives on the urban social structure   101
             The case of Birmingham   104
             The extent of racial disadvantage in housing
             in Britain   112
             Summary   116

Chapter 7   Race and education   118
             Perspectives on the education system   118
             The educational performance of minority
             children in Britain   120
             Explanations of differences in educational
             performance   126
             Multicultural education   142
             Summary   143

Chapter 8   Responses – The state, the mass media and
             racial minorities   145
             The role of the state   145
             The mass media   153
             The reaction of racial minorities   160
             Asian and West Indian youth   163
             Summary   171

Bibliography   173

1

The nature of sociology and race relations

The nature of sociology

The dominant perspective which pervades this book is a socio-logical one. What then is sociology? As the term implies, sociology studies societies. This does not, however, get us very far, for to study societies is to study relations between people and this is something a host of subjects do. What distinguishes sociology from these other subjects is not so much its subject matter as its perspective, its particular way of looking at human behaviour. It seeks to explain human behaviour in terms of 'people's membership of social groups and the ways these are related to each other' (Coulson and Riddell, 1980). Crucial to this definition is the notion of 'social groups'. When sociologists speak of a social group, they have in mind a collection of people with distinctive attitudes and distinctive patterns of behaviour. Frequently these people do not know each other personally. Any social group is of potential interest to the sociologist, however, provided its members exhibit regularities of attitudes and behaviour which can be most economically explained in terms of their collective shared experiences rather than by individual characteristics. This is a little abstract, however. Let us therefore try to clarify what the sociological perspective involves by contrasting it with three other perspectives on human behaviour.

The first perspective we shall contrast with sociology is a bio-logical one. Although this can take many forms, the one which has percolated everyday thinking most is one which seeks to explain human behaviour not in terms of people's membership of social groups, but in terms of instincts. This perspective is perhaps best exemplified in the work of Desmond Morris, Konrad Lorenz and Robert Ardrey who draw their inspiration from ethology, the study of animal behaviour in their natural habitat. Apparent similarities between human behaviour and animal behaviour suggest to such writers that much human behaviour can be explained on the same lines as animal behaviour.

Now animal behaviour can often be plausibly explained in terms of instincts. For much of it is inborn and unlearned, albeit triggered off by appropriate environmental stimuli; common to all members of a species; and relatively unmodifiable. Let us look at two examples. If we take the example of bees, we find that each worker bee is able very soon after birth to communicate to other bees where and in what quantity food is to be found. If we take the example of geese we find that each newly hatched bird follows the first object it sees moving. In both cases the pattern of behaviour is instinctive. Such behaviour does, however, have its disadvantages. Take the case of the gosling. In normal circumstances the first large moving object it is likely to see is the mother. In this situation, the instinctive behaviour is well suited to the gosling's environment. When the situation changes, however, and circumstances become unusual so that the first large moving object the gosling sees is a man, the gosling fails to adapt to its changed environment and follows the man.

By comparison with the bee and the gosling, the human infant is an extraordinarily helpless creature. The reason for this is simple. Whereas much of the bee's and gosling's behaviour is instinctive, little of the human being's behaviour is. In contrast to the bee and gosling, the human being has to learn what to do. This is not to say that animals cannot learn. They can and do. But by virtue of the human being's greater brain power and perhaps unique capacity for language, man can learn much more. This allows for greater flexibility of action and adjustment to widely differing environments.

The significance of the fact that most human behaviour is learned should now be apparent. We cannot explain human behaviour simply in terms of instincts. For although we can talk, as psychologists do, of the existence of certain basic drives such as the sex drive, these can be channelled in very different directions entailing as a result very different patterns of, for example, sexual behaviour. The existence of universal drives cannot therefore by themselves account for the tremendous variety of human behaviour which has been exemplified through time and space. In order to explain this variety, we need to take account of people's membership of social groups.

That most human behaviour is learned may be readily agreed. Whether the same can be said of a concomitant of this position is less certain. The concomitant is this: that we should be extremely sceptical of any talk about 'human nature'. When people take particular patterns of behaviour for granted, they often suggest they are in some way 'natural' and that, as such, there is little we can or should do to change such behaviour. Our idea of what is 'natural', however, is what we are used to. Take for example the situation of men and women in our society. Women still tend to have primary responsibility for housework, including the rearing of children, and tend to be employed in less well rewarded jobs than men, which they fit around their family responsibilities. As such, women's primary role in our society is a domestic one. Now from the vantage point of our society, the suggestion therefore that women are naturally domestic creatures is a not wholly implausible one. When, however, we take account of the situation in other societies, such a suggestion becomes implausible. Take for example the situation among the Mbuti pygmies, a hunting and gathering society who live in the rain forests of the Congo. Here 'there is very little division of labour by sex' (Oakley, 1972) with the result that the men and women both hunt together and share the responsibility for the care of the children. Now from the perspective of our society, these gender roles may seem unnatural. But the reverse also applies. From the perspective of their society, our gender roles may seem unnatural. This example illustrates the point that what we believe is natural is what we are used to. The manifest differences between the roles that men and women play in our society cannot in fact be accounted for simply in biological terms. In order to understand why women frequently take a primarily domestic role, we need to turn our attention to the way sex is seen as significant in our society and how we learn through socialisation the cultural expectations pertaining to men and women in our society.

What is true of sex is even truer of race. For not only are we unable to account for the differences in the role of, say, black and white people in biological terms, but serious doubt can be cast on whether it is meaningful to talk of race at all in a biological sense. Within biology two approaches to the study of race can be distinguished (Banton 1979). The first involves distinguishing people on the basis of various physical attributes such as skin colour, head shape and hair form, to arrive at a classification of the human population into a limited number of races. A popular classification for example has involved distinguishing the Caucasoid, Mongoloid and Negroid races. When the theory of race was first being put forward in the nineteenth century, human beings were considered to belong to such biologically distinguishable races and these biological differences were thought as determining human behaviour. That some races were superior to others was generally agreed. At first this was reckoned to be the result of original creation but later in the century, under the influence of Darwin's theory of evolution, this was felt to be the consequence of an earlier process of natural selection. Such a conception of race has now been shown to be false and a second approach from population genetics to the study of race has therefore been adopted. Man's physical characteristics are determined by a mass of genes, the distribution of which is so varied that people classified as similar in one respect often are not in other respects. The consequence is that it makes little sense to classify people into a limited number of races.

If biologists have become increasingly sceptical of the utility of the concept and have dispelled the notion that each individual belongs to a particular race and that behaviour is influenced by the special characteristics of that race, does this mean that there is no such phenomenon as race? Not at all. The idea of race might not hold any scientific water but if people believe it does and act accordingly, then race does indeed exist. As W. I. Thomas has put it, 'if men define situations as real, they are real in their consequences'. In the context of race relations, this means that physiological differences in skin colour, although in themselves as insignificant as differences in height, can become significant because of the importance attached to them by people's beliefs. Take for example the situation which has existed in the Southern States of America, as Griffin so graphically described (Griffin, 1964). Here being black has been seen as a significant indicator of ones role. The role itself is not one which can be changed – it has not been achieved – but is one which has been ascribed at birth. Griffin's experience as a white man, who artificially darkened his skin, indicates in a dramatic way how he was constrained to produce the appropriate behaviour as deemed such for a black person. Because the white people here believed he was black and that being black was a sign of a subordinate status, he was treated accordingly. His experience conveys the reality of race. Although in itself biologically insignificant, being black was here considered to be significant and as a result was. In other societies, characterstics other than colour have been taken to indicate ones race. Indeed the most horrifying recent instance, where race was seen as significant, did not concern colour. It occurred in Nazi Germany, where being labelled a Jew indicated that one belonged to an inferior race and therefore should be placed in a concentration camp under constant threat of extermination.

The second perspective we shall contrast with sociology is, like the biological one, again concerned with explaining human behaviour. Explanations are not, however, sought in terms of instincts or human nature but in terms of personality traits or other individual characteristics. This perspective is best exemplified in the work of many psychologists but, in a more vulgarised way, can be found at the heart of most commonsense explanations of human behaviour. Let us take as an example to clarify the difference between the two perspectives of sociology and psychology, explanations of the way people acquire jobs.

Two broad theories can be distinguished in this area (Speakman, 1980). The first which has been put forward primarily by psychologists is known as the individual-ambition theory. The starting point is that of the individual and the emphasis placed on the way individuals choose occupations from all those available in line with their ambitions. Children, it is argued, go through various stages in which they learn more about themselves and the opportunities open to them. The choice which crystalizes after this maturational process is inevitably a compromise between an individual's values, interests and capacities and the opportunities available. It is, however, one which is consonant with ones self image and ones ambition. Thus it is that an individual may have to adjust his or her earlier desire to become a doctor and become a dentist instead. The second theory which has been put forward primarily by sociologists is known as the structure-opportunity theory. The starting point is that of the structure of society and the emphasis placed on the way this structure operates to limit choice. Occupational ambitions are here not seen as a very significant determinant of ones eventual job for two reasons. Firstly, what jobs are available is outside the control of the individual and secondly, the ambitions themselves are frequently based on what the individual has been taught realistically to expect. Therefore while for some people the desire to work with people is exemplified by being a milkman, for others it is exemplified by being a teacher. The stress here is on the way the structure of society constrains the individual to develop ambitions which are based on realistic vocational aspirations and, if these are frustrated, to adjust them accordingly.

In order to understand the emergence of racial distinctions along colour lines, we need to take a sociological approach and examine how, as a result of the social development of the West, groups from white European countries were able to dominate other countries, many of which comprised people of a different colour. As Dunning points out, 'The social development of Western Europe, even as early as the Renaissance, made available means of transport (especially efficient sailing ships), scientific knowledge (for example, the knowledge that the world is round), and technical inventions (such as the lodestone and the sextant), which facilitated the exploration and circumnavigation of the earth. Growing economic surpluses enabled voyages of exploration to be financed and military developments, such as the invention of firearms, enabled Europeans to control and dominate newly discovered territories and people' (Hurd, 1973). The Spanish and Portuguese were the first to establish colonies in the New World and faced with labour shortages, they began importing slaves in the 16th century. In the 17th century, however, their monopoly of the New World was challenged by the British, French and Dutch with the British becoming dominant in the 18th century, the centre of a 'triangular trade'. This involved the purchase of black people in Africa with British manufactures, their carriage to the West Indies and the Americas for work on the plantations and the transport of cotton, sugar and tobacco back to England for processing. The slave trade which entailed the shipment of millions of Africans, many of whom died before reaching the New World during, for example, the infamous 'middle passage', lasted for three and a half centuries.

To justify this massive importation of black people and their subsequent treatment as slaves, Englishmen drew upon a variety of stereotyped images. As Walvin points out, 'The Negro was held to be peculiarly sexual, musical, stupid, indolent, untrustworthy and violent' (Walvin, 1982). Although the Englishmen's earlier encounters with Africans had been a source of such imagery (Jordan, 1982), the need to justify slavery reinforced these early impressions and beliefs emerged which classified black people as inferior. At first these beliefs were presented in theological terms but in the course of the nineteenth century scientific theories were drawn upon to point to the inferiority of all people who had been colonised. Black people were no longer merely heathens but members of an inferior race. In the process white domination of black people was justified and the latter's subordination by the European powers towards the end of the nineteenth century seen as not only necessary but also desirable.

While the domination by West European countries of many countries in which the inhabitants were of a different colour provides a crucial back-cloth to racial inequality along colour lines, such inequality has varied both over time and space. For an example over time, take the United States. Three broad periods can be distinguished (Farley, 1982). In the first period which began in the middle of the seventeenth century and lasted 200 years, black people were slaves on the plantations of the American South. Here a person's status was almost completely determined by race, with laws in most Southern States aimed at assigning slave status to all blacks. In this situation, where the roles of white and black people were clearly distinct, black people were constrained by the rules of racial etiquette to exhibit due deference. Because of the disparity in power between the whites and blacks, there was little overt conflict, however. The same could not be said of the relations between the South and North which led to the attempted secession of the South and thus in 1861 to the civil war which resulted in the abolition of slavery. In the second period, which followed an ineffectual attempt at reconstruction, what stands out is the lack of change. A person's status was again mainly determined by race, with laws upholding segregation. In this situation, where the roles of white and black people were not quite as distinct and where competition over jobs and other scarce resources existed, there was a greater potential for overt conflict. This mainly comprised periodic bursts of violence usually by frustrated whites. Since the Second World War a third period has been ushered in. The movement of black people into towns, including those in the North, during the previous period provided an opportunity for black people to organise themselves more effectively. Both peaceful protest and riots have resulted in black people acquiring more power. Although racial inequality is extremely persistent, legislation outlawing racial discrimination has been passed and race consequently has become a less important determinant of status. In this situation, where competition for scarce resource is relatively unrestricted, the potential for escalating conflict is high, however, with increasing militancy by blacks being matched by a white backlash.

While racial inequality has clearly varied over time, with, in the case of the United States, race relations becoming more fluid, it also varies over space. Take for example the cases of Brazil and South Africa which perhaps exhibit the most divergent extant patterns. Although the pattern is by no means uniform throughout Brazil, the tendency for people to be classified as white or black is less apparent than it has been in the United States (Banton, 1967). Rather there is a colour gradient in which while a darker skin colour is a disadvantage and is generally associated with lower status, it is not an insuperable disadvantage and can be compensated for by other factors such as wealth. This is illustrated very well by the popular Brazilian saying that 'money whitens', which, while it points of course to the dominance of whites, importantly indicates that racial inequality is less rigid than in the United States. This contrast has intrigued a number of writers puzzled by the fact that two countries which have experienced slavery should have such different patterns of race relations. Many have therefore been led to argue that slavery in the two countries was significantly different. Some have stressed how the Portuguese who colonised Brazil had different values from the planter aristocracy in the Southern States. They did not have such a negative stereotype of people with a darker skin. This, coupled with the fact that the settlers were overwhelmingly male, encouraged considerable intermarriage with Indian women and a considerable blurring of racial distinctions. In addition, the settlers' religion was Catholic rather than Protestant. Not only was the Church powerful but, in its stress on the possibility of all people being saved, encouraged a more humane treatment of slaves and their gradual emancipation. If some have stressed cultural difference, others have emphasised how the plantations in Brazil and the Southern States differed economically, with those in Brazil not being geared to an expanding industrial market so that the degree of economic exploitation was not as severe. Whether cultural or economic factors are highlighted to account for the different systems of slavery in Brazil and the Southern States, however, it does seem that the less rigid pattern of race relations in Brazil has deep roots (Genovese, 1976).

If Brazil represents the best surviving example of a fluid pattern

7

of race relations on colour lines, South Africa by contrast exhibits the most rigid system of racial inequality. The roots of this inequality originated in the middle of the seventeenth century when the Dutch began colonising the area. Although the Dutch suffered setbacks at the hands of the British in their quest for domination, the descendants of the Dutch settlers, known as Afrikaners, regained control in 1948 and established apartheid. Under this system, which in many respects represents a formalisation of what had gone before, racial inequality is institutionalised with laws upholding segregation. In contrast to the colour gradient with its lack of clear breaks in Brazil, the population is rigidly classified by race as black, white, Asian or coloured, with each category having different entitlements. The system of apartheid is justified on the grounds that it enables different races to develop separately. What is significant, however, is the fact that the white minority, comprising less than 20% of the population, has been allotted much the major share of the land, while the black majority has been settled in Bantustans or Homelands on the worst land. Since it is difficult to gain a living there, these areas provide a plentiful supply of labour when needed for the mines and more recently for other industries. Work in the mines involves leaving ones dependents in their Bantustans to live in compounds for a period of time, while work in other industries means living in black townships with very circumscribed rights. In both cases the black people are, contrary to the theory of apartheid, being exploited by white people (Rex, 1973). Clearly such a rigid system of racial inequality is likely to generate intense conflict. To understand the source of this conflict we need to note, as we did in the case of Brazil, the way the society attaches significance to race. The choices open to the individual in how he or she relates to people of a different colour is clearly less restricted in Brazil than South Africa and less circumscribed now in the United States than in the past.

The third perspective we shall contrast with sociology is, unlike the biological and psychological ones investigated so far, not concerned with explaining human behaviour so much as in solving social problems. This perspective is not peculiarly well illustrated by any particular academic subject but is often considered by lay people to be the province of sociology. The common belief that sociology is concerned with solving social problems stems from two sources: the subject matter of sociology and the way sociological work is taken up by policymakers. Let us take each in turn. The subject matter of sociology comprises any social relations, but in practise the focus tends to be on those relations which are considered, whether by the population generally or by people in a position of power, to constitute social problems. Policymakers interested in the solution of such problems often draw upon the work of sociologists in arguing for a particular policy. This is not always done consciously inasmuch as sociological ideas are to some extent incorporated into commonsense. Sometimes, however, the evidence of sociological studies is explicitly used by policymakers as evidence for their proposed policy change. Take for example educational policy and in particular the replacement of the tripartite system by the comprehensive system. Under the tripartite system, children in the State system went at 11 to a grammar school, secondary modern school or (relatively rarely) technical school. The grammar school was considered the most desirable destination, since it led to the more highly rewarded positions in society. Theoretically all children had an equal chance to enter it, the basis for entry being ones performance in the 11+ examination. This system, which had been established under the 1944 Education Act for all children whose parents did not opt out of the state system, came under severe attack in the 1950s and 1960s for failing to live up to its promise of ensuring equality of educational opportunity. In particular a mass of sociological research during this period detailed how a smaller proportion of working class children relative to middle class children were gaining entry to grammar schools. This research was taken up by policymakers, especially in the Labour party, as evidence for the need to abolish the 11+ and create a comprehensive system. Now although clearly of relevance to policymakers who were committed to the principle of equality of opportunity, such research was not able to establish the desirability of this principle. And this is in fact always the case. Although sociologists frequently produce information which is pertinent to the concerns of policymakers, they can never establish the desirability of a particular change. Their expertise lies in their ability to study human behaviour more systematically than the lay person. This is not to say that sociologists do not hold opinions about what ought to be done. Indeed those who pointed to the underrepresentation of working class children in grammar schools generally advocated comprehensivisation. What is more, even when sociologists do not make explicit their preferences, their values are apparent not only in the questions which are raised, the concepts which are employed and the assumptions which are made, but they also shine through the conclusions which are reached. It is in fact because of the value implications of the work which is produced that controversies can become so heated.

In the field of race relations, the debate about the consequences of slavery upon the personality of black people for example has become a very excited one. Criticism has in fact been directed in particular at those who have argued that slavery resulted in the destruction of the cultural beliefs and values which the slaves brought with them from Africa and the acquisition in their place of cultural beliefs and values which disparage black people (Lane, 1975). This apparently academic thesis has generated disquiet among some black activists because it contravenes their view that despite all the atrocities committed against black people, a continuous tradition of rebellion can be detected. But if the debate over the consequences of slavery has been a fiery one, this is nothing compared to the debate over race and intelligence, sparked off by the thesis that the differences in IQ scores, which purport to measure intelligence, between white and black children are primarily a result of genetic differences between the two populations. What has particularly irritated critics of this thesis is the apparent implication that little can be done to reduce racial inequality and the consequent justification of the status quo (Richardson and Spears, 1973).

To recognise that sociology cannot be value free is not to go back on the point made earlier, that the major concern of the sociologist, in his or her role as a sociologist, is to explain human behaviour. This activity demands a degree of detachment. It is only by examining how different groups see a situation that an accurate description of that situation can be forthcoming. And it is only through stepping back and comparing different theories of that situation that we shall improve our explanations of it. The attempt to be as objective as possible will often not be achieved, but this is not a compelling reason for not making the effort. Indeed it is only by providing accurate accounts of, for example, racial disadvantage that action can be taken to eradicate it. While sociology is not primarily concerned with solving social problems, the search for the causes of human behaviour in people's membership of social groups does have implications for those who are so concerned, enabling them to act more rationally.

By contrasting sociology with a biological, a psychological and what can be labelled a political perspective, it should now be clear what the sociological perspective boils down to. It is a way of looking at human beings which involves an attempt to explain behaviour in terms of people's membership of social groups and the ways these are related to each other. It does not believe that behaviour is simply the product of instincts or human nature but rather emphasises the way drives are channelled by the groups to which people belong. It does not agree that behaviour can be sufficiently understood by reference to personality traits or individual characteristics but rather suggests that behaviour can only be fully comprehended by locating it within a wider social context. It does not attempt to solve social problems but rather believes in the importance of taking a detached view in order to discover which groups have defined an issue as a social problem and in order to provide an accurate account of what is going on.

Defining a race relations situation

In the course of illustrating the sociological perspective, through examples of the way race has been defined in different societies, we have at the same time been discovering what 'a race relations situation' comprises. It emerges, as Rex points out (Rex, 1970a), when three conditions are fulfilled: (a) one group of people behaves to another group of people in a way which denies them equal access to social resources; (b) the groups of people involved are recognised by signs which are regarded as unalterable; (c) the unequal relation between the groups is justified by various deterministic beliefs. Let us briefly highlight what these three conditions involve. The first stresses the significance of inequality. Although there is probably a tendency for groups with different cultures to stereotype and look unfavourably upon other groups, especially if there is a degree of competition between them (Cohen, 1976), it is only when one group is in a position to impose its definitions on others that the situation becomes one which tends to be considered problematic. The second condition emphasises the importance of physical differences. A *race* is defined here as a set of people who are considered to be physically different in some way and where such physical characteristics are seen as socially significant. Almost inevitably a race becomes an *ethnic group*, a set of people who intermarry and share a similar set of beliefs and values. Ethnic groups can form, however, on the basis of a variety of characteristics, the most common perhaps being nationality, language and religion. Although a race relations situation has been characterised as one which involves inequality, it should not be assumed that the inequality pertaining between ethnic groups, which are physically indistinguishable, is insignificant. The relative position of Protestants and Catholics in Northern Ireland makes this amply clear. The third condition insists that the essence of the ideas which justify racial inequality lies in the claim that the subordinate group necessarily has those negative characteristics attributed to it. Although the prime example of such ideas is the theory of race which emerged in the 19th century with its belief in the biological inferiority of black people, other ideas can perform the same role.

In specifying further the three conditions which give rise to a race relations situation, we have implicitly distinguished racialism and racism. Racialism we met under the first condition. It comprises those practices which disadvantage people on the basis of their

11

supposed membership of a particular race. Racism we met under the third condition. It comprises those beliefs which consider that the disadvantaged group inevitably has those negative characteristics attributed to it (Rex, 1970b). The best example of a race relations situation, exhibiting as it does both racialism and racism, is imperialism, involving as it did the domination by white West European countries of countries in which most people were of a different skin colour. Indeed the period of colonisation from the 16th century is in crucial respects the source of contemporary race relations situations. Britain of course was centrally involved in this process. Since the Second World War, however, we have witnessed a new phenomenon.

Post-war immigration to Britain

A significant number of people emigrated from Britain's old colonies to settle in Britain, the majority being of a different skin colour. There have of course been significant waves of immigration before. Thus in the 19th century the combination of a rising population and bad harvests encouraged a major movement of the population from Ireland and around the turn of the century virulent antisemitism prompted the entry of Jews from Eastern Europe. And the population movements have not been one way. Millions of people have emigrated from Britain in the last two centuries to settle in new lands and indeed except for relatively short periods, more people have emigrated from Britain than immigrated into the country during this time. Migration therefore is nothing new. Nor is the presence of black people in Britain which goes back at least 400 years. Nevertheless the immigration of West Indians and Asians to Britain has been seen by many as creating a different situation. Whether it has meant that we now have a race relations situation within Britain will be a major concern of this book, with a start being made in the next two chapters which will consider one aspect of racialism, viz. racial discrimination and one aspect of racism, viz. racial prejudice respectively. Before, however, we examine the kind of reception black people have met in Britain, we need to find out why they came to this country in the first place. A precondition, of course, was British imperialism, the consequences of which we shall briefly draw out for the two major groupings of black people in this country.

People from the West Indies and Guyana were the first to migrate to Britain, with the majority coming from one of the islands, Jamaica. Like other West Indian islands, Jamaica was colonised by white people from Western Europe. By the time England had captured Jamaica from the Spanish in the 17th century, the original inhabitants, the Arawak Indians, had been wiped out so that the island therefore comprised mainly of immigrants from England who managed the plantations and slaves imported from Africa who worked on them. The economy was of course geared to the needs of Britain. Thus sugar was exported to Britain, but the profits made, not invested in Jamaica but transferred to Britain. The Jamaican economy was not able to develop. Instead a process of underdevelopment occurred, which still persists in spite of the country becoming self governing in 1944 and independent in 1962, with the domination of the island's economy by plantation agriculture and its continued dependence on a few multinational corporations (Pryce, 1979). Despite therefore the abolition of slavery in 1833, the majority of Jamaicans have seen little improvement in their situation. The paucity of adequate farmland and the lack of sufficient jobs have thus encouraged many Jamaicans to look to emigration as a way of improving their situation whether to South America, North America or most recently Britain (Foner, 1977).

In India, a similar process of underdevelopment occurred. After the setting up of trading posts by the East India company in the 17th century, the British gradually took power. With the defeat of the French in the 18th century and recognition by the government of the centrality of India in the 19th century, the stage was set for the British Raj. As in Jamaica, the economy was made to serve the needs of Britain. The local textile industry was destroyed as a competititor to the Lancashire based one and indeed India became a key market for cotton goods from Britain. Since a large market is necessary for industrialisation to take place, Hobsbawm argues, the possession of India and other colonies was critical for Britain's Industrial Revolution (Hobsbawm, 1969). There seems little doubt that as the 19th century wore on India became 'the jewel in the Imperial diadem' (Barratt Brown, 1970) which Britain increasingly leant on as other countries 'caught up economically'. This is not to say that Britain did not invest in India. In the course of the 19th century significant investments were made, for example, in communications, but these did not prevent the Indian economy from being under-developed and dependent on the metropolitan society. The consequence has been the inability of the economy to generate enough jobs to meet the needs of a rapidly increasing population. Many have therefore looked to migration as a solution. Some migrated to other parts of the British empire under a system of indentured labour, whereby they were contracted to work for a particular employer for a number of years. In some cases they stayed when the contract had expired and brought their families over to join them to be followed later by other immigrants. In this way Indian settlements developed for example in East Africa. Migration is therefore not a new phenomenon for Southern Asians. Indeed independence itself, which was only achieved in 1947 after a long struggle, entailed further migration. The struggle between the two major religious groups, the Hindus and Moslems resulted in the partition of India, with Pakistan comprising two territories at the extremities of Northern India being Moslem, and India being predominantly Hindu. Not surprisingly, given the intensity of the preceding struggles, many people migrated to join their coreligionists. It is in this context that migration to Britain needs to be seen.

Under the British Nationality Act of 1948, citizens of the British Commonwealth were allowed to enter Britain to seek work and settle here with their families. Many took up this opportunity. West Indians were the earliest to come followed by Indians and Pakistani/Bangladeshis (the latter of whom came from what had been East Pakistan, but after the creation of an independent state in 1972, is now Bangladesh). The most recent arrivals were those from countries such as Kenya and Uganda in East Africa who had opted on the independence of these countries for British citizenship viz. East African Asians. Of these four major racial minorities, Indians constitute the largest group, followed by West Indians, Pakistani/Bangladeshis and finally East African Asians (Ballard, 1983). If we take the racial minorities together, they constituted 1.4 million people in 1971, of whom 28% had been born in Britain. By 1977 this had grown to 1.85 million people, of whom 40% had been born in Britain. There is expected to be further growth until the end of the century when there will be 3.3 million people from the racial minorities. This means that black people who formed about 4.2% in 1981 will comprise about 5.9% of the total population, stabilising at about that level (Runnymede Trust, 1980). The major reason for the expected growth arises from the fact that there is likely to continue to be a higher proportion of black children born mainly because the black population is relatively young and the original imbalance in the sex ratio has only been reduced quite recently. All in all, immigration from the New Commonwealth and Pakistan since the Second World War has brought a significant increase in the proportion of black people in Britain.

We need however to get matters in perspective. An examination of the 1971 Census indicates that people from the New Commonwealth comprised well under half the overseas born population in Britain and that none of the racial minorities was as large as the Irish or the Europeans (Rees, 1982). What is more, immigration from the New Commonwealth and Pakistan is to all intents and purposes at an end. It reached a peak in the early 1960s but has been, with the odd temporary increase caused by the expulsion of East African Asians, on a downward trend since. Immigration Acts, beginning with the Commonwealth Immigrants Act of 1962 have made it increasingly difficult for black people in particular to emigrate to Britain with the result that the vast majority of citizens from the New Commonwealth and Pakistan now accepted for settlement are dependents, especially women. Altogether the black population is small relative to the total population size with 1 in 30 being black in 1977 and 1 in 17 expected by the year 2000 (Runnymede Trust, 1980).

In the course of discussing the entry of immigrants from the New Commonwealth and Pakistan into Britain, it will have been noted that the term 'black' has been used as a shorthand to refer to them. The reason colour has been picked out is because this has, for many of the indigenous population, been the most noticeable feature and effect of the immigration; in choosing 'black' to describe that colour, what has now become the normal convention is being followed. It should not be thought, however, that the people described in this way have much in common. The differences between the West Indians and Asians are, for example, particularly manifest. Those who came from the West Indies and Guyana were the first to migrate to Britain. The majority came from Jamaica but the remainder were from a group of islands often with different traditions 1000 miles to the east. These islands share the common legacy of slavery, a culture with a strong white bias. Although the extent to which black people have inculcated from this culture a negative image of themselves has probably been exaggerated (Amos, Gilroy, Lawrence, 1982), the dominant culture in which many have been brought up is a recognizedly British one. Those who came to Britain had often attended schools in which they had been taught in standard English about the Mother Country. Many in addition were Christians, who attended church regularly. As such, these people, who were frequently skilled by West Indian standards, came to Britain with a culture which was not appreciably different from the ones most of the indigenous population were familiar with (Deakin, 1970). The same is not true of most Asians.

Indians constitute the largest of the Asian racial minorities in Britain, having emigrated from two major areas, the Punjab and Gujarat. Most Gujaratis and a few Punjabis adhere to the major religion in India viz. Hinduism. For Hindus every individual is born into a particular caste. Four 'varnas' or kinds of caste are normally distinguished and ranked in a hierarchy with the Brahmins (priests) at the top followed by the Kshatriyas (warriors), Vaishyas (merchants) and Shundras (servants), but within each varna can be found numerous castes whose members are occupationally specialised and who intermarry (Selwyn, 1980).

Each person is obliged to fulfil the duties prescribed for that caste, which if done well, will mean that when that person dies he or she will be reincarnated in a higher caste, ultimately attaining union with God. Although the major religion in India, Hindus are heavily outnumbered in Britain by Sikhs, who mainly come from the Punjab. Sikhism began as a reform movement within Hinduism in the 16th century, its founder preaching the equality of all men. By adhering to the five Ks viz. to wear uncut hair and beard (Kesh), comb (Kangha), long underpants (Kachha), steel bangle (Kara) and to carry a dagger (Kirpon), Sikhs have mainted a distinctive identity. Nevertheless, despite a rejection of aspects of the caste system, castes can still be distinguished among Sikhs, with most of those coming to Britain being in fact from the castes of small farmers and craftsmen (Ballard R. & C., 1977).

The Pakistanis, like the Indians in Britain, have come from a limited number of areas, mostly from Mirpur but also from the Punjab and from North West Frontier Province. Almost all of them are Moslems, as indeed are the Bangladeshis who mainly come from Sylhet. Islam is a world religion, founded by the Prophet Mohammed in the 6th century, which gained adherents after the invasion of northern India by Moslem rulers in the 11th century. Moslems believe in one God, Allah, and that Mohammed was the last and greatest prophet sent by Allah to teach people how to live, the Koran setting down the central principles (Henley, 1981).

East African Asians have mainly come from Uganda, Kenya and Tanzania. Although some had been in East Africa for more than one generation, they tended to maintain their identity and retain contacts with the two areas of the Indian subcontinent they had originated from, Gujarat and Punjab. Most of those who have come to Britain are Hindus, predominantly from three castes, who were frequently engaged in trade in East Africa (Michaelson, 1979). As such they differ from most Asians who have come to Britain, in emanating from towns and not villages.

In outlining three major religions, it is not being suggested that the beliefs and values of the Asian minorities are static. Rather the stress is on the continuity of Asian cultures, a continuity which enabled most of them to withstand the white bias in the culture the British brought with them in the nineteenth century. This applies particularly to those who lived in villages from which most of the immigrants to Britain have come. The result is that the Asians have tended to come to Britain, unlike the West Indians, with clearly different cultural traditions. 'Almost all the migrants have been drawn from families of middling wealth and status, and none of them regarded their departure as permanent and final' (Ballard R. & C., 1977). In comparison to the culture the indigenous population in Britain is familiar with, the Asian minorities have different religions, different languages and above all a different family structure. In India, Pakistan and Bangladesh, the joint family is the framework within which marriage takes place. The result is that the nuclear family of parents and children is located in a wider area which includes the man's brothers' nuclear family as well as unmarried brothers and sisters (Hiro, 1973). When Asians first came to Britain, wives and children tended to be left behind under the tutelage of the eldest male members of the joint family, but over time many have come to Britain. The Hindus and Sikhs have done this more quickly than the Moslems, who place most stress on purdah, a set of beliefs which involves the segregation of women (Saifullah Kahn, 1977). In all cases, however, the family and not the individual is considered the key unit, so that marriage is not seen as merely the joining together of two individuals who are attracted to each other, but a connection between families. As a member of the family the individual will receive significant support, but such a right will be forfeited if family obligations are sacrificed for the sake of selfishness. It is in this context that the institution of arranged marriages needs to be seen.

What then caused Asians and West Indians to migrate to Britain after the Second World War? It is convenient to distinguish here between push factors and pull factors (Banton, 1972). Push factors refer to those factors which encourage people to leave their homelands and pull factors refer to those factors which encourage people to come to Britain. The principal push factor has been poor opportunities in the homelands where population growth has developed at a pace which their underdeveloped economies cannot sustain. This is not to say that there has been a mechanical association between the degree of poverty and emigration. Most of those who have emigrated have been people with some wealth from areas with a tradition of migration as a solution to their problems. Most have expected their stay to be temporary and have maintained close contacts with their homelands, including sending back remittances (Watson, 1977). Whether these original intentions are likely to be fulfilled is, as we shall see later, doubtful. The other major push factor relates to the East African Asians, who were in most cases forced to leave Africa as a result of the adoption of an 'Africanisation' policy by some governments. To point out these push factors does not, however, explain why such people have come to Britain. In order to understand this we need to turn to the pull factors. The first has been the closing of other avenues and particularly for West Indians the possibility of admission into the United States as a result of the McCarran-Walter Act of 1952. This has meant that those who wished to migrate had to go elsewhere. They chose to migrate to Britain because of two further pull factors – the connection with Britain which stems from the fact that their countries had been part of the British Empire and, most importantly, Britain's labour shortage at the time.

Although there was immediately after the war a substantial group of Polish immigrants and other refugees and displaced persons as European Volunteer Workers, the labour shortage which Britain, along with other West European countries, experienced when the economy began to expand, was met through immigration from the New Commonwealth. In a few cases people were recruited for specific jobs. More often they came to Britain having heard that jobs were available. Although the period of migration was generally a time in which the economy was booming and there was a shortage of labour, there were occasions when the demand for labour fell. Remarkably, West Indian movement to Britain seems to have responded with extraordinary sensitivity to the demand, with net migration tending to go down as unemployment went up in the period for which appropriate figures are available (Peach, 1968 and 1978/9). The only exception seems to have been from 1960 to 1962, immediately prior to the first Commonwealth Immigrants Act, when anxiety about impending immigration control led some to 'beat the ban'. What is true of West Indian migration has also been shown to be true although to a lesser extent, of Asian migration (Robinson, 1980). Labour demand has been an important determinant of Asian immigration into Britain.

Summary

In the course of this chapter, we have attempted to outline the nature of sociology, explain what a race relations situation involves and provide background information for an understanding of race in Britain. Sociology has been characterised by its perspective on human behaviour. It involves an attempt to explain behaviour in terms of people's membership of social groups and the ways these are related to each other. Such a perspective is essential for an understanding of race. For it is only when physical characteristics, for example skin colour, are seen as significant that one can talk of race. The extent to which such characteristics are seen as significant varies in relation to the society as a whole. It is when one group, which is physically distinguished, treats another group, considered inherently inferior, in an unequal fashion that we have a race relations situation. The entry of immigrants from the New Commonwealth and Pakistan since the Second World War has been seen by many as giving rise to a race relations situation in Britain. Whether this is so we shall now begin to examine.

Guide to reading

A. Pilkington, *What is Sociology?* chapter 1, and M. Coulson and C. Riddell, *Approaching Sociology* provide further instances of the sociological perspective. J. Rex, *Race, Colonisation and the City*, chapter 17 develops further the depiction of a race relations situation found throughout his work. An accessible set of readings, which includes a reading from Rex and presents examples of writings on the United States, Brazil and South Africa, is P. Worsley, *Problems of Modern Society*, part 9. A brief account which shares Rex's stress on the importance of imperialism and includes a discussion of race in the United States, Brazil and Britain is that by E. Dunning, in G. Hurd, *Human Societies*, chapter 11. Two good textbooks, one British and one American, which include examples of race relations in different societies, are M. Banton, *Race Relations*, and J. Farley, *Majority-Minority Relations*. In relation to race in Britain, very readable accounts, which include a discussion of the societies from which New Commonwealth and Pakistan immigrants come and the factors encouraging their movement to Britain, include D. Hiro, *Black British, White British*, parts 1 & 2, N. Deakin, *Colour Citizenship and British Society*, chapters 2 & 3, M. Banton, *Racial Minorities*, chapter 4, and J. Watson, *Between Two Cultures*, chapters 1–5.

Discussion points

1. How similar is the picture of sociology depicted with your prior expectations of the subject? Take any social problem with which you are familiar and compare the way sociology would look at it with the way the three perspectives mentioned in this chapter would. Are the perspectives invariably at loggerheads with each other, or can they be complementary?
2. Do you agree that people are constrained by the meaning race has in a particular society? Is this equally true of white and black people? To what extent can people choose to ignore the way race is defined in society? How does this possibility vary from society to society?
3. Why do you think sociologists consider it important to define terms like race, ethnic group, racialism and racism? Have you come across any examples of these terms being used differently?
4. Have you found any of the information provided about the immigrants from the New Commonwealth and Pakistan surprising? What has that been? Why did you find it surprising? Where do you

think you derived your previous 'information' from? How can you check out which information is more accurate?

5. What do you suspect has been the result of the entry of black immigrants to Britain? Do you think it is likely to have brought about a race relations situation as defined in this chapter?

2

Racial discrimination

Newcomers or Blacks?

In the previous chapter we noted the relatively recent nature of New Commonwealth immigration into this country and also the increasingly severe controls which have to all intents and purposes brought this era of immigration to an end. The question we now need to turn to is how these people have been received in this country.

Two broad answers have been put forward. One emphasises that black immigrants are immigrants; the other emphasises that black immigrants are black. Let us outline each view in turn.

The first position is well exemplified by Patterson (Patterson, 1965) but hints of it can be found in much of the early post-war writing on race in Britain. Immigrants, it is argued, have to go through two processes before they can be absorbed or assimilated into the society they have entered: they have to adapt themselves to and at the same time be accepted by the host society. Neither of these two processes is likely to take place in the life span of one generation with the result that the reception black people meet is temporarily a negative one. On the one hand, the immigrants find difficulty in making what is often, as we have already seen, a move from a rural to an urban existence and in many cases a transition from one culture to another, with all that this implies in terms of language, religion and family structure. On the other hand, the host society finds difficulty in coming to terms with people who don't show an understanding of the implicit norms governing behaviour and therefore seem strangers.

Although most of the writers who have taken this approach recognise that there is a degree of cultural antipathy to black people in Britain which makes their absorption more difficult, the overriding mood is one of optimism. The discrimination which 'dark strangers' presently confront will, with the passage of time, and a new generation, be transcended. As support for this thesis, attention might be drawn to the experiences of immigrant groups in the nineteenth and early twentieth centuries, for example, Irish and Jewish immigrants into Britain and European immigrant groups generally in the United States. Although later generations still tend to retain traces of their roots (Glazer and Moynihan, 1970), the two key processes pointed to, viz. adaptation on the part of immigrants and acceptance on the part of host society, have been to a large extent completed and the earlier hostility and discrimination overcome.

While this approach stresses the immigrant status of New Commonwealth immigrants, the second position stresses the low status attached to black people in our society. This view is well exemplified by Rex but hints of it can be found in much recent writing on the subject. Attention is drawn in this approach to imperialism which involved, as we have already seen, the domination of black people by white European countries. The social development of the West facilitated not only exploration of the world but also enabled it to control the newly discovered lands. In the New World, such colonialism involved the mass transfer of slaves from Africa to work on the plantations. Needing to reconcile their treatment of slaves as mere objects and their dimly recognised humanity, beliefs emerged which classified such people as inferior. Such beliefs spread from situations of slavery to other situations of colonialism so that the image of the inferior slave tended to be stamped on all men who were colonised. In the process, white domination of black people was justified. These beliefs, it is argued, are still endemic to our culture so that the arrival of black people from countries which had formerly been part of the British Empire was met with a degree of hostility which would not have been triggered by the entry of white immigrants.

For those who point to the prevalence of such beliefs, the passing of time and a new generation will not necessarily entail a dramatic diminution in racial discrimination. As support for this gloomy outlook, attention might again be drawn to the United States but this time to an early immigrant group forcibly taken there, notably black people. Unlike other immigrant groups most of whom arrived later, they find, over one hundred years after the abolition of slavery, that it is extremely difficult to receive equitable treatment.

In contrast to the European immigrants who entered the United States voluntarily, black people were taken there by force. As such, their experience has been fundamentally different. In Blauner's terms, black people constitute a 'colonised minority' rather than an 'immigrant minority' (Blauner, 1982). Although they were not conquered and controlled in their homeland but were captured, transported and enslaved in the Southern States, the basic fact remains that they were oppressed like the Indians and Chicanos. Their entry into American society was forced; the work they undertook was not freely chosen but involved various degrees of coercion; and their culture was attacked. The experience of being a colonised minority has been markedly different from that of immigrant minorities. Although the latter often fled oppressive conditions, they did choose to go to the United States; although commonly exploited at work, they were free labourers not subject to the control characteristic of the plantation or reservation; although discriminated against, they were able to reconstruct aspects of their culture. These differences have had long term consequences, resulting in black people not being assimilated into the society in the same way as the immigrant minorities.

The two accounts of the reception met by black immigrants in Britain involve a process of abstraction. They pick out and focus on what are taken to be the really significant issues and they ignore a great deal of detail. Both accounts agree on picking out discrimination as significant in the reception met by the first generation but they differ in their choice of what constitutes the basis for this discrimination. In the one case, their status as newcomers is highlighted and in the other case their status as blacks is highlighted. Although we might have an intuitive preference for one or other of these two accounts, both suggestions have a degree of plausibility. In order to assess which, if any, is better supported, however, we need to look at the evidence. Fortunately such evidence is available in the form of two Political and Economic Planning studies conducted in 1966–7 and 1973–4, the first under the direction of Daniel (Daniel, 1968) and the second under the direction of Smith (Smith, 1977). Although other evidence could be cited, these comprise the most extensive research projects on this issue.

The extent of racial discrimination in Britain

Daniel's research was carried out in 1966 and 1967 and was designed to assess the extent of discrimination in employment, housing and commercial services. The research consisted of three stages: firstly interviews with 1000 immigrants in six towns; secondly interviews with those people in a position to discriminate; thirdly situation tests. The first two stages highlighted what people felt the level of discrimination to be and the reasons for it. These stages were, however, unable to disclose the actual extent of discrimination. This is where the situation tests become important, in which actors apply for jobs, housing and commercial services in a series of carefully controlled circumstances. Here a black immigrant (West Indian or Asian), a white immigrant (Hungarian) and a white native Briton, matched in terms of age and appearance and claiming equivalent occupational qualifications or housing requirements applied (in that order) for a job, a house or a commercial service on offer to the public. Discrimination is defined as a case in which one tester was made an offer or a better offer and the other(s) none or a worse one. If both the black and white immigrants met discrimination then the first theory is corroborated; if only the black immigrant met discrimination then the second theory is corroborated. What did the evidence show then?

The tests corroborated the findings of the first two stages – discrimination was indeed widespread and was based on colour not immigrant status. Indeed the tests suggested that black immigrants underestimated the extent of discrimination and that discrimination particularly affected people the blacker they were. In short, Daniel's study corroborated the second theory and questioned the first theory.

Despite these findings, Daniel's report is optimistic. The reason for this optimism is Daniel's belief that the discrimination, although widespread, was not underlain by prejudice. We shall be looking at prejudice in some detail in the next chapter but what Daniel is getting at is this. A distinction can be made between behaviour and attitudes. Although black people were disadvantaged because of their colour, such discriminatory behaviour was not caused by strong feelings of hatred towards black people. Rather was it prompted by the belief that others would not accept them or a belief that they were unqualified. Since strong feelings did not underly discrimination, it was argued that it would be possible to get rid of discrimination through an Act of Parliament. It was such reasoning that led to the Race Relations Act of 1968 outlawing discrimination in employment, housing and commercial services.

How extensive then is racial discrimination since the act? Smith's research was carried out in 1973 and 1974 and was designed partly to assess the extent of discrimination in employment and housing since the act. The situation tests took two forms. Actors were again used, as in the earlier PEP study, to apply for jobs and housing in person and by telephone. In addition to such actor testing, another method which Jowell and Prescott-Clarke had pioneered in 1969 (Jowell and Prescott-Clarke, 1970) was utilised: correspondence testing, in which matched written applications were sent in reply to advertised vacancies.

What conclusions were reached? Discrimination was again found to be considerable and was again found to be based on colour. In contrast to previous studies, no significant difference was found in the level of discrimination confronting West Indians and Asians. When applications for non-skilled manual jobs, skilled manual jobs, rented accommodation and house purchase by the actors are put together, the following emerges:

Table 1

	West Indians		Indians		Pakistanis		Greeks	
No. of cases	104		111		109		84	
	No.	%	No.	%	No.	%	No.	%
Discrimination	28	27	31	28	25	23	9	11

Source: Smith, 1977

This table presents the results of the actor tests in terms of net discrimination against the immigrant viz. the total number of cases in which there was discrimination against the immigrant, minus the (small) number of cases in which there was discrimination against the indigenous member. As such, it probably under-estimates the extent of discrimination against the immigrant, since what is here counted as reverse discrimination may not be genuine but rather a result of the fact that in each of the tests involving a pair of applicants, the immigrant always went in first. The discrimination against West Indian and Asian applicants, relative to Greek applicants, recorded here is nevertheless considerable. Needless to say, doubts can be raised about the tests, as they indeed were after the first PEP study. Perhaps the black testers wanted to show that racial discrimination was extensive and therefore did not try as hard as the white testers? Perhaps the employers, estate agents and land-lords suspected the applications were not genuine? Perhaps personal qualities rather than racial differences were the criteria for selec-tion? Although no amount of facts can prove a theory to be true, so that there is always some room for doubt, Smith found no evidence to substantiate these reservations and therefore concluded that racial discrimination was indeed extensive.

A similarly disturbing picture emerges with correspondence testing in which what is being assessed is the extent to which dis-crimination occurred in the granting of job interviews to white collar jobs. Although this method almost certainly produces a minimum estimate of the level of discrimination in recruitment to white collar employment, Asian and West Indian applicants for white collar jobs faced discrimination in 30% of cases compared with only 10% for Italian applicants. The fact that both the methods employed concur 'confirms the conclusion', as Smith points out, 'that discrimination is based on generalised colour prejudice.' In most cases, however, the discrimination was hidden and the recipient unable therefore to prove its existence. Take for example these two letters which were received in response to two matched applications for a white collar job in Jowell and Prescott-Clarke's research:

25

Reply to British applicant:

Dear Mr. Robinson,
Thank you for your letter of 31st July in response to our advertisement for an electronics engineer.
We should like you to attend for interview so that we can discuss the position further, and would ask you to telephone . . . as soon as possible so that we can arrange this . . .
Yours sincerely,

Reply to Indian applicant:

Dear Mr. Singh,
Thank you very much for your letter of 31st July in connection with an advertisement for an electronics engineer. There was a big response to this advertisement and we have studied all letters carefully before making our final short list of candidates. It seemed to us that you were really a little too well-qualified for the type of job we were offering and therefore regret to inform you that we decided against including your name on the short list.
We would like to wish you every success in obtaining the type of position for which your qualifications fit you.
Once again, our thanks for your interest.
Yours sincerely,

In point of fact, Mr. Robinson and Mr. Singh had identical qualifications. Mr. Singh would, however, have had no grounds to suspect discrimination. There is some evidence in fact that West Indians and Asians meet particularly severe discrimination in the more highly rewarded white collar jobs. This discrimination cannot be explained away on the grounds that the applicants lack the necessary qualifications. On the contrary, a study of graduates from English universities concluded that 'coloured students meet with far less success than white students at all stages of seeking a job. The coloured students had fewer offers and almost half had none at all, while in contrast the majority of white students had a number of job offers, and were able to choose which job to take'. After checking other possible factors which might account for these differences, the authors were forced to conclude that 'it is the colour of the black students in our society which lies at the root of their difficulties in gaining employment' (Ballard and Holden, 1981).

Under the terms of the Race Relations Act, individuals who believed they had been discriminated against could make a complaint to the Race Relations Board which, if convinced that discrimination had been intended, would try to conciliate the two sides or, as a last resort, take the matter to the civil courts. In 1973 the Board received only 150 complaints of discrimination in relation to recruitment to employment. Clearly this represents only a small proportion of the acts of discrimination which occur, since Smith estimates there to be at least '6000 cases a year of discrimination against Asian and West Indian job applicants in the non-skilled field alone' (Smith, 1977). It is scarcely surprising, however, that so few cases were taken to the Race Relations Board when it is borne in mind that discrimination is rarely open, that proof of its occurrence is extra-ordinarily difficult and that the likely benefits relative to the costs incurred in pursuing the issue derisory. Although it may be granted that acts of discrimination vastly exceed the number of complaints received by the Race Relations Board, some have argued that the situation tests exaggerate the extent of discrimination because in practise black people tend to avoid situations in which they suspect they may meet discrimination. Certainly people do on the whole avoid situations in which they think they may be victims of discrimination, but whether it is appropriate to talk of discrimination only when people have been turned down because of their race is doubtful. Take South Africa where, as we have already seen, the superior status of the whites is sanctioned by the law. There black people may rarely be turned down because they know that no benefit can be derived from applying for a position reserved for whites. Acts of discrimination may therefore not be very common, although they would of course be massive if people were to forget their place. In order to have an indication of the strength of discrimination in a society we need to know not only the extent of acts of discrimination but also what it would be if people did not attempt to avoid being victims of it. What both PEP studies indicate is a continuing and substantial level of discrimination against black people.

Although discrimination is still widespread and still based on colour we must not conclude that the Race Relations Act has been a complete failure. A comparison between the tests conducted in the two PEP studies indicate that the level of discrimination had fallen in housing and probably also in employment. In the case of employment, the two tests are not strictly comparable because the testing in 1966–7 was of firms suspected of discrimination, while the testing in 1974 was of a random sample of firms. Nonetheless the probability of a decline in the massive levels of racial discrimination found in the mid 60s is confirmed by the results of the tests in 1967 and 1973 of the level of discrimination in the field of housing. In the case of house purchase, discrimination was defined as a case in which one tester was offered a different range of houses by the estate agent and in the case of rented accommodation, discrimination was defined as a case in which one tester was given a better offer than another by the landlord. Since the discrimination faced by Asians and West Indians is similar, the fact that the 1967 tests involved only West Indians while the 1973 tests involved both West Indians and Asians makes no difference. The results of the tests are thus comparable and point to a fall in the level of discrimination, as the following table indicates:

Table 2

	1967 % discrimination against West Indian tester	1973 % discrimination against West Indian & Asian testers
Rented accommodation (as a result of contact by telephone)	62	27
House purchase (as a result of personal contact)	64	17

Source: Smith, 1977

Certainly discrimination was less open with the result that black people were less aware of it and expressed less personal experience of it.

Summary

In the course of examining what kind of reception New Commonwealth Immigrants have met in contemporary Britain, we have at the same time been illustrating the value of the social scientific approach. The sociologist attempts to answer a question which he or she finds puzzling by putting forward an explanation or theory. This of course is something we all do in everyday life. Where the sociologist differs from the man or woman in the street is in attempting to subject his or her theory to systematic examination in relation to evidence, and not merely look for illustrative support. Such an approach has been exemplified in this chapter. The question arose as to the explanation for the negative reception faced by New Commonwealth Immigrants. Two theories have been put forward. One suggests that the negative reception is temporary and due to their immigrant status. The other suggests the negative reception is more endemic and due to the fact that being black constitutes for the host population a sign of negative status. Both theories have a degree of plausibility but what the PEP studies attempted to do was examine these two theories in relation to evidence. On the basis of a series of tests they showed the second theory to be the more corroborated one. Racial discrimination, albeit rather less extensive than in the past, is still very widespread in Britain.

Guide to reading

A. Pilkington, *What is Sociology?* chapter 2 outlines in more detail the social scientific approach. S. Patterson, *Dark Strangers* and J. Rex, *Race, Colonialism and the City*, pages 203–223 provide examples of the two explanations of the reception faced by New Commonwealth Immigrants. W. Daniel *Racial Discrimination in England* outlines how personal and telephone testing were successfully used in the first PEP study to assess discrimination, while R. Jowell and P. Prescott-Clarke, 'Racial Discrimination and White Collar Workers in Britain' (*Race*, Vol. XI) outlines how correspondence testing was successfully used to assess discrimination. D. Smith, *Racial Disadvantage in Britain*, chapter 5, utilises both methods in the second PEP study and provides the most recent evidence in this area.

Discussion points

1. Why is racial discrimination considered unjust? What other forms of discrimination would you consider unjust?
2. How would you assess the theory that New Commonwealth Immigrants have met discrimination not because of their colour so much as because of their culture?
3. How convincing do you find the tests of the theories?
4. What possible explanations of racial discrimination can you put forward?
5. How can racial discrimination be prevented? What arguments are there, for and against, positive discrimination? What can you as an individual do?
6. What kind of multiracial society do you consider most desirable and feasible? Can you detect different images of a multiracial society in the two theories put forward?

3

Racial prejudice

The relationship between racial prejudice and discrimination

Prejudice and discrimination, although often used interchangeably in ordinary speech, need to be distinguished. For they draw attention to an important distinction, notably between attitudes and behaviour, and in the process highlight the fact that attitudes are not necessarily expressed in behaviour, and that behaviour does not necessarily stem from predisposing attitudes. This is not to say there is not a connection between attitudes and behaviour. Attitudes are normally conceptualised as having three aspects – a cognitive aspect, i.e. a set of beliefs about the phenomenon in question; an affective aspect, i.e. a set of feelings (positive or negative) about it, and a conative aspect, i.e. a tendency to behave in a particular way towards it. By definition then there is a connection between attitudes and behaviour. The connection is not a mechanical one, however. Take race relations, in which prejudice is used to refer to attitudes which involve categorising people negatively on racial grounds and discrimination which is used to refer to behaviour which involves disadvantaging people on racial grounds. Although it is assumed that prejudice is likely to lead to discrimination, the connection is by no means automatic and there are other factors which can explain racial discrimation. One such factor is conformity to social norms.

All of us can be seen as occupying a variety of positions or statuses in society. Whether ascribed at birth, such as the status of being white, or achieved, such as the status of being a student, each status is invariably accompanied by a set of norms which define for the occupant of that status the appropriate behaviour expected. Each set of norms constitutes a role. As members of society occupying various statuses, we are expected to conform to the appropriate social norms and are indeed sanctioned to play our roles accordingly. To the extent to which people discriminate because they take that to be expected of them, their behaviour therefore indicates not so much their attitudes as their willingness to perform their roles.

In the United States, a series of experiments carried out by social psychologists indicates the extent to which people are willing to conform to the expectations held of them. The most dramatic example is Milgram's study (Milgram, 1974) which examined the extent to which people can be induced to inflict pain on others. The people, from different walks of life, who accepted an invitation to take part in an experiment at Yale University on memory and learning were, unbeknown to them, the subjects of the experiment. Each subject was paired with an accomplice of the experimenter and both told that they were about to take part in an experiment to investigate the effects of punishment on learning. Which role each played – teacher or learner – apparently depended on drawing lots, but was of course rigged. After the learner had been strapped into a chair and fitted with an electrode in his presence, the teacher was taken to another room, shown the shock generator and told to give an increasingly higher shock each time a wrong answer was given by the learner. The learner, who was of course not really receiving any shocks, did not respond to the fake shocks until they indicated that 300 volts had been reached. He then cried out apparently in obvious pain, requesting the experiment to be stopped and refusing to go on. The teacher was, however, asked to continue. Alarmingly the majority did. Of the forty subjects, only five refused to go beyond 300 volts and twenty six in fact completed the experiment, administering seemingly 400 volts. This is not to say that the subjects found their role an easy one to play. Far from it. Most did not relish their parts at all, exhibiting increasing signs of distress and anxiety throughout the experiment. Nevertheless, what is most remarkable is the fact that, despite knowing what they were doing, they still obeyed the experimenter whom they saw as an authority figure and fully complied with the expectations held of them. As such, the experiment illustrates in a very graphic way how ordinary people can engage in such a barbaric act as the systematic slaughter of six million Jews in Nazi Germany and how in a society like South Africa, in which racial discrimination is institutionalized, discrimination involves behaving in conformity with the norms of society and is not therefore necessarily motivated by personal prejudice.

The fact that prejudicial attitudes and discriminatory behaviour do not necessarily coincide, with the former leading ineluctably to the latter, provided the starting point for the development of a typology of the relationship between the two concepts by Merton (Merton, 1977). Four types can be distinguished – the unprejudiced non discriminator whom Merton labels the all weather liberal; the unprejudiced discriminator whom Merton labels the fair weather liberal; the prejudiced nondiscriminator whom Merton labels the timid bigot; and the prejudiced discriminator whom Merton labels the all weather bigot. Diagramatically these four types can be presented as follows:

31

Table 3

	Unprejudiced	Prejudiced
Does not discriminate	1. Unprejudiced non discriminator (all weather liberal)	3. Prejudiced non discriminator (timid bigot)
discriminates	2. Unprejudiced discriminator (fair weather liberal)	4. Prejudiced discriminator (all weather bigot)

Although people's attitudes and behaviour are not always consistent, with the result that they can't be simply located in one of these four types, most people are closer to one type than the others. Perhaps the most interesting types are types 2 and 3, where the behaviour and attitudes do not correspond with each other. In both cases social pressures influence behaviour, thus inhibiting attitudes from being expressed in practice. In the case of the fair weather liberal, discrimination may result from the fact that others expect him or her to act in this way and it is easier to go along with these expectations than to face possible sanctions for doing otherwise. In the case of the timid bigot, prejudice may not be translated into behaviour because of the possible costs involved in doing so.

The extent of racial prejudice in Britain

Having examined racial discrimination in the previous chapter, we now need to turn our attention to racial prejudice and in particular how extensive it is in contemporary Britain. In the course of examining the extent of racial discrimination, it will be remembered that Daniel argued the primary motive for widespread racial discrimination at the time was not prejudice but a belief of those in a position to discriminate, that black people were less well qualified or that while they would accept black people others would not. In terms of Merton's typology, British people were fair weather liberals. Daniel's argument is in fact supported by the major survey on the extent of racial prejudice in this country conducted by Abrams (Rose, 1969). A sample of about 2500 white residents, drawn equally from five areas of high immigration, were interviewed in 1966 and asked a series of questions, from which four social issues were chosen as crucial measures of prejudice.

(1) Whether they would avoid having coloured neighbours even if they were professional people.

(2) Whether they regarded coloured people as their inferiors solely on the basis of skin colour.
(3) Whether the authorities should refuse housing to coloured tenants even if they had been on the waiting list the required time.
(4) Whether a private landlord should refuse accommodation to coloured tenants even if he knew that they would care for his property.

Although Abrams is none too clear on this point, it seems that the answers were classified as follows: those who gave no hostile answers were classified as 'tolerant'; those who gave one 'tolerant inclined'; those who gave two 'prejudice inclined' and those who gave three or four 'prejudiced'. On this basis Abrams claimed 10% were 'prejudiced', 17% 'prejudice inclined', 38% 'tolerant inclined' and 35% 'tolerant'. In other words, prejudice was relatively rare. As Rose and Deakin put it in *Colour and Citizenship*, 'The extent of tolerance cannot be stressed too often and is indeed one of the major facts of the actual situation . . . what is needed is not an effort to make people unprejudiced but rather to remind them that they are unprejudiced' (Rose, 1969).

Such was the thinking behind the Race Relations Act of 1968 which it was felt would successfully curtail racial discrimination because it did not go in the face of people's attitudes. Since most people in a position to discriminate were fair weather liberals, only discriminating when such behaviour was rewarded, what was needed were counterpressures to encourage people not to discriminate. This, it was believed, was what antidiscrimination legislation could provide. As for the few bigots around, legislation would increase the costs involved in translating prejudice into action and with luck might change such people's attitudes. Certainly there is evidence of this happening in the Southern States of America where the outlawing of discrimination has been followed by a reduction in prejudice (Farley, 1982), a finding not unexpected in the light of cognitive dissonance theory. This theory indicates a tendency in people to want to believe that their behaviour is consistent with their attitudes, so that if an inconsistency does become apparent people unconsciously change their attitudes. Whatever the truth of this theory, great hopes were held out for the Act because it seemed to be encouraging behaviour consistent with most people's existing attitudes.

Now, there has indeed been, as we saw in the previous chapter, a decline in racial discrimination which lends support to the notion that racial prejudice is rare. We also saw, however, in the previous chapter, that racial discrimination is still very extensive, although operating in a more covert way. This suggests that the extent of prejudice may have been underestimated. Before, however, we can investigate this possibility further, we need to be absolutely clear what we mean by prejudice.

Racial prejudice has only been considered worth investigating relatively recently. Because the attitudes denoted by the term were considered legitimate, only the objects of such attitudes were studied. As ideas of human equality came to be reinforced by scientific evidence, however, so these attitudes themselves began to be considered objects worthy of study in their own right. One dominant approach to the study of racial attitudes flows from a tradition in psychology, which stems from Freud.

Freud pictured the human mind as a battle-ground comprising three interacting forces which he labelled the id, superego and ego. The chief protagonists were seen as the id, which contained our basic drives, and the superego or conscience, which developed in the course of socialisation and was the repository of social norms. The ego tried to reconcile these contradictory demands by guiding the needs arising from the id into socially acceptable channels. However, in the course of development, the necessary restraint of the id some-times went too far, with particularly severe repression having implications for the individual's personality later. In extreme cases, people became neurotic, exhibiting symptoms which indicated that painful memories had been repressed into the unconscious id but were seeking to find expression. Although Freud's ideas changed during his lifetime and his followers by no means accept much of what he wrote, a Freudian tradition in psychology can be dis-tinguished which shares a number of tenets: all behaviour, including for example seemingly meaningless dreams, has a reason; in searching for the underlying causes of human behaviour, we need to take particular note of the role of the unconscious and the impor-tance of our early upbringing (Brown, 1964). In the case of racial prejudice, writers in this tradition attempt to show how it can fulfil unconscious needs, such as aggression, which are generated in the course of socialisation. In doing this they are attempting to account for the extraordinary intensity in the attitudes often held towards racial minorities. We shall briefly look at two such writers: Dollard who was particularly concerned to explain the hostility towards black people in the Southern States of America between the wars (Dollard, 1957), and Adorno who was especially intent on accounting for the violent hostility towards the Jews characteristic of the Nazi regime in Germany (Adorno et al., 1950). Dollard put forward the frustration–aggression theory of prejudice. In its simplest form, this theory holds that when an individual's attempt to achieve satisfac-tion is frustrated, aggression is generated. If this cannot be released in an attack upon those responsible for his frustration, it is displaced onto a scapegoat which is visible, vulnerable and capable of symbolising the true source of frustration. Since the process of socialisation inevitably involves restraint of basic drives (id) and therefore frustration, aggression is generated. This cannot, however, be directed against ones parents because of dependence on them and because of prohibitions stemming from the conscience (superego). There is therefore always some aggression available which can be directed against a scapegoat and which accounts for the intensity of the hostility towards it.

This approach pioneered by Dollard was taken up further in a study conducted by Adorno. Appalled by the atrocities that had taken place in Germany, Adorno was intent on understanding prejudice against Jews. The argument of this study was that prejudice was determined more by the personality of the prejudiced individual than the characteristics of the group who were the target of prejudice. There is a tendency, it is suggested, for a child who is forced to submit to unexplained rules in an atmosphere which lacks the warmth necessary for the child to identify with his parent, to develop an authoritarian personality. He is anxious to do the right thing and is therefore very conventional but his resentment needs an outlet – hence his very authoritarian attitudes towards those who seem to break conventional standards. In venting his feelings of frustration on to a variety of outgroups and projecting on to such groups undesirable characteristics he unconsciously finds in himself, virulent hostility towards them can escalate.

Although there are differences between the theories of Dollard and Adorno, both view prejudice as an external manifestation of the personality needs of the individual. Some people are envisaged as having inadequate or disturbed personalities, because of the way they have been brought up, and as a result of their sickness exhibit hostile attitudes towards an outgroup. Prejudice, then, is considered to be a phenomenon which only those people with warped personalities are infected by. It is in just such a tradition that the work of Abrams needs to be located. Thus it is that he writes, 'Not all negative unfavourable attitudes towards a group and its individual members necessarily constitute prejudice. The essence of prejudice lies in the fact that the hostility . . . results rather from processes within the bearer of the hostile attitude'. Indeed Abrams goes even further and argues not altogether convincingly that those people who express the most hostile attitudes tend to be psychologically distinctive in the way Adorno suggested, particularly in their authoritarianism. Now Abrams may well be correct in his claim that such personalities form a small minority of the population and consequently that prejudice in this sense is relatively rare. But this is not what we normally mean by prejudice and the danger of defining it in Abrams' sense is that it may well suggest that unfavourable attitudes are rare.

Sensitive to this issue, a number of sociologists have recently urged us to free the concept from its tie with individual personality factors. One such writer is Lawrence who suggests that the term is more normally used to refer to 'those unfavourable attitudes which involve the pre-judgement of groups and members of groups regardless of how they have arisen' (Lawrence, 1973). Such a definition not only enables us to note other sources of prejudice than personality factors but also sensitises us to the possibility that prejudice is extensive. If we return to Abrams' survey, we do in fact find that the data can be interpreted in such a way as to indicate extensive prejudice. For 65% of his respondents expressed at least one hostile answer to the four key questions. This figure may in fact underestimate the extent of prejudice. For when Bagley examined the responses to six items in the survey, 85% exhibited prejudice on one or more items (Bagley, 1970). Nor is there evidence of a significant variation in prejudice over time or space. Unfavourable attitudes seem to be characteristic of all social groups and the only factor which is consistently associated with a significant reduction in racial prejudice is length of education. The persistent and widespread nature of prejudice means that its roots cannot be sought in the personality type of an abnormal minority but must be sought in the cultural framework of our society. As Hartmann and Husband put it 'Our whole way of thinking about coloured people, influenced by the colonial past, constitutes a built-in predisposition to accept unfavourable beliefs about them' (Hartmann and Husband, 1971).

We are not born prejudiced but rather learn such attitudes in the course of socialisation. Although such a process continues throughout life, the first few years of a child's life are normally seen as particularly crucial. For it is during this period that the child is totally dependent on others for the satisfaction of his or her needs, and fundamental attitudes are learnt. This is not to say that the period is one of indoctrination. Adult attitudes are picked up in multifarious ways – partly through 'direct tuition' in which rewards and punishments are used by adults to reinforce appropriate behaviour, but also through 'indirect tuition' in which adults are imitated and identified with and role playing develops. What is more, children do not merely passively receive information but are actively engaged in seeking it out, frequently finding in the process contrary ideas emanating from different sources. Nevertheless, although this period is not one of indoctrination, children do become aware of the attitudes of their parents and frequently internalise and reproduce them as their own. Milner points out that this is as true of racial as of other attitudes and that in our culture these attitudes tend to be unfavourable towards black people (Milner, 1975).

Because such attitudes are so much part of the cultural air that we breath and are picked up quite normally in the course of socialisation, we all tend to be touched by them to some extent. This is true even of those of us who believe that we are not prejudiced. One illustration will suffice, which concerns a friend. George, as we shall call him, is a man whose liberalism is more than skin deep. In addition to espousing the right causes, he is willing to dedicate his leisure time to further them including, for example, giving up two weeks of his holiday to help at a Summer School I was organising on behalf of the local Community Relations Commission. Here was someone seemingly without prejudice. One Saturday, after visiting his mother in London as usual, he got in his car to drive back home only to find that it would not go. After gently pleading with the car and doing all the normal things one does in such a situation, he became steadily angrier. Even kicking it did not make any difference, with the result that it ultimately had to be towed to the nearest garage. Fuming by this stage, he took the train home, only to find that a bunch of football supporters whose team had just lost, chose his carriage to vent their ire. They were drunk; they were teenagers; they were lads; they were dressed in a distinctive way and so forth, but what George noticed above all was that most of them were black. By itself such an observation was unimportant but, disturbingly, it was accompanied by a series of negative images. The stereotypes which had been intellectually rejected came flooding back in his mind. George was shocked to discover that he still carried such prejudicial baggage around with him.

The point of this story is not to suggest that we are all equally prejudiced, but to indicate the power of race imagery and the pervasiveness of unfavourable attitudes towards black people in our society. In view of this it is scarcely surprising that such attitudes are drawn upon by people to make sense of their daily experience. Indeed, the stereotypes these attitudes embody seem to many to be confirmed by what they see and hear. They encounter black people in subordinate work roles and thus find that their image of them as being inferior is confirmed. They note that the entry of New Commonwealth immigrants into the inner cities has been associated with the decline of such centres and consequently draw clear inferences as to which group is responsible for urban decline. They hear that the children born here are doing badly at school and involved in street crime, again reinforcing their picture of black children as inherently lacking in ability and tending towards criminality. Although these phenomena and can will be interpreted differently, it nevertheless remains the case that many people feel their experience indicates the validy of these beliefs. The salience of such beliefs of course varies, but although those, for example, who are living alongside black people, feeling they are in competition with them, may find the beliefs more salient (Phizacklea and Miles, 1980), we are all seen to some extent as being affected by them.

For those who believe that prejudice is indeed widespread in this way, the thinking which lay behind the Race Relations Act of 1968 seems overly optimistic. Since widespread prejudice underlies and legitimates discrimination, it is scarcely surprising that an Act which was designed primarily to provide a moral lead should prove only partially successful. This is not to say that the Act of 1976, with its stronger provisions, is doomed to failure.

Unfavourable attitudes are extensively held but are not on the whole very rigid. It is still only a small minority (12%) of the population, as Marsh points out on the basis of a national survey in the mid 70s, whose attitudes seem totally beyond rational persuasion (Marsh, 1976). As for the vast majority, prejudice here coexists with more positive attitudes. Thus while most people make prejudicial remarks and exhibit little sympathy for black immigrants, at the same time, Little and Kohler (Little and Kohler, 1977) point out they exhibit sympathy for black people born in this country and believe in equal rights. Such apparent inconsistencies are not a peculiarity of people's racial attitudes. They stem from the fact that people are touched by different value systems, which are not themselves wholly coherent. Thus the dominant values in our society exhibit both racist attitudes and egalitarian attitudes with immigration legislation exhibiting the former and Race Relations Acts the latter. Is it any wonder then that people's attitudes are not themselves wholly consistent? Be that as it may, people's attitudes in this area are to some extent malleable and open to persuasion. A stronger act, if rigorously pursued, might therefore have some further effect in curtailing discrimination. Smith sums up the position well: 'In most organizations, the proportion of people who are active and vociferous in their opposition to the minority groups is small, but the majority feels some sympathy for these attitudes, or at any rate is prepared to tolerate them. Because these feelings exist, acts of discrimination are likely to occur unless steps are taken to prevent them – not because it is the positive wish of the majority that they should, not because discrimination is the active policy of management or unions, but because the pressures to discriminate, however weak they are, will eventually have their effect unless they are opposed' (Smith, 1977).

Summary

In the course of examining how extensive racial prejudice is in contemporary Britain, we have at the same time been illustrating how the adoption of a social scientific approach does not usually produce the clear-cut results presented in the previous chapter. Social science involves, it will be remembered, testing theories against the facts. Thus we saw in the previous chapter how the facts produced by the PEP studies refuted the theory that the discrimination faced by New Commonwealth and Pakistan immigrants is primarily bound on newness (Theory 1) and at the same time corroborated the theory that the discrimination is primarily based on colour (Theory 2). Diagramatically our findings can be presented as follows:

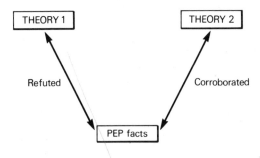

In this particular case, the facts were considered to be relatively unproblematical. Facts do not, however, lie around pure and unsullied. They have to be interpreted and they tend to be interpreted differently in the light of the theory one holds. Our examination of the extent of racial prejudice has exemplified this point. Some writers have argued that racial prejudice is relatively rare in contemporary Britain, whereas other writers have argued that it is extremely widespread. Their disagreement is not over the facts, but over their interpretation of the facts. Whereas some interpret the facts in the light of their view that prejudice is a product of a particular personality type (Theory 1), others interpret the facts in the light of their view that prejudice is a product of growing up in our culture (Theory 2). Diagramatically our findings can be presented as follows:

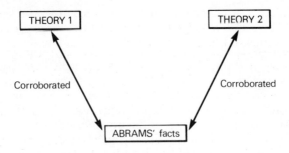

To show that each theory interprets the facts somewhat differently and in such a way that the proponents of each theory are able to claim that the facts fit their respective theory may suggest that there are no reasons for preferring one theory to another. This is not the case. Theories can be evaluated in terms of two broad criteria – in terms of their internal coherence or logical consistency and in terms of their correspondence to the facts. Take the very common notion that biology is the cause of racial divisions. Such an explanation can be criticised in terms of both our criteria. It is incoherent because it is unable to show how physical differences lead to racial divisions; assertion replaces a carefully delineated set of steps connecting the two. It does not correspond to the facts because it is unable to account for the fact that it is the meaning placed on particular physical differences which results in racial divisions and that these meanings vary from society to society. But what about the two theories of prejudice examined in this chapter?

Both the theory put forward by Abrams, that prejudice is the product of a particular personality type, and the theory put forward by Lawrence, that prejudice is a result of growing up in a racist culture, seem logically consistent and thus coherent. Key terms are defined, and the connection between the factors which are isolated as important, are carefully delineated. Thus, one easily understands the steps connecting extremely hostile attitudes, an authoritarian personality and specific child-rearing practises as outlined by Abrams, and the steps connecting unfavourable attitudes, a racist culture and British colonialism as outlined by Lawrence. In terms of the criterion of coherence then, there seems little to choose between the two theories. The same at first sight seems to be true, if the theories are evaluated in terms of the other criterion of correspondence to the facts. For, as we have already seen, both theories are able to interpret the facts produced by the 1966 survey in such a way that they are consistent with them. Thus, the theory put forward by Abrams, leads to the prediction that prejudice is rare and in terms of the definition adopted it is found indeed to be rare, while the theory put forward by Lawrence, leads to the prediction that prejudice is extensive and in terms of the definition adopted, it is found indeed to be extensive. Before, however, we can conclude that both theories are equally valuable, we need to compare the two to ascertain whether one is more comprehensive than another and is thus able to account for a greater range of facts.

Each theory highlights a different set of factors and connections between them and, in doing so, is able to account for some facts but not others. Thus one theory, by linking causally child-rearing practises, an authoritarian personality and extremely hostile attitudes, is able to account for the intensity of hatred towards a particular group, but not why that particular group was the target of hatred (Blalock, 1982). The other theory, in contrast, by linking causally British colonialism, a racist culture and socialisation into such beliefs and values, is able to account for the extensiveness of unfavourable attitudes towards that particular target but not the intensity of hatred felt by some. Now, in this particular case, both theories may be correct. Intensive prejudice, which is unamenable to rationality, may be a product of a particular personality type while a diffuse prejudice is indeed very widespread. This is not to say, however, that both theories are equally valuable. For the second theory is not only able to explain why prejudice in Britain takes a racial form, but is also able to account for more of the variations in the extent of such prejudice than the first theory. On the basis of a comparison of matched samples in England and Netherlands, for example, Bagley and Verma conclude that the greater racial prejudice in England stems from its culture rather than from psychological factors (Bagley and Verma, 1979a). This means, as Hartmann and Husband point out, that 'only after the underlying cultural predisposition to prejudice has been taken into account does it make sense to ask how variations in prejudice relate to other factors' (Hartmann and Husband, 1971). There is no doubt that one such factor accentuating hostility is 'authoritarianism' but this must be seen in the context of the wider culture. Where does this leave us then? Both theories of prejudice are corroborated, but the second is more comprehensive and as such is more valuable.

Guide to reading

A. Pilkington, *What is Sociology?* chapter 3 and conclusion highlights the difficulties involved in interpreting the facts and thus the problems entailed in subjecting sociological theories to empirical test. For those interested in exploring further the relation between theory and fact, Open University, *Social Sciences: a foundation course, D102*, Unit 18 constitutes a good starting point. Open University, *Making Sense of Society, D101*, Unit 21 provides an introduction to psychological approaches to the study of attitudes. On racial prejudice, E. Rose, *Colour and Citizenship*, chapter 28 reports Abrams' study, pointing out that racial prejudice in Britain is relatively rare, being a product of a particular personality type, while N. Deakin, *Colour, Citizenship and British Society*, chapter 12, reinterprets the same data to suggest that racial prejudice is more widespread. D. Lawrence, *Black Migrants, White Natives*, chapter 3, takes this suggestion further and presents a scathing attack on Abrams' study. Writers who accept the validity of this critique and argue that racism pervades our culture include D. Milner, *Children and Race*, chapters 1–4. C. Bagley and G. Verma, *Racial Prejudice, the Individual and Society*, chapter 6 provides a useful summary and synthesis of the research in this field.

Discussion points

1. Why is racial prejudice considered unjust? What other forms of prejudice would you consider unjust?
2. How valid do you think surveys are in indicating people's attitudes?
3. Do you think both theories of prejudice have equal merit? Why do you think sociologists prefer the second theory put forward?
4. What possible explanations of racial prejudice can you put forward?
5. What beliefs do you hold about different minority groups? Where did you pick up these beliefs? Can you justify them? Are you always consistent in your attitudes? Can you detect any prejudices here?
6. How can we curtail racial prejudice? What can you as an individual do?

4

Perspectives on race

Sociology involves an attempt to explain human behaviour as scientifically as possible in terms of people's membership of social groups. As such it comprises a distinct perspective on man and society. Within this broad perspective, however, can be detected different approaches which incorporate divergent assumptions about man and society. Such differences have existed since the emergence of sociology as a separate discipline and can be located in the work of the three writers who above all others have established the principal frames of reference of modern Sociology (Giddens, 1971). It is to these – Marx, Durkheim and Weber – we now turn.

Classical sociology and social inequality

'Surprisingly enough they were relatively silent about race' (O'Callaghan, 1980). Indeed it has often been argued that 'none of the major sociological theorists . . . paid much attention to questions of race relations' (Banton, 1967), a deficiency which is less perplexing when it is recognised that 'no racial problem at all comparable to that of the present day presented itself in the historical situation in which the basic structure of sociological theory took shape' (Lockwood, 1970). Such a claim clearly exaggerates the failure of the sociological tradition to discuss race, and ignores, for example, the perceptive discussion of race and ethnic relations by the classical sociologists in three major and overlapping areas: slavery, imperialism and nationalism (Stone, 1977). Nevertheless, there is little doubt that while noting the significance of race in particular societies, their analyses of modern societies led them to believe that it would cease to be an important basis of inequality or source of identity. Although they were mistaken in this particular case, the work of Marx, Durkheim and Weber has been taken up by later writers and their different approaches applied to race relations. In order to understand the roots of these different approaches, therefore, we shall examine the writings of the three classical sociologists.

43

Since we saw earlier that a race relations situation involves inequality, attention will especially be focused on their conceptions of social inequality in modern society. After this temporary detour, we shall then be in a position to return to our main path and outline the major approaches and perspectives on race, which will be taken up in the following chapters.

Working as they were in the nineteenth century, with the effects of the French and Industrial revolutions still ringing in their ears, Marx, Durkheim and Weber were particularly interested in discovering what fundamental changes had taken place in society and what fundamental changes were likely to take place.

For Marx, the most fundamental change which the revolutions signalled was the emergence of a new kind of society – capitalism. Capitalism can be defined in terms of two interrelated features: a) the production of goods and services is primarily geared to the search for profits which accrue to those people who own the means of production and b) the process is organised in terms of a market upon which commodities, including labour power itself, are bought and sold. In contrast to the situation in pre-industrial societies, where the production of goods and services is directed towards the needs of the locality, this tie between production and consumption is broken in a capitalist society and replaced by the market. The market not only allows commodity production to occur, but with the dispossession of the producers from the means of production, turns labour power itself into a commodity. As a consequence, capitalism is characterised by two classes – those who own the means of production (the bourgeoisie) and those who do not own the means of production and are therefore forced to sell their labour power and work for the bourgeoisie (the proletariat). The relation between these classes on the surface is less exploitative than in a pre-industrial society in which people were obliged, for example, to hand over a definite amount of produce to the lord of the manor or to work unpaid on the lord's land. For in a capitalist society, workers hire out their energies and skills, in order to produce the goods and services which are eventually sold on the market, in exchange for wages. The exchange, however, is not on inspection a fair one. The wages invariably represent less in terms of value than the value realised through the sale of the products of proletarian labour and the difference between the two, which Marx called surplus value, is appropriated by the bourgeoisie as profit. The relation between the bourgeoisie and proletariat is clearly, therefore, one of exploitation, and has caused, as a consequence, the increasing alienation of the proletariat.

'In what does this alienation exist?' Marx asked. 'First, that the work is external to the worker, that it is not a part of his nature, that consequently he does not fulfil himself in his work but denies himself, has a feeling of misery, not of well being, does not develop freely a physical and mental energy, but is physically exhausted and mentally debased. The worker, therefore, feels himself at home during his leisure, whereas at work he feels homeless. His work is not voluntary but imposed, forced labour. It is not the satisfaction of a need, but only a means for satisfying other needs. Its alien character is clearly shown by the fact that as soon as there is no physical or other compulsion, it is avoided like the plague. Finally, the alienated character of work for the worker appears in the fact that it is not his work but work for someone else, that in work he does not belong to himself but to another person' (Bottomore and Rubel, 1961).

As capitalism develops, Marx argued, so the conditions for its transcendence become more apparent. Driven by the need to maintain the rate of profit, the bourgeoisie adopts increasingly sophisticated technology, thus making it possible for the population as a whole to enjoy a high standard of living and for members to fulfil themselves. Such an outcome is, however, not possible so long as the bourgeoisie continues to appropriate surplus value for itself. In Marx's terms, the 'relations of production' in a capitalist society prevent the promise of shared material abundance, which the developing 'forces of production' point to, from being fully realised. What is more, the existence of a fundamental imbalance between production and consumption results in periodic crises when the market is unable to absorb all the goods and services which have been produced. The bourgeoisie of course, respond to such crises by seeking new markets and 'the need of a constantly expanding market for its products chases (it) over the whole surface of the globe' (Avineri, 1969) encouraging in the process European colonial expansion. Economic crises, however, recur and invariably result in bankruptcies. In order to counteract these tendencies to overproduction, capital becomes more concentrated, thus making it increasingly possible for production to be centrally coordinated and oriented to people's needs. Such an outcome is again, however, not possible so long as the bourgeoisie compete with each other to make profits. For these possibilities, which emerge in a capitalist society, to be realised, the revolutionary action of the proletariat is needed.

At first the proletariat's resistance to bourgeoisie domination is only sporadic. Members are not united but struggle among each other as well as against the bourgeoisie. Over time however, a combination of circumstances promotes the class consciousness of the proletariat. The development of capitalism tends to mean the demise of classes characteristic of the former pre-industrial society – landowners and peasants – and therefore the emergence of a more simplified class structure. The existence of a particularly vulnerable and unorganised sector of the labour force, which can be tapped during a boom but disposed of during a slump, described by Marx as 'a reserve army of labour', tends to mean that wages remain around subsistence levels and the relative disparity in wealth between the bourgeoisie and proletariat increases. The introduction of machinery tends to mean the erosion of traditional craft skills and the elimination of skill divisions within the proletariat. A process of class polarisation occurs, in short, in which the proletariat, less divided and subject to increasing relative poverty, face a clearly distinct bourgeoisie. As they live through the economic crises of capitalism with their attendant increases in unemployment and decreases in wages and as they work concentrated together in large factories, so members communicate to each other their increasing dissatisfaction with bourgeoisie exploitation. They organise themselves to begin with on a local level, later on nationally, to improve their wages and conditions until finally they are strong enough to oust the bourgeoisie and set up a new society. In the process they transform themselves from a mere category of people who happen to share the same conditions, to a group of people who, realising they share the same conditions, organise themselves to change them. In Marx's terms, they make the passage from a 'class in itself' to a 'class for itself'.

The bourgeoisie of course does attempt to prevent the proletariat from making this transition from a 'class in itself' to a 'class for itself'. Although its power rests ultimately on ownership of the means of production, such economic dominance is translated into political dominance with the result that the bourgeoisie becomes a ruling class. The state, considered by Marx to be 'the executive committee for managing the common affairs of the whole bourgeoisie' represents the interests of the class as a whole, managing its common affairs in two major ways. The first relies on its control of the means of coercion and involves being repressive. Examples here include legislation inhibiting the formation of trade unions and the use of the army to quash strikes. The second depends on its significance in the dissemination of beliefs and values through society and involves propagating, along with various other organs, ideologies which purport to show the justice and necessity of bourgeois domination. Particularly because, as Marx put it, 'the ideas of the ruling class are, in every age, the ruling ideas: i.e. the class which is the dominant material force in society is at the same time its dominant intellectual force' (Bottomore and Rubel, 1961), the development of class consciousness may be delayed. Ultimately, Marx argued, the proletariat will see through the fog of bourgeois ideology and become revolutionary, however. For the revolution is inevitable. Marx went further to claim that the proletarian revolution will be unique. For whereas past revolutions have been made by a minority for the benefit of a minority, the proletariat's revolution will be made by the majority for the benefit of the majority. This will enable a classless society to be formed in which the ideals put forward during the French Revolution will be fully realised: freedom will replace alienation; equality inequality and fraternity self-interest. Such a society Marx called communism.

To move from Marx to Durkheim and Weber is to move from an earlier to a later generation of social thinkers. It is also to move to two critics of Marx. For the work of both Durkheim and Weber must be seen partly as an attempt to refute Marx or at any rate a very common interpretation of Marx which stressed the determinacy of economic factors and the irrelevance of cultural and political factors. This was considered important because by the last quarter of the nineteenth century there had arisen revolutionary movements which claimed to practise what Marx had preached and in the case of the Social Democratic Party in Germany, held to a form of economic determinism. According to this doctrine, society can be likened to a building, composed of a base and superstructure. The base, consisting as it does of a contradiction between the forces and relations of production, forms the economic foundation on top of which political and cultural levels arise. In line with the analogy, the economic base is envisaged as the primary determinant of social relations, the superstructure reflecting its effects. Such a doctrine, in suggesting that cultural and political factors are unimportant, was rejected vociferously by both Durkheim and Weber.

For Durkheim, the most fundamental change which the French and Industrial revolutions signified was the growth of 'organic solidarity'. To understand this phenomenon more clearly he contrasted two types of society – 'primitive' society and 'advanced' society. Primitive societies, he argued, have little division of labour. They consist of a number of groups, called clans, which closely resemble each other. Such societies are bound together by the fact that the members of the various clans all adhere to the same beliefs and values, these beliefs and values being embodied in religion. This situation Durkheim called one of 'mechanical solidarity'. It could not last, however. For population increases in primitive societies produce more interaction among its members and the resultant increase in competitiveness is only solved by the development of the division of labour. This does not, however, mean the end of solidarity. For in advanced societies, where the division of labour has gone furthest, a new type of solidarity arises, 'organic solidarity'. Such solidarity does not depend so much on acceptance of a common set of beliefs and values. It depends, rather, upon the fact that specialisation makes people more dependent on one another. Now, since it is organic solidarity which binds the members of advanced societies together, it is advanced societies which see the development of individuality. For as organic solidarity replaces mechanical solidarity, the strength of common beliefs and values becomes less pervasive with the result that people are able to hold different beliefs and are able to perform different activities. This is not to say that common beliefs and values disappear in advanced societies. In fact, in one case they become stronger. For, alongside the development of the division of labour, there emerges a common belief in the dignity and worth of the individual. Advanced societies do not therefore collapse into disorder with the development of the division of labour and with the growth of individuality Instead, organic solidarity replaces mechanical solidarity. Despite his insistence on this point, Durkheim was well aware that advanced societies face grave difficulties. This is borne out by his analysis of suicide.

Durkheim distinguished three main types of suicide – altruistic suicide, egoistic suicide and anomic suicide. Altruistic suicide is found predominantly in primitive societies. In such societies, it is a duty for an individual, when placed in certain circumstances, to take his life. In doing so, he will be showing his commitment to the shared beliefs and values of his society. The decline of such shared beliefs and values, however, means that altruistic suicide is rarely found in advanced societies. In its place there emerges, Durkheim argued, two other types of suicide. Egoistic suicide is an offshot of individualism. As individualism develops so does the tendency for the individual to think primarily of himself. Unless this tendency is tempered, Durkheim argued, through membership of a strongly integrated group, the individual may be temped to commit suicide. Anomic suicide is an equally modern phenomenon. It springs from anomie – a situation in which the individual is no longer controlled by a moral code. The result is not freedom for the individual but a condition in which he is a prisoner of his own inexhaustible desires, a condition which is conducive to suicide. Durkheim went further than this, however, and in doing so came into direct conflict with Marx. For he argued that it is anomie which explains class conflict.

Class conflict, he insisted, is not a permanent attribute of advanced societies but results from a temporary failure of these societies to develop an adequate moral code. What is needed, therefore, is not revolution, as Marx has suggested, but a moral code which will restrain individuals, show them their dependence on one another and make them willingly accept different jobs and different rewards. The Church cannot provide such a moral code, for its beliefs no longer command universal assent. It is therefore necessary for the state and the occupational associations to support a new moral code. This will be centered around the emerging common belief in the dignity and worth of the individual. Its development presupposes equality of opportunity. The reason for this is that it is only when individuals are able to fill the occupational positions which accord with their natural talents that they will accept the unequal rewards which attach to these positions as legitimate. When this situation is reached, Durkheim argued, advanced societies will be able to enjoy organic solidarity without the threat to social order which comes from anomie.

Weber echoed Durkheim's stress on the importance of moral values. But his emphasis was different. For while Durkheim pointed out the crucial role that values play in restraining individuals and in producing social solidarity, Weber pointed out the crucial role they play in motivating individuals and in changing society. This is borne out in his analysis of the origins of the 'spirit of capitalism'.

A crucial element in the rise of capitalism, Weber argued, was the acceptance by a number of groups of a new set of attitudes towards work and money. Such a set of attitudes he called 'the spirit of capitalism'. This spirit contrasted sharply with the attitudes towards work and money prevalent in the past. For it encourages the individual to systematically accumulate wealth, it forbids him to use his income for personal enjoyment and, most important, it persuades him to work as hard as possible in his chosen 'calling'. The source of this spirit, Weber argued, lay in certain Protestant movements which emerged during the Reformation. Particularly important was Calvinism, a movement led by John Calvin. According to Calvin, God had irrevocably predestined every human being either to everlasting salvation or to everlasting damnation. Such a doctrine produced in Calvin's followers, Weber argued, a sense of 'unprecedented inner loneliness'. For how could they be sure they were one of the chosen? Calvinist pastors responded to such doubts by advising believers to engage in 'intense wordly activity' in order to attain the confidence of being one of the chosen. Thus it was that there emerged within Calvinism a unique religious ethic. This ethic enjoined the individual to work as hard as possible in his chosen vocation and yet forbade him to use the income derived from such work on personal enjoyment. Such an ethic, Weber argued, in contrast to the ethics of other religions, was conducive to the spirit of capitalism.

Weber's thesis has been interpreted by some commentators as constituting a direct refutation of Marx's analysis of the rise of capitalism. For, it is argued, whereas Marx tried to show that the conflict which resulted from the relations people established in the economy – in short, class conflict – was the cause of the rise of capitalism, Weber showed that a particular set of ideas – in short, the Protestant ethic – was the cause of the rise of capitalism. Such an argument is, however, unjust to both Weber and Marx. Weber did not claim to show that Calvinism was the cause of capitalism. In fact, he specifically stated that before we could tell what caused what, it would be necessary to investigate the factors which influenced Calvinism. All he did claim was that Calvinism had some significance for the rise of capitalism. As for Marx, he did not claim that ideas were of no significance. What he did claim was that a particular set of ideas would not become at all prominent in a society unless they were congruent with the interests of one of the conflicting classes. In short, the views of Weber and Marx on this issue were not widely divergent. Both agreed that in analysing the rise of capitalism or any other situation it was necessary to investigate people's economic situations and people's ideas; both agreed that it was necessary to investigate how people's economic situations affected their ideas and how people's ideas affected their economic situations.

If Weber and Marx were not in fundamental disagreement in their accounts of the emergence of capitalist societies (Giddens, 1979), they were, however, over other issues. Their respective analyses of the modern state bear this out. For Marx, the modern state represents the interests of the economically dominant class, the bourgeoisie, and therefore will disappear when capitalism is transcended by communism. Weber completely disagreed. For him, a much more important characteristic of the modern state is its 'rational legal' basis of legitimacy which he contrasted with two other bases of legitimacy, 'traditionalism' and 'charisma'.

Acceptance of domination, Weber argued, is often based upon a belief by subordinates in the legitimacy of their subordination. In the past, subordination was usually based upon a belief in 'the sanctity of age old rules and powers'; the feeling was 'That's the way things have always been'. At times, however, a new kind of authority emerged, temporarily sweeping away traditional authority. This, Weber called charismatic authority. In this situation, subordination was based upon a belief of both leader and followers in the authenticity of the leader's exceptional qualities and mission. The prototype of this situation was a leader who said, 'It is written, but I say unto you . . .'.

If the past has seen the alternation of traditional and charismatic authority, the modern world, Weber argued, had seen the emergence of a new kind of authority – legal rational authority. Here subordination is based upon the acceptance of certain laws or rules. In contrast to the situation under traditional and charismatic authority, superordinates are not obeyed out of personal loyalty but because they happen to be the individuals entitled by the rules of the organisation or the laws of the land to give orders.

The rational legal authority characteristic of the modern state is associated, Weber argued, with a bureaucratic form of organisation. Such an organisation has a number of basic characteristics which distinguish it from organisations found in the past. It has a system of rules which govern the conduct of officials in the pursuit of their official duties; it is organised hierarchically with a strict chain of command from top to bottom; it has a rigid division of labour which makes it important for recruitment of officials to be based upon demonstration of specialised competence; and it maintains the dependence of officials by not allowing them to own the resources necessary for the performance of their duties.

Weber did not deny that capitalism involves the emergence of a class system based upon capital and wage labour. But this was not for him as critical as the process of bureaucratisation. Rather than generalising from the economic to the political, Weber generalised from the political to the economic. Bureaucratisation, which is first and foremost characteristic of the rational legal state is spreading and will continue to spread because it is the only organisation capable of coping with the tasks of coordination necessary to modern capitalism. Despite his insistence on the technical superiority of bureaucracy, however, it should not be thought that Weber particularly welcomed the trend towards increasing bureaucratisation. Far from it. He lamented the fact that bureaucratisation was making us into 'specialists without vision, sensualists without heart' and asked 'what can we oppose to this machinery in order to keep a portion of mankind free from this parcelling out of the soul, from this supreme mastery of the bureaucratic way of life?' (Bendix, 1966). To Weber, Marx's answer seemed utopian. Bureaucratisation will not disappear with the transcendence of capitalism by communism. Instead it will increase as the state takes over the means of production. What is needed instead, Weber argued, is a charismatic leader, generated by the mass franchise, to guide the fortunes of the state.

Weber's stress that cultural and political factors may be as significant as economic factors is well brought in his discussion of social inequality. For Weber, inequalities in power and advantage take three main forms – those of class, status and party (Runcimann, 1978). Class pertains to inequalities in power and advantage which have their source in the workings of the capitalist market. Status pertains to inequalities in power and advantage which have their source in the way people evaluate each other. Party pertains to inequalities in power and advantage which have their source in the fact that people form organisations to pursue their interests. By making a conceptual distinction between these three dimensions of stratification and by pointing to three possible bases of group formation, Weber was again able to question Marx's emphasis on the economic as the source of inequalities in power, advantage and classes as the key groups. Although Weber's distinction between class, status and party does not preclude the possibility of an increasing congruence between them, the overriding importance attached to class is questioned. Enough has already been said of organisation, or party as Weber called it, in our discussion of Weber's account of bureaucracy. Let us therefore look in a little more detail at status, which, Weber argues, had been historically more significant as a basis of group formation than class.

Status is, as we have already pointed out, formed out of the tendency of human beings to evaluate each other, to express respect for some human attributes and contempt for others. The result is the existence of prevalent beliefs and values concerning the criteria of social worth. What human attributes are evaluated and how they are evaluated will vary from society to society, but the consequence is that some groups will be able to benefit from and actively exploit such beliefs and values (Goldthorpe and Bevan, 1977). Thus, in our society, race is seen as a significant criterion of social worth, a criterion which clearly disadvantages black people. Those who are seen as having the same social worth, Weber argued, are in the same status situation. Being invariably conscious of their common position, they normally constitute a status group, manifesting their distinctiveness through following a particular life style and placing restrictions on the manner in which others may interact with them. In some cases a status group is able to secure legal and institutional recognition for its privileges. Such stratification may be thought of as achieving its most developed form in the caste system; there one finds the closest approximation to what Goldthorpe calls an 'integrated status hierarchy' in which everyone knows their place and consequently defer to their superiors, accept their equals and derogate their inferiors (Goldthorpe and Hope, 1972).

Status stratification has not always coincided with stratification by class. Thus, Weber argued, it historically restricted the spheres of economic life which were allowed to be governed by the market and even now possession of material property is not always a sufficient basis for entry into a dominant status group. But although membership of a dominant status group cannot be secured simply by the pretensions of sheer property, nevertheless property is usually regarded as a status qualification in the long run. The 'nouveaux riches' may not be accepted into the dominant status group but their children are likely to be. The reason for this is that different forms of advantage and power, tend to be convertible so that economic advantage can be translated for example into a public school education which itself may constitute an entitlement to high status. But if there can be a coincidence of class and status as a result of the influence of class on status, the reverse also applies; there can be a coincidence of class and status as a result of the influence of status on class. Thus if racial discrimination results in black people being placed in those occupations which are characterised by low pay, poor job security and few promotion prospects, status disadvantages are being translated into class disadvantages.

Whether status stratification or class stratification is more prevalent in society is influenced, Weber argued, by how far the society in question is subject to economic transformation. Whereas status groups flourish during periods of relative stability, classes flourish during periods of economic change. The implication seems to be that in capitalist societies, class stratification is likely to be the more significant. To this extent Weber's disagreement with Marx revolves around the significance he attached to status groups in the past rather than the present. Although both Weber and Marx were mistaken in their supposition that ethnicity would lose its salience, Weber's insistence that class and status constitute alternative bases of group formation at least leaves open the possibility that ethnic groups may be as significant as classes in a way Marx's stress on the overriding importance of class does not.

Let us finally then turn to Weber's theory of class. Class, for Weber, as we have already mentioned, pertains to inequalities in power and advantage which have their source in the capitalist market. As such, class is defined as an aggregate of people who share a similar market situation and therefore similar life chances. People's chances to acquire scarce resources, be they goods such as a house or services such as medical care, he argued, are determined by the degree of power they wield in the market. Whether people own or do not own the means of production, Weber argued, remains crucial, for possession of this attribute enables people to wield a great deal of power in the market. But although he believed like Marx that property and lack of property constitute the most fundamental class situations, his primary emphasis was a pluralistic one (Giddens, 1973). Far from thinking that capitalist development would lead to the polarisation of classes, Weber saw bureaucratisation as leading to a differentiation among the nonpropertied between manual and non-manual workers. Although there are other relevant attributes which people bring with them to the market advantaging some more than others, Weber emphasised in particular the attribute of educational qualifications which enables those who possess this attribute to wield more power in the market than those who do not on the whole. But if Weber's definition enables us to talk of more than two classes, in a way that adherence to Marx's distinction between ownership and nonownership of the means of production as the sole criterion of class does not, in itself it does not enable us to specify a limited number of classes.

Now the main concern of a theory of class is not to distinguish a number of economic categories by, for example, classifying people into a number of aggregates on the basis of their similar market situations. The main concern is to connect economic categories with the key social groupings in society, by, for example, discovering which market situations, if any, lead people to adopt similar norms and similar patterns of relationships. It was this concern to locate the key social groupings which partly lay behind Marx's distinction between 'class in itself' and 'class for itself' and it was the same concern which lay behind Weber's distinction between 'class' and 'social class'. Although Weber did not provide an adequate account of the relation between class and social class, he did suggest that common mobility chances limit the number of social groupings forming on the basis of similar market situations. Thus while a worker may fairly easily move from an unskilled to a semi-skilled manual occupation and the son of a semi-skilled worker may fairly easily become a skilled worker, the chances of intra or inter-generational mobility into non-manual occupations may be much less. In capitalism, Weber in fact distinguished four main social classes: the manual working class, the petty bourgeoisie, the propertyless white collar workers and those 'privileged through property and education'. Of these social classes, the most significant are the working class, the propertyless middle class and the propertied upper class. For with capitalist development, Weber admitted, the petty bourgeoisie is declining. Whether these groupings become class conscious depends, however, on a variety of factors and is by no means inevitable.

Where does this leave us then? Marx believed in the primacy of the economic and, as such, agreed that the most distinctive feature of modern society is its capitalist mode of production. Class inequality is the central characteristic of a capitalist society but it gives rise to a revolutionary movement which will in the end create an egalitarian society. Durkheim and Weber disagreed with much of this. Durkheim questioned Marx's emphasis on the primacy of the economic and stressed instead the cultural. Organic solidarity constitutes the most distinctive feature of modern society. It entails inequality but, as long as this arises from a situation in which people have equal opportunities, the emergence of an appropriate moral code will ensure its acceptance and the continuation of organic solidarity. Weber also questions Marx's emphasis on the economic and therefore the overriding importance of class conflict. He saw the most distinctive feature of modern society as having first arisen in the political realm i.e. bureaucratisation and noted that inequality can arise from non economic factors and thus take the form of status, for example race, and party as well as class. Class conflict is characteristic of modern society but far from ushering in an egalitarian society is likely to create further bureaucratisation.

Classical sociology, race and ethnicity

All theories involve abstracting from the complexities of the real world certain features which are considered to be central. The analyses of Marx, Durkheim and Weber are no exception. Although aware of the significance of racial and ethnic inequality as a source of identity and a generator of conflict in particular societies, their emphasis on those features which are characteristic of all capitalist or industrial societies led them to discount race and ethnicity as of central importance. (Lockwood, 1970). Indeecd all three 'social theorists tended to regard ethnicity as a spent force' (Parkin, 1979). This applies both to Marx who pointed to capitalism as the key factor behind the erosion of racial and ethnic identity and conflict and to Durkheim and Weber who regarded features of industrial society (Giddens, 1982) as the central variables underlying the declining significance of race and ethnicity.

While appreciating and indeed fulminating against the dehumanising consequences of capitalism, Marx considered the system to be a progressive stage in the history of mankind. Its expansion over the whole world and its destruction of what Marx considered to be archaic attachments to a particular ethnic group was therefore thought to be a necessary prelude to human emancipation (Avineri, 1969). Durkheim and Weber likewise thought that certain features of industrial society were inimical to race and ethnicity, with the need for efficiency, for example, demanding the replacement of ascription by achievement. Despite the initial plausibility of such views, 'as applied to the actual racial situations in our recent and present world the view that industrialisation moves ahead naturally to dissolve the racial factor is not borne out by the facts' (Blumer, 1977). This is not to say that the substantive ideas of the classical sociologists in the field of race and ethnicity are of no value. Indeed Marx's ideas on imperialism, Durkheim's critique of biological reductionism and Weber's insistence on status as a form of inequality have been taken up and developed by later writers. It has been, however, less their substantive ideas in this area so much as their general approaches which have been taken up and applied to race relations.

Before we move on to examine their general approaches, let us draw together the main points of our discussion so far in tabloid form:

Table 4   Classical sociology and race: Marx, Durkheim, Weber

	Marx	Durkheim	Weber
Main institutional sector stressed	The economy	Culture	The Polity
Central feature of modern society	Capitalism	Organic solidarity	Bureaucratization
Dominant form of social inequality	Class inequality which increasingly overrides other forms of inequality as capitalism develops.	A meritocracy in which individuals acquire positions through their own achievements.	Different forms of inequality coexist; but with the increased pace of life and the stress placed on specialized competence in an industrial society, class inequality becomes more pronounced.
Future of race inequality	Of diminishing importance	Of diminishing importance	Of diminishing importance

Our perusal of the work of Marx, Durkheim and Weber was not prompted by mere antiquarian interest. It was triggered off not only by the fact that these three writers perceptively recorded some of the significant features of our society which we now take for granted at a time when our society was only emerging (Kumar, 1978) but also by the fact that modern sociologists frequently refer back to their work, sympathising with the approach of one rather than another. Marx, Durkheim and Weber, although in agreement over many issues, highlighted, as we have seen, different features of modern society. To some extent this follows from the different assumptions they held. We shall briefly outline the key differences in their assumptions about the nature of society and the nature of man because these have formed the foci of major disputes among later sociologists and in the process we shall be able to distinguish different sociological approaches.

Contemporary sociological approaches to race: consensus and conflict

We shall begin by contrasting two conceptions of society. The first regards a consensus over basic values as an essential feature of society while the second regards conflict over basic interests as an essential feature of society. Of the founding fathers, Durkheim tended to accept the first conception and Marx the second conception.

For Durkheim, an agreement over basic values is considered a central attribute of society because it provides an answer to 'the problem of order'. Society is able to persist because its members share in common certain values. Durkheim of course recognised that conflicts did occur but believed these stemmed above all from the fact that people did not adhere to an adequate moral code. For Marx, conflict over basic interests is considered a central attribute of society because it accounts for the shift from one form of society to another. In Marx's terms 'The history of hitherto existing society is the history of class conflict'. Marx of course recognised that a cultural consensus could occur but believed this stemmed above all from the success of the dominant class in persuading the subordinate class of the legitimacy of its domination.

These two conceptions of society, which can be located in the work of Durkheim and Marx, still tend to distinguish sociologists, with some tending to favour a consensus approach and others to favour a conflict approach. Let us examine the two approaches in relation to a specific issue, that of medicine (Pilkington, 1980) before applying them to the field of race.

The consensus approach sees our society as fundamentally agreed over its economic and political arrangements. This means that, in the context of medicine, doctors and patients are visualised as sharing the same interests. Given such a congruence of interests, the doctors should be left to regulate themselves. After all, doctors as professionals, have a body of expert knowledge which they apply to diagnose and treat a range of illnesses; they are concerned primarily with the health of their patients rather than their own self interest and they are controlled by the Hippocratic oath which, should they break, can mean that their association strikes them from the register and bans them from practising medicine. The high regard in which doctors are held because of their value to society is reflected in the high rewards they attain and the high degree of satisfaction patients exhibit with them. Conflicts can and do of course occur but they stem primarily from a failure of communication.

The conflict approach sees our society as characterised by a plurality of groups with each group having different interests. Some groups are in a better position than others to enhance their interests. In the case of medicine, professionalism is a strategy doctors have succcessfully used to further their own interests. Restricting entry into an occupation whose members alone are allowed by the state to provide certain services entitles doctors to maintain a high demand for their services and so gain high rewards; professional self regulation allows them to forestall public scrutiny and thus maintain the disinterested image they project of themselves. The high rewards doctors receive is not so much an indication of the value of their work as evidence of power. The decisions they make go far beyond any expertise they have and in fact by treating the individual rather than the environment doctors not only do little to prevent illness but also direct attention from measures which could prove more effective. Consensus does of course occur but this is seen as stemming from the power of this group.

The two approaches have been depicted in an extreme form above. People often don't hold exclusively to one approach, let alone to one approach in an extreme form. Nevertheless people do tend to picture society in a way which approximates closer to one approach than another. Diagramatically the approaches can be visualised as lying in their extreme forms at opposite ends of a continuum: CONSENSUS ←——→ CONFLICT. Most writers cannot be placed at either extreme but are closer to one end than the other.

Although it was not made explicit at the time, we have already encountered the two approaches earlier in chapter 2. For they underly the two theories which attempt to explain why immigrants from the New Commonwealth have met a negative reception in Britain.

The first theory, it will be remembered, laid emphasis on the immigrant status of such people. An implicit assumption of the theory was a picture of the host society as characterised by a fundamental agreement on basic values. Since cultural consensus is deemed necessary, the chief onus is on the immigrants themselves to change. The will allow cultural differences to be minimised and will result in assimilation.

This host-immigrant framework was developed in the United States to account for the assimilation of immigrants into American society. Although the process was not a smooth one, entailing to begin with reliance on an ethnic community as a source of identification and protection, over time individuals were able to enter the wider society and gain mobility within it. Park, whom Bowker and Carrier argue 'was perhaps the first to produce a comprehensive and systematic theory of race relations from the standpoint of modern sociology' (Bowker and Carrier, 1976) generalised from the American experience to argue that 'in the relations of races there is a cycle of events which tends everywhere to repeat itself . . . (and) . . . which takes the form of contacts, competition, accommodation and eventual assimilation . . . (and) . . . is apparently progressive and irreversible' (Park, 1976). A similar picture has been presented by many other writers. One such is Eisenstadt, who, in the course of examining immigration into Israel, concluded that 'the absorption of the immigrants within the social and cultural framework of the new society' was the ultimate outcome of 'every migratory movement' (Eisenstadt, 1976). These writers exemplify a consensus approach and it is this which underlies the host-immigrant framework. Such a framework is criticised, however, by exponents of the second theory to account for the reception of immigrants from the New Commonwealth and Pakistan.

The second theory, it will be remembered, laid emphasis on the status of being black in our society. In contrast to the United States, Britain was pictured as a society divided above all on class lines (Rex and Moore, 1967). Since there are already distinct cultures in Britain, the chief onus is not on the immigrants themselves to change. Indeed, to do so would scarcely result in assimilation since the primary responsibility for the negative reception which they have met lies with the racism of the wider society. Such racism needs to be resisted so that integration becomes possible. Assimilation in this view is neither desirable nor practical. It is not desirable because it may not be sought and it is not practicable because, even when it is sought, the extent of racial prejudice and discrimination prevents its actualisation. Integration is therefore preferred, a status defined by the Home Secretary at the time of the 1968 Race Relations Act, Roy Jenkins, as 'not a flattening process of assimilation but equal opportunities accompanied by cultural diversity in an atmosphere of mutual tolerance' (Cheetham, 1982).

This approach was developed in the United States to account for the situation of black people there. An early exponent was Lloyd Warner (Warner, 1976) who argued that 'the social organisation of the Deep South consists of two different kinds of social stratification': a class system and a caste system. Although there were class differences among both whites and blacks, Warner pointed out that there was a more insurmountable barrier between whites and blacks. This meant that improvements in the economic situation of some blacks did not result in the barrier being breached but in the barrier being tipped diagonally. Diagramatically the situation can be presented as follows:

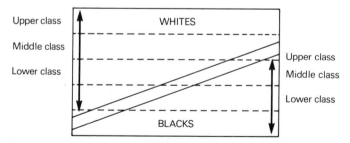

While movement was possible for both whites and blacks up and down the class structure, Warner argued that there was another division between white and black people which prevented any movement. This barrier, which had been almost horizontal at the end of the Civil War, had been tipped up but had not been breached. In attempting to conceptualise it as a caste system, Warner hoped to draw attention to its similarities with the Indian caste system with its taboos on intimate association between castes especially in the field of marriage. The use of this analogy has been heavily criticised however. Three criticisms will suffice. The first points to the fact that in India inequality was accepted while in the United States it was rejected as a central value: 'the Indian system is a coherent social system based on the principle of inequality, while the American 'colour bar' contradicts the egalitarian system within which it occurs and of which it is a kind of disease' (Dumont, 1977). The second accentuates this stress on picturing castes within an overall system, by pointing to the occupational specialisation of castes and the resulting interdependence between them, a feature not present in the United States (Leach, 1976). The third emphasises how, despite the fact that ones racial status in the American South and ones caste position is ascribed at birth, there are nonetheless significant differences. As Cox points out, 'In race relations it is almost always sufficient merely to look at a man to identify him; in caste relations his status must be inquired into' and 'A man could be expelled from his caste and forgotten; he cannot be expelled from his race' (Cox, 1948). In view of these criticisms, it is doubtful whether the concept of caste is of value in analysing black-white relations. Nevertheless, an appreciation of the distinctiveness of the experience of black people in the United States has been maintained in the work of Cox himself and more recently, as we have already seen in chapter 2, in the work of Blauner. These writers exemplify a conflict approach and it is this which underlies the explanation of the negative reception of black people in Britain in terms of white racism.

The consensus and conflict approaches to racial inequality are clearly value laden. For one attributes primary responsibility to the cultural characteristics of the disadvantaged group while the other attributes primary responsibility to the actions of the dominant group or the structure of society as a whole. One thus believes the disadvantaged group itself should change while the other believes the power of the dominant group should be challenged and resources redistributed accordingly. A particularly graphic illustration of the controversial nature of these approaches was the debate generated by the Moynihan Report, a government report on black poverty in the United States (Valentine, 1968).

Moynihan concluded that the fundamental cause of continuing black poverty in the 1960s was the structure of the black family. In his own words, 'Obviously not every instance of social pathology afflicting the Negro community can be traced to the weakness of family structure . . .. Nevertheless at the centre of the tangle of pathology is the weakness of the family structure. Once or twice removed it will be found to be the principle source of most of the aberrant, inadequate or antisocial behaviour that did not establish but now serves to perpetuate the cycle of poverty and deprivation'. According to this view, the black poor have acquired what Oscar Lewis called a 'culture of poverty'.

Distinct beliefs, ideas and values, originally developed as a response to poverty included 'the absence of childhood as a specially prolonged and protected stage in the lifecycle, early initiation into sex, free unions or consensual marriages, a relatively high incidence of abandonment of wives and children, a trend towards female – or mother – centred families (Lewis, 1966). In addition to these family and sexual practises at variance with the wider society, Lewis argued that both the failure to participate in the institutions of the wider society and the existence of a syndrome of attitudes which included a sense of helplessness and a tendency to live purely for the present constituted central features of the culture of poverty. Such a culture emerged among the poor to cope with the difficulties of poverty but, once developed, this distinct culture is passed on to the next generation in the course of socialisation. As a result of the acquisition of such beliefs, ideas and values, the children are incapable of taking advantage of any improved opportunities which may be open to them and poverty persists.

The implication of this line of reasoning, which Moynihan applied to black poverty, is clear. Since it is above all the cultural characteristics, and in particular the family structure of the black poor, which are primarily responsible for their continuing poverty, this culture and family structure need to be changed so that they fit more closely the standard of the wider society.

Needless to say this consensus approach to black poverty has been severely criticised by exponents of the conflict approach, who have pointed out that not only did the report fail to show that female headed families were harmful in the ways indicated, but, by putting the blame on the black family, also helped to justify doing nothing to reduce poverty. Black poverty persists, it is argued, primarily because of continuing disadvantages to which black people are subject. Such writers are sceptical of the view that the poor black has a self perpetuating and distinct culture. Behaviour which apparently contravenes the standards of the wider society is better understood in terms of a failure to fulfil mainstream values than as indicative of an adherence to a distinct set of values. Thus, on the basis of a study of black streetcorner men in a poor area of Washington, Liebow argues that the men's entry into marriage signified their adherence to mainstream values, that the failure of these marriages indicated that the men's income was too little to sustain them and that the justification of such failures on the streetcorner represented an attempt to cover up a sense of inadequacy. In Liebow's terms, 'the streetcorner man does not appear as a carrier of an independent cultural tradition. His behaviour appears not so much as a way of realising the distinctive goals and values of his own subculture . . . but rather as his way of trying to achieve many of the goals and values of the larger society, of failing to do this, and of concealing his failures from others and from himself as best he can' (Liebow, 1976). For proponents of this conflict approach, the alleviation of black poverty demands not a change in black culture but a major redistribution of resources.

In accounting for the persistence of black poverty in the United States it may be quite widely accepted that the consensus approach, which tends to place primary responsibility on the cultural characteristics of the poor, needs at the very least to be complemented by the conflict approach, which tends to place primary responsibility on the structure of society. In other areas of racial disadvantage, however, there is almost a reflex tendency to adopt a consensus approach and see the problem in cultural terms. As Ahmed puts it in the course of discussing social work, 'the most popular trend in diagnosing problems of Asian clients is to seek cultural explanations' (Ahmed, 1981). What is more, these cultural explanations often involve a negative picture of the cultures in question. Thus, in the process of examining the significance of race for health care, attention has been placed on the practise of some Asians in applying 'surma', a cosmetic material, on the eyes of young children, when it has been shown to contribute to lead poisoning, while the tendency of the same people to abstain from tobacco and alcohol has been less frequently commented upon (Davis and Aslam, 1981).

Although there is a tendency for practitioners to take a negative view of different cultures, 'there are of course cultural differences between the indigenous and immigrant populations which can have medical implications' (Cheetham et al., 1981). One example will suffice and concerns differences in the way illness is defined. Rack, a psychiatrist, argues that Asians tend to focus on bodily complaints and identify illnesses in terms of the extent to which they can play their customary roles rather than in terms of mental distress (Rack, 1981). If he is right, it means that the medical practitioner 'needs to be sensitive not only to the differences in prevalence of disease but also to different ways of experiencing and reporting illness if he/she is to avoid misdiagnosis' (Cheetham et al., 1981). For proponents of a consensus approach to medicine then, the cultural distinctiveness of some racial minorities gives rise to problems of communication. So long as practitioners are sensitive enough to cultural differences, however, these problems will be overcome. The primary role for the practitioner in this view is to integrate patients into the Western system of medicine. This objective is best achieved when there is a heightened sensitivity to cultural differences, thus allowing for more effective diagnosis and treatment on the one hand and health education on the other. Such a conception of the medical practitioner's role emerges very clearly in an article earlier cited on the special health care needs of Asians: 'Many of the problems presently confronting us could be overcome by better *communication*. Other problems may require one or two generations to pass before Asian immigrants are totally *integrated* into the Western system of medicine' (Davis and Aslam, 1981; my emphasis).

For proponents of the conflict approach to medicine, the stress on the cultural distinctiveness of racial minorities can obscure the fact that many of the health problems faced by black people stem from the social and economic conditions they confront. Take for example the question of Asian diet, which is seen by Scrivens and Hillier as failing to provide enough Vitamin D. In their own words, this makes Asians 'culturally vulnerable, through their dietary customs to . . . illness' (Scrivens and Hillier, 1982). The implication is that health education programmes should be aimed to encourage Asians to improve their diets and thus prevent their children from contracting rickets in a country with much less sunshine. There is, however, an alternative way of solving the problem of Vitamin D deficiency put forward by advocates of the conflict approach. This is for the government to supplement, as it does already with margarine, a staple element in the Asian diet with Vitamin D. Requests by black organisations to this effect have, however, so far been turned down by the D.H.S.S. and attention instead been directed to health education. Such programmes, it is argued, implicitly blame Asians for the health problems they meet. As one Community Health Council put it, 'White mothers are no better informed than Asian ones about the need for Vitamin D in the diet. Yet all the publicity about the inadequacy of Asian diets creates the impression that Asian mothers do not know how to feed their children properly' (Brent Community Health Council, 1981). For proponents of the conflict approach to medicine then, the arrival of black people in this country has brought to the surface racism and, it is this, above all, which needs to be confronted. This involves not only an attempt to combat racism in ones own practice but also suggests to the practitioner the importance of a new role, working with black organisations on various campaigns to ensure that the special needs of racial minorities are met. We have already mentioned the campaign to persuade the D.H.S.S. to supplement a staple part of the Asian diet with Vitamin

D but there are others which include, for example, attempts to persuade health authorities to put vegetarian diets on hospital menus (Slack, 1981).

Before we move on to look at two further sociological approaches, let us summarize the main differences between the consensus and conflict approaches in tabloid form.

Table 5 Contemporary approaches to race: consensus and conflict

	Consensus	Conflict
Main source	Durkheim	Marx
Image of society	Composed of individuals who share the same fundamental values.	Characterized by groups which have different interests and tend therefore to conflict with each other.
Explanations of racial inequality	Race inequality persists primarily because of the cultural characteristics of the minority group. Thus poverty continues to afflict many black people in the USA mainly because they live in a culture of poverty.	Race inequality persists primarily because of the actions of the dominant group or the structure of society as a whole. Thus poverty continues to afflict many black people in the USA mainly because they are subject to racism and deprivation.
Policy implications	The minority group should change its culture to fit that of the wider society. Thus, minorities should fit into the 'Western' system of medicine.	The power of the dominant group should be challenged and resources redistributed in favour of the minority group. Thus, the 'Western' system of medicine should adjust to meet the needs of minorities.

Contemporary sociological approaches to race: systems and action

If the different assumptions, held by the classical sociologists, about the nature of society lie at the root of the consensus and conflict approaches, the same is true of the different assumptions held about the nature of man. We shall again contrast two conceptions of man. The first emphasises that human beings are a product of society and their behaviour consequently determined by their membership of it. The second emphasises that society is a product of human beings and that what they do is dependent upon the decisions they make. Of the founding fathers, Durkheim tended to accept the first conception and Weber the second conception. We are advised by

Durkheim to 'treat social facts as things'. Human behaviour in this view is on a par with the subject matter of the natural sciences and, as he exemplified in his study of suicide, needs to be explained in the same way. The emphasis here is on the way human beings are dominated by society. We are advised by Weber, on the other hand, to take note of the fact that human beings attribute 'subjective meaning' to their actions. This means that the subject matter of the natural and social sciences is inherently different and that in the latter we need to understand, as Weber did in his Protestant ethic thesis, the reasons which guide people's behaviour. The emphasis here is on the way human behaviour depends on the beliefs people choose to adhere to.

These two conceptions of man, which can be located in the work of Durkheim and Weber, still tend to distinguish sociologists, with some tending to favour a systems approach and others to favour an action approach. Let us examine the two approaches in relation to a specific issue, that of the operation of a social work agency (Open University, 1978) before applying them to the field of race.

The systems approach sees society as comprising a number of systems, with human behaviour being determined by the needs of these systems. A social work agency is one such system, designed in this particular case to fulfil certain welfare goals. The members of this organisation are visualised as role players whose behaviour is determined by particular norms and their position in the hierarchy of command as epitomised in the formal organisational chart. From this point of view, social workers are considered to have little autonomy and to be constrained to operate in particular ways.

The action approach sees human behaviour as guided by the meanings which people give to various phenomena. Instead of seeing a social work agency as designed to fulfil clearly defined objectives, advocates of the action approach visualise it as the outcome of tensions and conflicts between different actors. The latter do not mechanically act out their parts but decide what to do in the light of the meanings they give to their activities and those of others. After all, the goals of the organisation are vague and the norms not so specific that there is no room for different interpretations of how appropriately to play ones role. What is more, situational exigencies often ensure that in the course of human interaction roles are modified so that the receptionist, for example, does not merely perform a clerical function as laid down in the formal organisational chart. It is of course true that some actors are in a more powerful situation than others in the agency to have their meanings upheld, but their power is never total so that meanings are often negotiated in the course of interaction. From this point of view, social workers cannot abrogate all moral responsibility for their actions by claiming that their behaviour is determined by the demands of their role, for ultimately it is they who decide what to do (Berry, 1974).

The two approaches have been depicted in an extreme form above. People often don't hold exclusively to one approach, let alone to one approach in an extreme form, however. Take for example our earlier discussion of the social meaning of race in chapter 1. The significance of race, it was argued, depends on physical differences being defined as significant. The social meaning of race varies from society to society, however, so that it is clearly different, as we saw, in the United States now than in earlier periods and different again in Brazil and South Africa. This means that the social systems do not constrain relations between the races in the same way. While some severely limit opportunities for individuals to act in terms of their own meanings, others provide much greater opportunities for individuals to do this. From this point of view people are neither wholly determined nor wholly free. The extent to which people are constrained and the extent to which people are free varies from social system to social system. Nevertheless, people do tend to picture society in a way which approximates closer to the systems approach or the action approach. Diagramatically the approaches can be visualised as lying in their extreme forms at opposite ends of a continuum: SYSTEMS ⟵⟶ ACTION. Most writers cannot be placed at either extreme but are nonetheless closer to one end than the other.

Take the case of the social services. It has now become increasingly and more widely recognised that the existing provision does not meet the needs of racial minorities. Thus in 1978 the report of the Association of Directors of Social Services concluded 'that the response of social services departments to the existence of multiracial communities has been patchy, piecemeal, and lacking in strategy' (A.D.S.S. and C.R.E. 1981). Because of the pervasiveness of racism (Husband, 1980) and the cultural distinctiveness of some racial minorities (Ballard R., 1979), it has been argued that these groups have special needs. Take for example the question of the fostering and adoption of black children. Some have insisted that racial matching is needed here for three main reasons: 'that it preserves a child's heritage; that white parents are unable, despite their best efforts, to teach black foster and adoptive children to cope with discrimination; that a black child cannot develop a proper sense of identity in a white home' (Cheetham, 1982). Although the evidence pertinent to this issue is not clearcut (Bagley and Young, 1982), there seems little doubt that the needs of racial minorities have in many cases not been met and that existing practises will have in many cases to be modified if they are to be met. Another example concerns the issue of day nursery places. Normally priority is given to children of single parents but in the process the needs of Asian families in which both parents need to work are neglected (Horn, 1982). Instances of this kind suggest to some social workers the utility of adopting what was earlier called a campaigning role. To be able to play such a role presupposes of course an action approach to social work. Proponents of a system approach by contrast argue that the constraints of the social work agency or of systems impinging on the agency do not allow such a choice of roles.

The differences between the two approaches we have just been exploring are brought out in the diagram below.

Table 6   Contemporary approaches to race: systems and action

	Systems	Action
Main source	Durkheim	Weber
Image of human beings	People are the product of society, and their behaviour is therefore determined by membership of it.	Society is the product of people and what the latter do is dependent upon choices.
The meaning of race	People are constrained by the meaning of race, which is prevalent in society.	The meaning of race is negotiable, and people have some choice over how they act toward each other.
The possibility of change	Individuals are constrained to take up particular roles so that the possibilities of combatting racial inequality are limited. Thus, the social worker is obliged to play an integrative role and encourage minority clients to fit into the needs of the 'system'.	Individuals have some freedom which roles to take up so that the possibilities of change are considerable. Thus, the social worker has the option to play a campaigning role and seek changes in the way the 'system' normally operates.

The approaches, which we have distinguished – the consensus and conflict approaches, on the one hand, and the systems and action approaches on the other hand – cannot be compared in such a way that one is deemed true and another false. For they do not themselves constitute theories, but sets of assumptions about the nature of society and the nature of man which give rise to theories. The approaches can, however, be evaluated in terms of their relative usefulness in generating well substantiated and coherent theories.

In order to highlight the fact that adherence to one approach or another is not an all or nothing matter but one of degree, it will be remembered that we earlier presented the approaches diagrammatically in terms of two continua. By placing these continua at right angles to each other, we acquire the following property space and are in a position to locate the major theoretical traditions in sociology (Robertson, 1974):

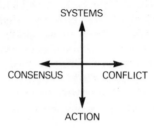

Perspectives on race: functionalism, Marxism and conflict theory

Three theoretical traditions or sociological perspectives are commonly distinguished: functionalism, Marxism and interactionism (Haralambos, 1980, Bilton et al., 1981, O'Donnell, 1981). It is possible, however, to make finer distinctions and, for example, not only subdivide interactionism into two traditions but also depict a separate tradition, conflict theory (Brown, 1979). Of these traditions, three have been particularly influential in the study of race: functionalism, Marxism and conflict theory. In distinguishing them we need to be careful not to imply, however, that these traditions are hermetically sealed off from each other and that sociologists can invariably and unequivocably be placed in one tradition rather than another. The situation is better visualised instead as one in which sociologists tend to work within one tradition rather than another, albeit one which is frequently in debate with others. The purpose of distinguishing three broad traditions at this stage is to provide an aerial map of sociological perspectives on race. These are taken up and applied to particular topics in other chapters. Needless to say, as one moves closer to the ground, distinctions, which can be ignored from above, become more apparent and a more detailed map becomes necessary.

Functionalism is the easiest of the three traditions to locate. With its picture of society as a consensual system, it is located in the top left hand quadrant of the property space (as above). Of the founding fathers, it was Durkheim who tended to espouse this perspective, but the most influential recent exponent of functionalism has been Parsons. The functionalist perspective is based on a biological analogy. Just as the human body consists of a number of interdependent parts which work together to enable the body to survive, so it is argued human society consists of a number of interdependent parts which work together to enable the society to survive. Thus, just as the heart pumps blood around the body and, in doing so, performs a key function for the body, so the institutions which characterise a modern society tend to specialise in meeting different needs and as a result enable the social system to survive. The economy, for example, specialises in meeting the needs of the social system to adapt to its environment, by providing goods and services. It is regulated by the polity, which is primarily concerned with setting goals and sorting out priorities for the system as a whole. These goals are in turn consonant with wider social norms. The law enforces them and, in doing so, helps integrate the different parts of the social system. The norms are themselves dependent on certain common values which the family, the educational system and religion pass on from generation to generation. This is not to say that the social system is static. Indeed the tendency for the parts of the social system to be in some sort of balance means that a disturbance in one part results in corresponding adjustments in others. Over time a process of social evolution has in fact occurred, with distinct institutions emerging in modern society to specialise in different functions.

For Parsons, an agreement on certain values is an integral feature of human society. For not only are the needs of the social system met in line with such common values, but it is these values which underpin the specific norms which govern people's behaviour in the different roles they play. As such, cultural consensus is seen as critical to the maintenance of social order.

We have already met an example of a functionalist perspective on race earlier in this chapter viz. the immigrant-host framework, in which it is assumed that immigrants enter a society characterised by a set of common values. In pointing to such consensus as an integral feature of society, exponents of the immigrant-host framework are adopting a functionalist perspective. According to this perspective, the need for consensus means that a group with different beliefs, ideas and values is generally considered not only strange but also inferior. If this group is in turn distinguishable in terms of its physical characteristics, then racial inequality emerges. Although social inequality is considered to be necessary in order to motivate talented people to acquire the requisite skills and fill the jobs which are most critical to the functioning of society (Bendix and Lipset, 1967), racial inequality is deemed to be 'dysfunctional'. There are two reasons why this form of inequality is thought to lead to problems for the social system. The first arises from the fact that talented individuals from the racial minorities are prevented from filling key jobs so that the system as a whole is inefficient. The second arises from the fact that racial inequality gives rise to conflict so

69

that the system as a whole is disrupted. Functionalists are, however, optimistic that in time measures to further equal opportunities allied to an adherence to a common set of values will result in the erosion of racial inequality (Parsons, 1969).

Marxism is characterised by three central beliefs: a belief that in some sense the economy is of primary importance, that class conflict is consequently central and that ultimately this will result in a more desirable form of society. With its picture of society as conflictual, it is located in the right hand side of the property space previously depicted. In being unwilling to locate it in one of the right hand quadrants as opposed to the other, we are being faithful to Marx's dictum that history is made by men but not under conditions that they choose. Nevertheless there has been throughout the history of Marxism a major tension between those who wished to stress system constraints and those who wished to stress the possibility of action.

A recent example of a Marxist perspective which adopts a systems approach is found in the 'structuralist' position of Althusser and his followers. According to this position, the capitalist mode of production comprises three levels – the economic, the political and the ideological. Although the economy is 'determinant in the last instance', the political and the ideological are not mere reflections of the economy, but have 'relative autonomy'. This means that they are visualised as having effects on the economy and in particular are seen as playing a key role in maintaining fundamental economic relations. Thus the state is concerned generally with the 'reproduction of the relations of production' while ideology is concerned particularly with ensuring that people are socialised appropriately and thus fill their allotted places in the relations of production (Althusser, 1971). Such a position constitutes an extreme systems approach. For it views actors merely as occupants of positions and occupants at that who have so imbibed the dominant ideology that they automatically carry out their roles. Needless to say this position has been severely criticised by Marxists who tend to adopt an action approach (Thompson, 1978).

The tension within Marxism between the systems and action approaches is exemplified in different approaches to the study of race. For those who take a structuralist position, the function of the state is to 'reproduce the relations of production'. In acting on behalf of capital to maintain the rate of profit, the state has thus dominated other countries, contributed to their underdevelopment and encouraged sections of their population to migrate and play a subordinate role in the host society (Sivanandan, 1982). Whether state personnel have intended it or not, the consequences of such state policies have entailed racialism and a corresponding racism. For those who are more sympathetic to an action approach, however, state policies cannot be seen as ineluctably determined in this way by the needs of capital but are the outcome of choices (Ben-Tovim and Gabriel, 1982). An example of a somewhat conspiratorial form of this approach can be found in the work of Cox. For Cox, prejudice is defined as 'a social attitude propagated among the public by an exploiting class for the purpose of stigmatising some group inferior so that the exploitation of either the group or its resources or both may be justified' (Cox, 1948). According to this view, prejudice is used by the bourgeoisie to justify exploitation and to fragment the proletariat. Racialism and racism are fully intended.

Despite the fact that there is a tension within the Marxist perspective on race between systems and action approaches, there is general agreement that a Marxist analysis 'begins with the concepts of capitalism and class' (Phizacklea and Miles, 1980). An example which starts there 'and then proceeds by introducing the concept of migrant labour' has been developed to account for the entry and reception of black people in Britain since the Second World War (Phizacklea and Miles, 1980).

The expansionist nature of capitalism led it to seek out new sources of profit throughout the world. One form such a search took was that of colonialism which entailed the conquest of noncapitalist countries. The exploitation of the colonies fostered Britain's economic development but at the same time disturbed their development. In this situation, sections of the population turned to migration to improve their economic situation. While a negative image of black people predated this period of colonialism, such an image was reinforced by the experience and ideas pointing to their inherent inferiority taken up and used to justify further colonialism so that by the end of the nineteenth century 'racism . . . had a circulation throughout the class structure of Britain' (Miles, 1982b). When therefore migrants from what were now ex-colonies responded to the demand for labour after the Second World War and chose Britain as their destination, they were confronted by racism. Such ideas have been taken up by sections of the working class who wanted a simple explanation for the material decline of their areas. This has meant that, despite the fact there was little competition for jobs, because the migrants were taking up jobs being vacated by whites, a further source of division within the working class has opened up.

Although such an analysis does recognise that people who have been categorised as belonging to a particular race are seriously disadvantaged, we are urged to move beyond 'the way in which the social world appears immediately to the observer' to 'the essential relations which, in turn, can be used to explain why the social world appears as it does' (Miles, 1982a). These relations are of course the relations of production and thereby class relations. The implication of such an analysis seems to be that 'racial' disadvantage can only be solved as a result of a unified working class creating a revolution and inaugurating a society in which there are different relations of production.

The final theoretical tradition we need to turn to is that of conflict theory. According to this perspective, society consists of a number of groups who, in the course of pursuing their interests, come into conflict. The form this conflict takes depends on a number of factors, but a key factor is the relative power of the groups involved (Rex, 1981a). Although this perspective, like Marxism, takes a conflict approach to society and does therefore owe something to Marx, it tends to differ from Marxism in two important respects: firstly, in its insistence that the culture and state of a society can be as significant as the economy in generating conflict and secondly, in its advocacy of an action approach. Both of these points are emphasised by Weber and it is this stress which is echoed by the proponents of conflict theory who, being sceptical of the distinction drawn in the Marxist account between appearance and reality, are more willing to recognise the possibility of racial and ethnic conflicts being as significant as class conflicts. This readiness to accept the actors' definitions means that conflict theory tends to be located in the bottom right hand quadrant of the property space earlier depicted.

Although conflict theory does differ from Marxism, it is more clearly opposed to functionalism. We have already in fact noted some differences earlier in this chapter when we contrasted consensus and conflict approaches to, for example, the immigration of black people into Britain. The conflict approach, it will be remembered, believes 'that it is misleading to assume that immigrants enter[ed] a homogeneous society based on consensus . . . immigrants entered a society in which conflict between indigenous groups was endemic, because goods and services were unequally distributed' (Sherman and Wood, 1982). Conflict theory is similarly opposed to functionalism over the question of the origins of racial inequality. Rather than pointing to the tendency of people who belong to one group to see other groups as strange and inferior as the explanation for the emergence of racial inequality, conflict theorists stress instead differences in power between groups in situations in which one group can benefit by subordinating another. A recent analysis which sees inequality as generated by competition in this way has been put forward by Parkin in 1979. Groups who benefit from existing inequalities in power and advantage, he argues, seek to maximise their rewards by restricting access to resources and opportunities to a limited circle. In short, they attempt to use their power to promote their own interests at the expense of others. Which attributes are used as criteria for exclusion varies from society to society, being dependent to a large extent on the policies of the state. In a capitalist society, the two main devices generally used to restrict access to resources and opportunities are the ownership of property and the possession of educational qualifications. The beneficiaries of these exclusionary devices comprise the dominant class but are opposed by those who do not benefit from existing inequalities in power and advantage and wish to win for themselves greater resources and opportunities. While such class conflict is a normal feature of capitalist society, it is not necessarily the most significant form of conflict. For other characteristics can serve as criteria for restricting benefits to a particular section of the community. One such characteristic is skin colour. Its use as an exclusionary device means that there can be significant racial conflict which cuts across class and in an extreme case, such as that in South Africa, can mean that it is the dominant form of conflict.

Summary

Where does this leave us then? While the first three chapters attempted to spell out the perspective on human behaviour which sociologists share, this chapter has focused on differences among sociologists: the different analyses of modern society put forward by the classical sociologists; the different assumptions about the nature of society and the nature of man held by sociologists; and the different theoretical traditions still found among them. In pointing to the way, say, functionalism, Marxism and conflict theory raise different questions, highlight different facets of society in their explanations and put forward different policies, there is a danger, however, of implying that they have equal value. This implication is not intended. Indeed in the following chapters, explanations suggested by these broad perspectives will be compared and contrasted in terms of both their internal coherence and their correspondence to the facts.

The major differences between the theoretical perspectives which we have been exploring are summarized in the table overleaf.

Guide to reading

C. H. Brown, *Understanding Society* constitutes a brief and clear introduction to sociological theory, distinguishing usefully five theoretical traditions. Of the recent textbooks, M. Haralambos, *Sociology Themes and Perspectives* is the most systematic in examining the contribution of the major traditions to different topics, but

Table 7 Three theoretical perspectives on race

	Functionalism	Marxism	Conflict theory
Main source	Durkheim	Marx	Weber
Perspective on Society	Society consists of interdependent parts which work together to enable society to survive, with each institution functioning to meet society's needs in line with common values.	Class conflict is the most fundamental feature of society, and this will ultimately result in a more desirable form of society.	Society consists of several groups which, in the course of pursuing their interests, tend to come into conflict. Whether racial or some other form of conflict is more significant varies from society to society.
Explanation of racial inequality	The need for consensus means that people with a different culture are seen as strange and inferior. If they are in addition seen as physically distinct, racial inequality emerges.	Whatever the origins of race inequality, its persistence is due to the fact that it benefits the dominant class.	Groups invariably seek to promote their interests at the expense of others and restrict benefits to a limited circle. If the exclusion of people of a different skin colour helps to maximize a group's rewards, race inequality results.
Future of race inequality	Race inequality does not fulfil important functions and will gradually disappear as individuals are increasingly judged by their achievements.	Since race inequality benefits the dominant class, it will only disappear when the working class has abolished capitalism.	Race inequality will persist unless attempts are made to combat it directly.

unfortunately neglects race. There are, however, two useful readers in this area. J. Stone, *Race, Ethnicity and Social Change*, part 1 contains material on the contribution of both classical sociologists and more recent writers, while G. Bowker & J. Carrier, *Race and Ethnic Relations*, part 1 includes further articles on these more recent approaches. Of the three theoretical traditions on race distinguished in this chapter, functionalism has been so severely attacked that the major disputants now comprise Marxism and conflict theory. A useful comparison of these two perspectives on race can be found in a unit written for the Open University by J. Allen, notably *Social Science: a foundation course, D102*, Unit 11 and two recent examples in R. Miles, *Racism and Migrant Labour*, chapter 7 and F. Parkin, *Marxism and Class Theory*, chapters 3–6. Those interested in relating different approaches and perspectives on race to social work and medicine will find the two readers edited by J. Cheetham useful, viz. J. Cheetham et al. (ed), *Social and Community Work in a Multiracial Society*, and J. Cheetham (ed), *Social Work and Ethnicity*.

Discussion points

1. While we were examining the different assumptions about the nature of society and the nature of man, did you find yourself tending to favour one set of assumptions rather than another? Using 'race' as an example, how would you try to defend your assumptions to other people who do not share them?
2. Taking an issue not examined in this chapter, say, the process of socialisation, how do you think the different approaches would examine it? What about the different theoretical traditions?
3. What are the implications of the different sociological approaches and perspectives for social policy in the field of race relations? What do you think can be done to combat racial inequality?
4. With specific reference to the social and community services, in what sense do you think that the racial minorities have special needs? To what extent do these derive from their cultural distinctiveness or from racism? Do you find that the beliefs you hold about minority cultures tend to be negative? How well substantiated are these beliefs? Why do you think the needs of the racial minorities are not being met? What are the arguments for and against (a) the view that the provision of services should ignore people's race and ethnicity and (b) the view that the needs of racial minorities require special treatment and provision? Is it, in your view, politically possible to take race and ethnicity more into account? Is this desirable? What would it involve?
5. Why do you think the functionalist perspective on race and ethnicity has become less popular among sociologists? How would you try to choose between Marxism and conflict theory as perspectives on race and ethnicity?

5

Race and employment

In the first chapter we pointed out that, although black people have been resident in Britain since Elizabethan times, the vast majority of the present black population stems from immigration since the Second World War. They initially came in response to Britain's labour shortage to fill job vacancies and have remained a small but increasing proportion of the labour force. Already by 1971, of the 6% or so of economically active people who had been born or both of whose parents had been born outside the United Kingdom, those from the New Commonwealth comprised a third, slightly outnumbering those from Ireland. Because a far higher proportion of blacks are below retiring age, black people are more likely to be economically active than white people with the result that their growth as a proportion of the labour force is likely to have continued (Runnymede Trust, 1980). In the second and third chapters, we noted, however, that the reception black people have met has been a primarily negative one, involving extensive discrimination and prejudice. The question therefore arises as to the consequences of such discrimination and prejudice for their employment. This is a particularly pressing question because employment is a crucial determinant of life chances and in relation to black people is seen by the Home Affairs Select Committee to be 'the most important immediate cause that limits their chances in life' (Home Affairs Committee, 1980).

Because occupation is such a central influence on people's life chances, it has frequently been used as an indicator of social class. Indeed in some cases social class has been defined in terms of occupation, for example, as 'a grouping of people into categories on the basis of occupation' (Reid, 1980). Classifying people in this way into social classes enables one to distinguish people in terms of their economic position and thus to highlight inequalities between people. A major concern of sociologists, however, has been to show how those who share a common economic position tend to constitute a distinct social grouping. Here too, however, occupation has often been seen as important. Thus for those, like Halsey, who follow Weber in seeing key groupings arising from the way rewards are distributed, 'the anatomy of class is displayed in the occupational structure' (Halsey, 1978) so that classes comprise 'those occupational groups and their families which share similar ... market situations.' In this particular case, three major classes are distinguished: a class comprising 'professional, managerial and administrative occupational groups,' an intermediate and 'heterogeneous' class and, finally, a class consisting of manual workers. For those who follow Marx in seeing the major groupings arising from people's relationship to the means of production, what is significant above all is whether one owns and controls the means of production or not. Nevertheless, with the realisation that the anticipated polarisation between the bourgeoisie and proletariat has not happened, occupation has even here sometimes been used as a proxy for class. In the case of Westergaard and Resler, three classes are distinguished: a class comprising 'directors, managers, high officials and members of the established professions,' 'an intermediate cluster' and 'the broad mass of ordinary earners' (Westergaard and Resler, 1975). Although debates continue both within and between the two major traditions of class theory, the picture each presents of the class structure is often, as in the examples above, not dissimilar.

Underclass or working class?

For writers who take a conflict approach and see British society as characterised by class divisions, the entry of black people into the United Kingdom presents a challenge. How do racial divisions relate to the pre-existing class divisions? How do the racial minorities fit into the indigenous class structure? Three major theses have been put forward: the 'unitary working class thesis,' the 'divided working class thesis' and the 'underclass thesis' (Miles, 1982b).

According to the first thesis, black people are an integral part of the working class. They are manual wage earners and, as such, suffer the same disadvantages as other manual wage earners. Racial discrimination may intensify these disadvantages but, overriding any special disabilities, is a common class position. This is the traditional Marxist position but it has also been put forward by conflict theorists. We shall not, however, elaborate on this thesis since it is clearly 'contradicted by the available evidence' which indicates that the thesis underplays the significance of racial discrimination (Miles, 1982b). Let us therefore turn to the other two theses, beginning with the most widely held one.

The underclass thesis argues that racial discrimination is so extensive that black people occupy the most disadvantaged positions in society, being concentrated at the bottom of the economic order.

Although they share some disadvantages with other manual wage earners, their subordinate position is distinctive enough to warrant the label 'underclass', a class beneath the working class. This position has been put forward by Marxists (Sivanandan, 1982) but we shall focus here on the arguments which have been put forward for the thesis by conflict theorists.

Two main lines of argument have been put forward to suggest that black people form an underclass. The first starts off from a recognition of the significance of racism in British society. The existence of widespread prejudice means that black people tend to have, in Weber's terms, low status. As a result they meet severe discrimination and find themselves 'heavily concentrated amongst the lowest paid occupations, or . . . chronically unemployed or semi-employed' (Giddens, 1973). Evidence which supports this line of argument comes from a local study in Nottingham which points to the continuing significance of racial discrimination since the last Race Relations Act. Here the authors emphasise in particular how managers and employers still tend 'to reject black applicants for higher status jobs with promotion prospects' (Hubbuck and Carter, 1980).

The second line of argument which has been put forward to suggest that black people form an underclass stresses that the disadvantaged positions which black people have filled existed before they took them. It starts off therefore from an appreciation of the way the economy generates a particular kind of occupational structure. Such a starting point tends to play down the significance of racism in the formation of an underclass but is not incompatible with an appreciation of its role in accounting for the way racial minorities comprise an underclass.

For the main proponents of this second line of argument, a major and developing feature of Western economies has been the emergence of what has become known as a 'dual labour market.' Such economies are increasingly divided into two sectors: a monopoly sector in which the occupations which characterise the primary market are to be found and a competitive sector in which the occupations which characterise the secondary market are to be found.

The monopoly sector consists of large firms and organisations with the following characteristics: they are technologically advanced, capital intensive and bureaucratically organised. The workers, who are highly unionised, enjoy the advantages which pertain to occupations within the primary market. They receive relatively high economic returns, security of employment and some chances of promotion. The latter is consequent upon the emergence in such firms and organisations of internal labour markets, whereby the low level jobs are filled from outside but the remainder are filled by promotion from within.

In contrast to the monopoly sector, where companies have a degree of control over the markets they are operating in, the competitive sector consists of small firms and organisations, operating in competitive markets, and with the following characteristics: they are technologically backward, labour intensive and lack a bureaucratic form of organisation. The workers, who tend not to be unionised, incur the disadvantages which accrue to occupations within the secondary market. They receive a low rate of economic return, little job security and few chances of promotion.

The concept of a dual labour market emerged in the United States to account for 'a measured disparity between the earnings of white male workers on the one hand and of female or black workers on the other' (Morgan and Hooper, 1982). White male workers, it was argued, were predominantly located in the primary market, while female and black workers were mainly found in the secondary market.

Explanations for the emergence of such a dual labour market have, however, differed. Some have emphasised how technological developments within the monopoly sector necessitate a stable labour force. The specialised and costly nature of the machinery in this sector demand an experienced workforce, a demand which is met by developing an internal labour market. Firms within the competitive sector, by contrast, who operate in a fluctuating market require a disposable labour force. While firms in the first sector look then for stable employees, firms in the second sector look for 'unstable employees', in particular women and black people. If some writers highlight the role of technology in generating a dual labour market, others have emphasised instead the control exerted by employers or workers. Those who point to employer control argue that managers in the monopoly sector have developed internal labour markets as part of a strategy to bribe and divide a potentially unified workforce, while managers in the competitive sector have continued to rely on coercive means of control. Women and black people predominate in the latter sector because of their allegedly weaker work orientations. Those who prefer to stress the power of white male workers suggest on the other hand that employers are constrained to discriminate against women and black people as a result of union pressure. The dual labour market is not in the interests of employers, who prefer to hire labour as cheaply as possible, but is foisted upon them by white male workers.

Although there is disagreement as to whether the dual labour market emerged because of technological demands, employer strategies of control or union pressure, it is argued that the result is a stratified labour market, with black people and women disadvantaged in relation to white men. As yet, however, the dual market theorists 'have produced very little hard data to support their arguments, which are really interesting hypotheses rather than established fact' (Blackburn and Mann, 1979). Despite this, the notion of dual labour market has been taken up by some theorists in order to account for the apparent fragmentation of the working class in West European societies.

One of the earliest users of the notion was that of Giddens, who suggested that the division between the primary and secondary markets could be found within firms. The growth of planning, which Western European economies have witnessed, necessitates a stable labour force which can be relied upon. Firms have therefore attempted to gain the loyalty of the workers considered to be central to their plans by extending to them the advantages of the primary market. This has inevitably entailed increased labour costs so that at the same time they have attempted to create a secondary market characterised by a pool of cheap and disposable labour. Such positions, it is argued, have tended to be filled in Britain by women (Barron and Norris, 1976) and racial minorities (Rex and Tomlinson, 1979). In being so reliant on immigrants to take up these secondary occupations, Britain has not been exceptional. For North Western Europe has witnessed, since the Second World War, a massive migration of labour from underdeveloped regions, such that by the 1970s, the migrants taken together would comprise the seventh largest nation in Europe (Berger and Mohr, 1975). As Giddens puts it, 'In many contemporary European societies, the lack of an indigenous ethnic minority leads to a 'transient' underclass (which turns out to be not so transient after all) being imported from outside' (Giddens, 1973). Such a situation has proved acceptable to the indigenous working class, enabling them to move into more desirable occupations at the expense of people considered to be inferior.

Evidence which supports the argument that the development of a dual labour market in Britain has led to the formation of a black underclass comes from a local study in Handsworth, Birmingham. Here, the authors argue, 'immigrants are employed predominantly in less attractive industries and in less rewarding jobs.' Hence it is that both the West Indians and Asians tend to suffer a higher rate of unemployment, work longer hours often involving shifts, receive lower than average earnings and are offered fewer chances of promotion, relative to white workers. While it is accepted that Handsworth 'is relatively speaking a lower-class area for any group . . . there is a greater preponderance in each ethnic group here of unskilled and semi-skilled manual workers.' The authors conclude that the evidence which they have produced supports the dual labour market thesis, being 'consistent with the notion of two kinds of job situations with whites predominant in one and blacks in the other' (Rex and Tomlinson, 1979). As a result, it is argued, black people constitute an underclass at work. Since their interests are to some extent at odds with the more advantaged working class, they may respond to their disadvantaged situation in a different way. Indeed this is more than likely because their disadvantages at work are matched by disadvantages in housing and in the education system. With the formation of an underclass across all these sectors, the likelihood of black people operating 'as a separate class or an underclass in British society' is increased.

Although the two lines of argument, which we have outlined, do differ in their emphases, with one stressing the centrality of racism and the other the centrality of a dual labour market, both converge in seeing the situation of black people as one which is most usefully conceptualised as that of an underclass, filling those occupations with the most disadvantaged market situations.

While the underclass thesis is the most widely held account of the class situation of black people in Britain, some Marxist writers have put forward an alternative thesis. The divided working class thesis argues that the situation of black people can only be understood in the context of the need of advanced capitalist societies after the Second World War for 'migrant labour'. Migrants from underdeveloped areas of Southern Europe and the Third World have entered Western European societies to undertake the most undesirable jobs, which has resulted in a new source of division within the working class. Let us turn to the work of the most well known exponents of this thesis.

Castles and Kosack argue that the attempts by capitalist regimes since the Second World War to promote economic growth and achieve full employment have made it increasingly difficult to maintain a 'reserve army of labour.' The latter, however, is crucial if wages are to be kept down and profits up, and so a reserve army had to be found. With the drying up of internal sources, migrants from underdeveloped regions outside Western Europe began filling this function, being imported during an economic boom and being obliged to return home during a recession. In the process, these workers have fulfilled important functions for capitalism. Economically, their concentration in unskilled work has kept wages down and profits up. Socially, 'immigration has brought about a split in the working class of Western Europe' (Castles and Kosack, 1973). Like other workers, they do not own or control the means of production and are therefore members of the working class with the same long term interests, but they are not spread across the working class. Rather, they 'form the lowest stratum of the working class carrying out unskilled and semi-skilled work in those industrial sectors with the worst working conditions and/or the lowest pay' (Castles and

81

Kosack, 1981). Their disadvantageous position both at work and outside is unlikely to be eradicated since it is not in the interests of the ruling class to eradicate discrimination and provide adequate educational opportunities when 'this would remove the supply of cheap unskilled labour which is at present so profitable' (Castles and Kosack, 1973). The persistence of two distinct strata within the working class, with the indigenous workers in a more favourable position than immigrant workers, means that their short term interests diverge. The indigenous workers often feel themselves to be superior and exhibit prejudice towards the immigrants (most of whom on the Continent are white), a process which the ruling class deliberately encourages. 'The result is that class consciousness is weakened, and tends to be replaced by a sectional consciousness, based on real and apparent conflicts of interest between the two strata within the working class' (Castles and Kosack, 1973). Politically, this decline in class consciousness reduces the strength of the working class. In addition, the denial in many instances of political rights to immigrants means that they are inhibited from taking action to improve their situation. This weakens the class as a whole.

The suggestion that migrants constitute a distinct part of the working class has been taken up more recently and applied to the position of black migrants in Britain. Economic growth in Western Europe after the Second World War led to shortages of labour in certain sectors of the economy, which were met by migrant labour. Such migration did not, however, bring about a split in the working class of Western Europe because, as the authors point out, 'the working class was not, prior to the migration of labour, first united and then divided by its arrival' (Phizacklea and Miles, 1980). Migration instead entailed a new division within the working class. Rather than see the working class as divided into two strata, it is preferable, therefore, to see it as comprising a number of fractions. From this view 'migrant labour constitutes a distinct fraction of the working class.' It occupies a specific economic position being 'not only concentrated within the manual working class, but in semi- and unskilled sections of the working class' with 'a parallel position in the housing market.' In addition to its inferior economic position, migrant labour has a subordinate political position, with few rights, its subordination being justified ideologically. Although it is recognised that the situation facing migrant labour on the continent is not identical with that facing labour in Britain, it is argued that the latter does constitute a distinct fraction of the working class.

Economically, black migrants in Britain 'are concentrated within the manual working class and, compared with all workers, concentrated within the semi- and unskilled sections of the working class.'

Politically, and, despite the fact that their rights exceed those of their colleagues on the Continent, in practise they are in a subordinate position. The subordinate position they occupy is in turn justified through the propagation of racist ideologies.

Although there are differences between the positions of Castles and Kosack, on the one hand, and Phizacklea and Miles, on the other hand, they agree that black people, like their counterparts on the Continent, were initially a form of migrant labour. They constitute a distinct section of the working class and, as such, may respond to their subordinate position in a distinct way.

How different are the two theses which we have been examining? Miles argues that they are 'mutually exclusive' (Miles, 1982b). In doing so however, he underplays the similarities between the two theses. Although they do of course differ over the factors which they choose to highlight as primarily responsible for the situation of black people, the difference tends to be one of emphasis.

Take, for example, the two factors which are seen as critical to the formation of an underclass by proponents of the first thesis, viz. racism and the emergence of a dual labour market. Miles not only accepts their importance but also attempts to incorporate them into his own account of the class position of black people. Although he ultimately prefers the second thesis and thus conceptualises the position of black people as a fraction of the working class, he (and Phizacklea) point(s) to similar differences between black and indigenous workers to those highlighted by proponents of the underclass thesis. The differences between the two theses do not therefore seem to be in the substantive conclusions which they reach. Thus, in the field of employment, there is agreement that black workers are employed in predominantly nonskilled work, that they are locked into such work with few chances of escape and that this tends to segregate them from the indigenous workforce. The disadvantages faced by black workers are thus stressed by the proponents of both theses, as is the possibility of such disadvantages leading to distinct forms of consciousness and action. Whether to label the position of black people in terms of an underclass or a fraction/stratum of the working class depends ultimately on ones preferred definition of class (Moore, 1977).

The extent of racial disadvantage in employment in Britain

In order to assess whether black workers are employed in predominantly nonskilled work, with few chances of improvement and segregated from the white workforce, as the two theses suggest, we need to examine the empirical evidence. Let us take each of these three points in turn. To begin with, then, are black workers employed in predominantly nonskilled work?

The most recent and comprehensive evidence from a national survey is the PEP survey of racial minorities in 1974, in which 'all those who were economically active (that is working, looking for a job or registered as unemployed) and who had had a job at some time since coming to Britain, were classified according to the level of their present job, if working, or their last job, if unemployed' (Smith, 1976). In the following table, the job levels of men from five ethnic groups are compared. For each ethnic group, the proportion of men at each job level is as follows:

Table 8   Job level analysed by country of origin – men

Men in job market who have worked	White	West Indian	Pakistani/ Bangladeshi	Indian	African Asian
Job level	%	%	%	%	%
Professional/ Management	23	2	4	8	10
White collar	17	6	4	12	20
Skilled manual	42	59	33	44	44
Semi-skilled manual	12	23	38	27	24
Unskilled manual	6	9	20	9	2
Unclassified	1	1	1		

Source: Smith, 1977

A comparison of the job levels of whites and racial minorities indicates that the job levels of the latter tend to be skewed towards lower levels so that they all tend to be underrepresented in non-manual jobs, especially the higher ones, and overrepresented in manual jobs, especially the lower ones. 'The job levels of Asian and West Indian men are,' in short, Smith points out 'substantially lower than those of white men.' Their concentration in manual work stems partly from their newness to the country – in particular the fact that they tend to have lower qualifications and, in the case of some Asians, an inadequate command of English – but it also reflects racial discrimination. Hence it is that qualifications tend to bring racial minorities a lower rate of return than white people, so that whereas 79% of the latter with qualifications to degree standard are in high level nonmanual jobs, only 31% of minority men with similar qualifications are in such jobs. To point to the lower job levels of black men is not to say, however, that racial minorities are all in the same position. Smith goes on, 'The gap between Pakistanis and whites is the widest, West Indians come next, followed by Indians, while the gap between African Asians and whites is comparatively small' (Smith, 1977).

But do the figures confirm that black workers are to be found predominantly in non-skilled work? If we add together the proportions in semi- and unskilled work, for each racial minority what do we find? 32% of West Indian men, 58% of Pakistani/Bangladeshi men, 36% of Indian men and 26% of African Asian men are found in this kind of work. Compared to the 18% of white men in this kind of work, each of the racial minorities is overrepresented at this level, but in only one case – that of the Pakistani/Bangladeshis – are a majority of men in such jobs. Westergaard and Resler's conclusion on the basis of an analysis of the 1966 sample census still seems to be true: 'Migrants from Pakistan apart, in short, the majority of men from the coloured Commonwealth were in jobs classified as skilled, or in some form of nonmanual work' (Westergaard and Resler, 1975). Indeed it is likely that Smith's survey overstates the proportion of men in each ethnic group in nonskilled work. For the national sample was selected in such a way that it was representative of 76% of the British population who belong to one of the four ethnic groups (West Indian, Pakistani/Bangladeshi, Asian and African Asian) we have been looking at. The 24% who had to be excluded for practical reasons because they lived in districts where they formed a very small proportion of the population, Smith points out, are less likely to have an occupational distribution so skewed towards the lower levels. If he is correct, in suggesting that his sample understates the proportion of Asian men in middle class occupations and West Indian men in skilled working class occupations (Smith, 1976), then the conclusion that black workers are not in predominantly non-skilled work is reinforced even further.

Once it is accepted that both the underclass thesis and the divided working class thesis have heavily overstated the concentration of black immigrants in nonskilled work, then it follows that they are not overwhelmingly locked into such work. But has the situation deteriorated over time so that they are now more likely to find themselves in such work?

The most obvious source of information is the national Census which takes place every 10 years. Over the period we are interested in, a Census was conducted in 1961, 1966 when there was a 10% sample Census, 1971 and 1981. Unfortunately the information we need to compare the situation of racial minorities over time is not fully available. In 1961, 1966 and 1981 the only information collected, which was relevant to placing people into different ethnic groups, related to people's country of birth. This means, however, that, especially in the earlier years, those who were classified as Indians or Pakistanis included a high proportion of white people who had been born in the Indian subcontinent. In the case of the most recent Census, in which after much heated debate it was decided not to include an ethnic question, there is the added problem that those who are classified as belonging to particular ethnic groups will exclude many of those who see themselves as belonging to such groups but have been born in Britain (Bulmer, 1980). This leaves us with only one Census in which the information collected gives us a reasonably accurate estimate of the numbers belonging to different ethnic groups. But if collecting information on people's parents' country of birth in 1971 provides us with a more accurate picture, the inaccuracy of other years 'means that only broad trends can legitimately be identified' (Field et al., 1981). With this caveat in mind, three tables are presented over on the job levels of men from different ethnic groups in order to identify broad trends. The first two, which are derived from the 1966 and 1971 Censuses, show, for each ethnic group, the proportion of men at each job level in Britain as a whole. The third, which is derived from the large scale National Dwelling and Housing Survey in 1977 (and was carried out for the Department of the Environment following the cancellation for economic reasons of the 1976 Census) shows, for each ethnic group, the proportion of men at each job level in England. Information on the groups to which people belonged was derived by asking each household directly, rather than by making inferences from their country of origin.

The tables tend to confirm the conclusions we reached earlier on the basis of the survey of racial minorities in 1974. In each of the three years, 1966, 1971 and 1977, the job levels of the racial minorities tend to be lower than the rest of the population, with the Pakistani/Bangladeshis in the worst position followed by the West Indians and finally the Indians. The position of the latter in fact is not markedly different from that of the population as a whole. Indeed in 1966, its position was superior. This is probably attributable, however, to the fact that this category includes a large proportion of white people who may have been disproportionately represented in the higher level jobs. The Indians aside, the job levels of the racial minorities are substantially lower in each of these years. Nevertheless we again find that it is only among the Pakistani/Bangladeshi men that a majority are employed in nonskilled work so that our previous criticism of the view that black workers are predominantly employed in nonskilled work is confirmed. But has the situation deteriorated over time?

Table 9   Job level analysed by country of origin and ethnic group – men 1966, 1971, 1977

1966

Job level	West Indies	Country of birth India	Pakistan	Great Britain
Professional/ Management	2.2	17.7	5.9	15.4
White collar	5.8	19.4	5.7	17.5
Skilled manual	42.2	28.3	22.2	40.3
Semi-skilled manual	27.6	22.9	34.9	18.3
Unskilled manual	22.2	11.7	31.3	8.5

1971

Job level	West Indies	Country of birth India	Pakistan	Great Britain
Professional/ Management	2.7	15.9	7.0	18.0
White collar	7.6	15.2	5.1	18.1
Skilled manual	45.1	32.1	25.2	39.7
Semi-skilled manual	27.2	23.9	38.1	16.0
Unskilled manual	17.3	12.9	24.6	8.3

1977

Job level	West Indies	Ethnic origin India	Pakistan/ Bangladesh	White
Professional/ Management	3.6	19.4	8.5	22.2
White collar	8.0	14.9	5.9	18.5
Skilled manual	50.1	34.7	31.2	39.9
Semi-skilled manual	25.5	20.8	38.0	13.7
Unskilled manual	12.9	10.1	16.4	5.7

Source: Field et al., 1981

If we take the West Indians and Pakistani/Bangladeshis, we can see an improvement in their overall employment situation over the period. In the case of the West Indians the proportion of nonmanual workers increased from 8% to 10.3% to 11.6% and the proportion of higher level nonmanual workers from 2.2% to 2.7% to 3.6%. As far as manual work is concerned, the proportion of skilled workers rose over the period and the nonskilled fell. In the case of the Pakistani/ Bangladeshis, the same situation pertains with the proportion of nonmanual workers increasing from 11.6% to 12.1% to 14.4% and the proportion of higher level nonmanual workers from 5.9% to 7% to 8.5%. As far as manual work is concerned, the proportion of skilled workers rose over the period and the nonskilled fell. When we turn to the Indians we find an apparent move in the opposite direction between 1966 and 1971 which is probably, as we pointed out above, a result of there being a high proportion of white Indians in high level positions at the beginning of the period. Between 1971 and 1977, however, we find much the same overall improvement as we did with the other two minorities.

Since 1966, the composition of the minority labour force has changed so that the overall improvement in the job levels of West Indians and Asians indicates not only the fact that some individuals have gained promotion but also the effects of new people taking up jobs. Of particular importance here is immigration since 1966 and young people reaching working age. The former is likely to have led to improved job levels for men from the racial minorities because the immigration legislation from the 1960s has put a premium on skill, making it extremely diffiicult for those who do not have special skills, or are dependents, to enter the country. Whether young people reaching working age are being employed in higher level jobs than their parents is too early to say, but on the basis of an analysis of the 1971 Census of the occupational distribution of West Indians born in Britain and abroad, Lomas and Monck point to 'some progression up the job "ladder"' (Lomas and Monck, 1977).

The improvements we have been talking about have been shared by white people as well so that although there has been 'some progress towards socio-economic parity with the majority . . . the gap is still wide' (Field et al., 1981), especially for the Pakistani/ Bangladeshis and West Indians. Field et al., after examining the period from 1961 to 1981, sum up the position well, 'The twenty years . . . show, therefore, important absolute advances in the employment . . . conditions of West Indians and Asians . . . but . . . the amount of relative progress has been small' (Field et al., 1981). If the improvements have not been as substantial as one would like, at least the situation has not deteriorated in such a way that the racial minorities find themselves increasingly in nonskilled work.

To question the notion put forward by both the underclass thesis and the divided working class thesis that black workers are predominantly locked into nonskilled work means of course that they are not, as the dual labour market theory claims, segregated in such secondary occupations. Nevertheless it could be that the occupational classification that we have relied upon, and is used in the

Census, is so crude that it camouflages key differences between occupations which are grouped together. Perhaps many of the jobs which are grouped together as skilled manual are in reality no different from those classified as semi- or unskilled? Perhaps a finer occupation classification would indicate significant segregation?

That the black and white workers are not in an identical situation, even when classed as being at the same job level, becomes clear when average earnings are compared for workers at each job level. The PEP survey of racial minorities indicates that, except for nonskilled workers, the earnings of minorities are lower and that this discrepancy increases the higher the level of the job.

Table 10 Earnings analysed by job level – white and minority men

Median gross weekly earnings	Professional/ Management	White collar	Skilled manual	Semi-skilled manual	Unskilled manual
White men	£53.50	£41.70	£38.10	£34.40	£29.70
Minority men	£46.20	£36.10	£37.50	£35.90	£33.70

Source: Smith, 1977

Indeed the difference in earnings between the two groups is more marked than the table indicates. People's earnings tend to be at their lowest either when they are young or when they are old. Because the proportion of old workers in particular is so much smaller among the minorities than the whites, the differences are therefore understated. When only those aged 25–45 are compared, we find that 'white men at the higher job levels earn substantially more than minority men at the same levels; at the middle levels, the difference is smaller, but still marked; at the lowest job levels, minority and white men earn the same' (Smith, 1977). To maintain even these income levels, however, minority workers have to undertake substantially more shift work than white men. Thus in 1974, 31% of minority men were working shifts compared with 15% of whites (Smith, 1976).

That minority workers often have to work in undesirable conditions for their money is borne out by a very detailed study of the labour market for male manual workers in Peterborough. The study examined not only workers who are classified as 'semi-' and 'unskilled' but also the 'skilled', excluding in fact from the sample only the minority of 'skilled' workers who need a formal apprenticeship for their job. But despite the inclusion of many who are classified as 'skilled', the authors argue that most manual work is so unchallenging that workers exhibit more skill driving to and from work than at work itself. What is the situation of minorities here?

Since the majority of immigrants in Peterborough are not from the New Commonwealth and Pakistan, Blackburn and Mann do not specifically focus on racial minorities. Nevertheless they point out that 'immigrants must work harder, either for longer hours or on piecework, in order to reach the same wage' (Blackburn and Mann, 1979). Although their average earnings may be higher than those born in Britain, this is at a cost. Blackburn and Mann, after examining the intrinsic nature of the jobs undertaken by the white immigrants, conclude 'that immigrants have worse jobs: they expend more effort but use fewer manual and mental skills, they are less autonomous in their work, and their working conditions are more unpleasant.'

The fact that there are average differences in earnings and other rewards for workers at the same job level confirms our earlier suspicion that workers classified together are not in an identical situation. Indeed the differences we have pointed to show that within each job level, racial minorities tend to be disadvantaged. The differences do not, however, show 'actual segregation between the jobs and job rewards' of black and white workers. National studies have not pointed to a 'high concentration' of black workers in particular occupations and have indicated that the 'overlap between the two groups is considerable.' Blackburn and Mann's own local study looks at the situation of immigrants more generally, but concludes that 'the majority of immigrants are sharing jobs with the nativeborn' and that 'although immigrants receive less on average, their conditions overlap very considerably with those of native British workers.' Nevertheless they did discover a 'minority of just under a third (and just over a third in the case of the coloured Asians) are occupying clearly segregated low level jobs.' An obvious example of such segregation would be the employment of Pakistanis and Bangladeshis on permanent night shifts in the textile industry (Allen et al., 1977). While a finer occupational classification does allow us to note some segregation, it cannot be said that racial minorities are overwhelmingly segregated from other workers at work.

Where does this leave us then? The underclass thesis and the divided working class thesis argue that black workers are engaged predominantly in nonskilled work, with few chances of improvement and segregated from the white workforce. Each of these points we have questioned on the basis of an examination of the evidence. In the case of only one of the racial minorities is even a majority of men engaged in non-skilled work. There have in fact been improvements over time in the job levels of black workers. On the whole black workers work alongside white workers. In short the evidence we have produced fails to corroborate the two theses.

So far we have examined only male workers. This has been because the two theses, which we have been assessing, believe that women generally tend to constitute part of an underclass or a stratum/fraction of the working class. To explore possible differences in the employment situation of black and white women is therefore not as pertinent to an assessment of the thesis. Nevertheless the economic activity of black women is of critical importance to the life chances of the racial minorities and needs therefore to be investigated.

When we look at the economic activity of minority women, two phenomena stand out. The first is the much higher proportion of West Indian and Asian women workers who are employed full time compared with white women workers. A major reason for this difference is undoubtedly the fact that black women are more likely to come from low income households and therefore have more economic need to work full time. The second phenomenon, which stands out, is the way the racial minorities have varying rates of economic activity. In 1974, for example, while 43% of women generally were economically active, at one extreme stood the West Indians where 74% were active, while at the other extreme stood Moslem Asians, where 17% were active; non Moslem Asians lay between them with 45% active (Smith, 1977). How do we explain these differences? Two sets of factors can be distinguished. The first relates to people's relative newness to the society. West Indian women tended to arrive in this country much earlier than Pakistani/Bangladeshi women, many of whom are Moslems. The latter have in most cases only followed their husbands to Britain relatively recently and have thus not only had less time to build up job contacts but also often have an inadequate grasp of English (Smith, 1976). In this context, it is perhaps not so surprising that the activity rate of Moslem Asians is so much lower than that of the West Indians. Also of key importance, however, to an understanding of these differences is a second set of factors, which relate to people's cultures. Many Moslems in Britain observe purdah. Adherence to a system which maintains a distance between men and women clearly restricts the possibility of economic activity outside the home (Saifullah-Khan, 1976) and thus goes some way to explaining their relatively low rate of activity. At the same time it ought to be pointed out that the official figure may understate the real activity, when account is taken, for example, of homeworking (Allen, 1982a). In relation to the high rate of activity of West Indians, note needs to be taken of the fact that they are 'highly motivated to achieve a degree of financial independence and their conception of 'motherhood' entails an economic aspect' (Phizacklea, 1982).

What kind of jobs then does the economic activity of the racial minorities lead to? The most recent and comprehensive evidence from a national survey again comes from the PEP survey of racial minorities in 1974. In the following table, the job levels of women from four rather than five ethnic groups are compared, since the number of Pakistani/Bangladeshi women workers was too small to warrant separate analysis. For each ethnic group, the proportion of women at each job level is as follows:

Table 11   Job level analysed by country of origin – women

Women in job market who have worked	White %	West Indian %	Indian %	African Asian %
Job Level				
Professional/ Management	5	1	2	2
White collar	50	41	26	38
Skilled manual	16	8	14	12
Semi-skilled manual	24	41	49	41
Unskilled manual	5	6	9	7
Unclassified		3	1	

Source: Smith, 1976

A comparison of the job levels of whites and racial minorities indicates that the job levels of the latter tend to be skewed towards lower levels so that they all tend to be underrepresented in non-manual jobs and overrepresented in manual jobs, especially the lower ones. Thus, in contrast to the situation among white women, a majority of the women in each racial minority are in manual work. Their relative newness to the country partially accounts for this, but recognition also needs to be taken of racial discrimination. Hence it is that black girls can leave school with similar qualifications but end up in inferior jobs to white girls (Allen and Smith, 1975).

Although the job levels of minority women are 'distinctly lower than for white women . . . the differences are less striking than they were in the case of men' (Smith, 1977). Moreover, 'the earnings of minority and white women are much the same' even when 'separate comparisons' are 'made for women in nonmanual and for those in manual jobs.' How do we account for these less striking differences between minorities and whites among women than men? Smith suggests that 'for those who already suffer the disadvantage . . . of being women, there is little scope for racial disadvantage to have a further, additive, effect.'

The role of women in our society still tends to be a primarily domestic one so that women are frequently viewed as actual or potential wives and mothers. Although they constitute a large proportion of the labour force, their work outside the home is often considered secondary and they are, therefore, expected to fit it around the requirements of their primary role (Phizacklea, 1982). The result is considerable occupational segregation, with women heavily over-represented in poorly rewarded low level jobs. In this context, there is indeed less 'room for racial discrimination to have an additional impact' so that it is not surprising to discover that the PEP survey of racial minorities indicated that 'women seem to face less discrimination than men in the more junior jobs in which they have traditionally worked' (Smith, 1977). Nevertheless, racial discrimination does have some additional impact so that, as we have seen in our comparison of job levels of black and white women, 'in general, race interacts with gender further to depress occupational status' (Webb, 1982).

Where does this leave us then? We have pointed to significant racial disadvantage in employment which, in the case of minority women, reinforces the effects of sexual disadvantage. The disadvantage is not, we have argued, so extensive that black people constitute an under-class or a subordinate stratum/fraction of the working class but it is nevertheless clear that black people do face special problems and that a common class position with white workers does not invariably override the special disabilities they face. If these three theses, which we distinguished earlier, are not corroborated, how are we to concept-ualise the relation between race and class? One possibility is to see two forms of inequality at work, with black people facing a series of disadvantages within the class they belong to. Take, for example, the class to which most black people belong—the working class. In this case the minorities share some disadvantages with their white colleagues but in addition face further disadvantages. Thus while members of the working class have a higher risk of unemployment than those in the middle class, black members are especially vulner-able, in particular at times of rapidly rising unemployment.

While total unemployment increased between 1972 and 1981 by 138%, black unemployment increased by 325%. In short 'the relative position of black workers deteriorated progressively through the 1970s' (Rhodes and Braham, 1981) with the result that the population of the unemployed who were black jumped from 2.4% in 1972 to 4.0% in 1981. How do we account for the fact that black people face a higher risk of unemployment? There are two broad reasons. The first revolves around the fact that they are overrepresented in those categories which are most at risk. They are, for example, now overrepresented among the young and in particular school leavers and thus share the higher risk to unemployment the young and in particular school leavers generally face. Most importantly, they are overrepresented, as we have already seen, in semi- and unskilled manual work. People who are employed in such work are much more liable to be made redundant than others so that black semi- and unskilled workers share a common liability with their white colleagues. For Smith in fact this is the major reason for the deterioration in the relative position of black workers. As he puts it, 'the extra risk of being unemployed that arises from being an Asian or West Indian is small compared with the extra risk from being an unskilled manual worker rather than a senior manager or university professor' (Smith, 1981). Nevertheless, being black does make a difference, as he recognizes, and constitutes the second reason for the higher risk of unemployment met by black people. Evidence of its importance can be found in the National Dwelling and Housing survey which investigated the characteristics of the unemployed in ten English cities. In seven of them, comprising roughly 10% of the black population in England, ethnic origin did not seem to have any bearing on unemployment, but in three towns (London, Birmingham and Leicester), which accounted for 56% of the black population in England, it did. As Barber put it, 'taking account of skill and age, the proportion of economically active men (and in London, women) of minority ethnic origin who were unemployed were generally significantly higher overall than those for people of white ethnic origin' (Barber, 1980).

On the basis of a national survey conducted in 1968–69, Townsend indicates that, among the racial minorities, 'there was some suggestion from our limited numbers that more were living in income units in poverty, or on its margins' (Townsend, 1979). The survey was conducted at a time when 'the rate of unemployment among black workers – at about 2½% – was roughly equivalent to their numbers in the total workforce' (Rhodes and Braham, 1981). Since black workers are still overrepresented in low paying occupations and still have to support a higher than average number of dependents, the greater risk of unemployment they now face is likely to have contributed to an even 'higher prevalence of poverty amongst ethnic minorities than amongst whites' (Field et al., 1981) and meant that race is increasingly 'a powerful indicator of poverty in our society' (Edmonds, 1982). The rise in unemployment threatens, in short, to wipe out the gains made by racial minorities.

To argue, as we have done, that black people in Britain are disadvantaged but not so extensively that we are entitled to conceptualise their situation as one of an underclass or a subordinate stratum/fraction of the working class, is not to say that migrants generally in Western Europe are not appropriately conceptualised in either of these ways. How does their situation in fact compare with that of black immigrants in Britain?

The position of migrant labour in Europe

To begin with, one must note the context within which the migration took place. It has been numerically a very significant migration. As Braham puts it, 'migration into the industrialised countries of Western Europe from the less developed countries of Southern Europe, and even further afield, has become the largest mass migration since the USA ended unrestricted immigration' (Braham, 1975) and has meant that 'by 1970 there were about eleven million immigrant workers and their dependents in the industrialised countries of North-West Europe' (Open University, 1980). The migrants came to fill the 'less desirable' jobs which had been vacated by indigenous workers during the economic boom after the Second World War. The recruitment of foreign labour was not the only possible option open to Western Europe governments faced by labour shortages but, according to Böhning, it seemed 'the easiest way out' (Böhning, 1981). The alternatives of coaxing indigenous workers back into undesirable jobs by paying higher wages or coercing them back by creating unemployment seemed unacceptable. Since the economic boom was not expected to last and the labour shortages were thought therefore to be temporary, migrant labour recommended itself as a cheap solution to a short term problem. Bilateral agreements were therefore made with other countries and agencies set up in these countries to recruit labour. This meant that particularly in West Germany and Switzerland, 'migration was: by permit only; for specific jobs; for specific periods, and without any right to bring dependants' (Braham, Rhodes and Pearn, 1981). Whether the countries exporting labour have gained from these agreements is debatable, but at least migration does relieve their unemployment problems and provide through the remittances sent back by the migrants an added source of income. What is clear, however, is the fact that migration has brought advantages to the countries which have imported labour. Castles and Kosack argue that the migrants' occupancy of nonskilled jobs contributed to keeping wages down in these jobs. This helped in turn to boost profits, encourage investment and thus promote economic growth. Britain's relatively poorer economic performance than other countries is, in this context, seen to be a consequence of the fact that 'the migration to the UK from the New Commonwealth was matched by a migration from the UK to the Old Commonwealth so that the total labour force did not expand to the extent that was evident in Germany, France or Switzerland' (Braham, Rhodes and Pearn, 1981).

What kind of reception have the migrants generally met then? They have on the whole been confronted, like the immigrants from the New Commonwealth and Pakistan, with prejudice and discrimination. Their pattern of employment, however, has been even more

95

restricted than immigrants in the UK. Thus, a study comparing the situation in Britain, France and Germany pointed out that, in the case of the latter two countries, 'foreign workers are disproportionately concentrated in the manufacturing industry sector,' especially 'the metal manufacture and construction industries' and that the proportion of foreign manual workers in semi- and unskilled manual occupations was as high as 'eight out of ten in Germany and seven out of ten in France' (O'Muircheartaigh and Rees, 1976). In these two countries, migrants are indeed concentrated in nonskilled work as the following table adapted from Castles and Kosack indicates:

Table 12   Job level of immigrant workers analysed by country

Job level	France (1967) Both sexes %	Germany (1968) Men %	Germany (1968) Women
Nonmanual	6.3	8.0	12.0
Skilled manual	25.2	20.0	3.0
Semi-skilled manual	36.6	36.0	30.0
Unskilled manual	31.9	34.0	53.0
Unclassified		2.0	2.0

Source: Giner and Salcedo, 1978

While there are enormous problems in comparing the employment situation across different societies, so that the figures from different sources don't always concur, we can still discover the broad similarities and differences between the employment patterns in Britain as opposed to France and Germany. What is apparent is that 'the economic position of migrant/immigrant workers in Britain has been less unfavourable than in France and Germany' (O'Muircheartaigh and Rees, 1976).

Two main reasons can be put forward for the more favourable employment situation of black immigrants in Britain. The first is because immigrants in Britain were needed in a wider range of occupations. Allen and Smith put this point well, 'Black workers fulfilled two sorts of manpower requirements. During the period 1952 to 1965, the need for a mobile labour force to fill jobs at low levels of skill, status and rewards in particular industries was partially met by the use of migrants from Asia and the Caribbean. Throughout this period and continuing to the present, highly skilled and professional workers in certain categories have come from Asia and the West Indies to meet specific shortfalls in manpower' (Allen and Smith, 1974). What is more, successive immigration legislation since 1962 has meant that more recent immigrant workers from the New Commonwealth and Pakistan have been more likely to be accepted if they have special skills or qualifications. Since a high proportion of Asians who were forced to leave East Africa were also highly skilled, there has not, as elsewhere, been a tendency to recruit predominantly unskilled workers in Britain. The second major reason for the more advantageous occupational position of black immigrants in Britain is 'the much more favourable civil status of Commonwealth migrants to Britain as against migrant workers in France and Germany' (O'Muircheartaigh and Rees, 1976). Until the 1962 Immigration Act, immigrants from the New Commonwealth were free to seek work in Britain, settle with their families and enjoy the same political rights as the indigenous population. Although legislation since then has eradicated this right so that most new workers, who migrate from the New Commonwealth and Pakistan, are now subject to control by work permit, the vast majority of black immigrants were 'not restricted in terms of types of work or ability to bring in dependants and settle' (Braham, Rhodes and Pearn, 1981). The situation in other North European countries was often very different. Thus migrants who had been recruited for a specific period and for a specific job found that 'at the end of a contract, if not before, [they] could be expelled to their own countries, strengthening employer control in the workplace and adding a new tool of economic regulation – reducing unemployment by exporting it.' An instance of this occurred in West Germany in the minor recession of 1966–67, when 'some 30 per cent of the non German immigrant workforce, 400 000 workers, were obliged to return home' (Rhodes and Braham, 1981). Here 'the role of the foreign labour force as an "industrial reserve army" is quite clear' (Giner and Salcedo, 1978).

We must be careful, however, not to exaggerate the differences between the situation in Britain and elsewhere in Northern Europe. For there has been a certain convergence between them. On the one hand, since 1971, Britain has had a 'contract labour system' not dissimilar to that found on the continent. It is true that Britain has not had much need to use the system during a period of rising unemployment but its development has brought it closer to the European system. On the other hand, there has been increasing evidence that the transition from temporary migrant to permanent settler, which happened earlier in Britain, is now being replayed on the continent. Böhning points to two reasons for migrants becoming immigrants. The first arises from the fact that the indigenous population continues to refuse to undertake the undesirable jobs even at a time of high unemployment so that 'over here foreign workers become a more and more indispensible part of the labour force' (Böhning, 1981). The second arises from the fact that 'the migrant absorbs at least superficially some of the norms and values of the host society' with the result that he continually puts off returning home. The opportunity of becoming an immigrant is made possible not only by the fact that workers are needed to fill the less desirable jobs but also because governments find it difficult to resist the desire of migrants to stay 'given the context of interstate relations and a desire to maintain the semblance of open, tolerant and democratic societies' (Braham, Rhodes and Pearn, 1981).

Despite a degree of convergence in the situation of migrant/immigrant labour in Britain and the rest of Europe, the notion of an underclass or subordinate stratum/fraction of the working class, which we previously rejected as inappropriate to describe the situation of black people in Britain, does seem to have some applicability to the situation of migrants in Europe. For, after all, they are predominantly located in nonskilled work with relatively few political rights.

Summary

In the course of this chapter, we have distinguished three accounts of the class situation of black people in Britain: the unitary working class thesis, the divided working class thesis and the underclass thesis. The first is easily disposed with. A cursory examination of the evidence indicates that racial disadvantage is too significant to assume that a common class position will invariably outweigh disadvantages specific to black people. We must be careful, however, not to infer therefore that racial disadvantage is so extensive that the minorities are condemned to occupy nonskilled jobs, segregated from the indigenous workforce and with few chances of escape. Although advocates of the second and third theses present some plausible arguments which lead us to expect such an outcome, the evidence indicates that this has not happened. Migrant workers elsewhere in Europe are more appropriately characterised as forming a subordinate stratum/fraction of the working class or underclass than black people in Britain.

Guide to reading

In a series of units for the Open University, P. Braham has presented useful overviews of the employment situation of black immigrants in Britain, in the wider context of migrant labour in Europe.

Particularly pertinent are the following: *An Introduction to Sociology*, D207, Unit 14 and *Ethnic Minorities and Community Relations*, E354, Block 1 and 4. A useful and complementary set of readings is P. Braham, E. Rhodes and M. Pearn (ed), *Discrimination and Disadvantage in Employment*. Examples of the two major theses examined in this chapter are J. Rex and S. Tomlinson, *Colonial Immigrants in a British City*, especially chapters 1 and 4, which argues that black people constitute an underclass and R. Miles, *Racism and Migrant Labour*, especially chapter 7, which argues that black people constitute a fraction of the working class. Systematic evidence on the employment situation of racial minorities can be found in D. Smith, *Racial Disadvantage in Britain*, Part 2 and S. Field et al., *Ethnic Minorities in Britain: a study of trends in their position since 1961*, chapter 4. S. Castles and G. Kosack, *Immigrant Workers and Class Structure in Western Europe* constitutes a useful source of information on the situation in Europe generally.

Discussion points

1. What similarities and differences can you detect between the accounts of the class situation of black people examined in this chapter? Do you agree that the evidence tends to contradict these theses? What doubts can be raised about this evidence?
2. How would you characterise the class situation of racial minorities? Do they share the same class situation? What do you understand by 'class' here? Is your position closer to that of Marxism or conflict theory?
3. How clarifying do you find the dual labour market thesis? Is it helpful in explaining the employment situation faced by women and migrant workers in Europe?
4. Examine critically any study, eg. the one by Castles and Kosack, looked at in this chapter.
5. What do you consider the likely future of the employment pattern of black people to be? What are the key factors upon which your anticipated outcome depends? How possible do you think it is to ensure that progress is made? What do you anticipate the response of racial minorities will be, if racial disadvantage persists? What can employers/unions/government do to eradicate such disadvantage? Are policies, which are designed to combat disadvantage generally, more feasible and desirable than those aimed at racial disadvantage specifically? How effective do you think these policies are likely to be?

6

Race and housing

The immigrants from the New Commonwealth who came to Britain
in the 1950s and 60s settled in areas where there was a demand for
labour. This has meant that while black people form only a small
proportion of the population as a whole, 'in certain regions, cities and
wards there are visible concentrations' (Runnymede Trust, 1980).
Thus most of the racial minorities are living in the South East and
West Midlands and within each region are concentrated in the conur-
bations. In 1971, for example, while only 36.6% of the population as a
whole were living in such areas, as many as 76.7% of West Indians and
61.5% of Asians were living there (Runnymede Trust, 1980). If
smaller areas are distinguished, greater concentration is apparent so
that 'within each conurbation area, they are concentrated in particular towns or local authority areas; within the local authority
areas they are concentrated in a few wards, usually the central ones
having a mainly nineteenth century housing stock, and even within
wards they are concentrated in particular streets' (Smith, 1977).

Although the indigenous population may pay overriding attention
to the colour of the racial minorities, the latter have not necessarily
settled in the same areas. Rather, 'migrants who share a common
background in the homeland tend to settle together in Britain'
(Banton, 1972). Thus in Yorkshire and Humberside, for example, are
to be found 30% of Pakistani/Bangladeshis but only 4% of West
Indians, 11% of Indians and 5% of African Asians (Smith, 1977).

These differences in settlement patterns are not so surprising when
it is recognised that the movement to Britain of Indians, Pakistanis
and, to a lesser extent, West Indians has taken the form of 'chain
migration', whereby 'a man from a particular village in, say, Gujarat,
settles in Britain and then brings kinsmen, friends and the friends of
friends from the home district to his new place of residence' (Banton,
1972). Such a process of migration has meant that many of the South
Asian and, to a lesser extent, West Indian settlements have passed
through 'distinct phases of development'. Using the Sikhs as their
prime example, the Ballards have pointed to four such phases.

The first phase was a pioneering one, in the course of which some
ex-seamen began to settle. This led to the establishment of extremely

small settlements, between the wars, composed of people who were able to act as a 'bridgehead' for later arrivals. The second phase developed after the Second World War. It involved a 'mass migration' of male workers to fill the job vacancies which had arisen because of Britain's labour shortage. This was a period of extreme austerity in which the migrants, oriented to their villages of origin, were anxious to maximise their income so that they could return home as quickly as possible. During this phase, 'most of the workers lived in densely packed all-male households in inner-city areas' (Ballard and Ballard, 1977). Such extreme austerity could not last, however, so that 'as the migrants' social relationships in Britain intensified and as viable ethnic colonies emerged, it became increasingly attractive for a man to consider bringing over his wife and children'. The third phase was therefore 'marked by the large-scale entry of wives and children, a move to less crowded housing conditions and a general consolidation of the ethnic settlement'. Cheap houses were bought and more money spent on them as the migrants began to orient themselves less to their villages of origin and more to other settlers. With the re-establishment in Britain of traditional institutions and the proliferation of businesses, this period therefore witnessed further development in the creation of a distinct 'social world' and inaugurated the fourth phase, characterised by the emergence of a second generation.

A key feature, which distinguishes the second and third phases of development, is housing, the central concern of this chapter. In order to see how the housing situation of racial minorities has changed, we shall take as our case study the city of Birmingham which 'has the largest black population outside London' (Ward, 1978). Our reason for choosing Birmingham is that it has been the subject of two major studies concerned with race: *'Race, Community and Conflict'* (Rex and Moore, 1967), probably 'the most widely read book on race relations within a British context' (Eldridge, 1980) and *'Colonial Immigrants in a British City'* (Rex and Tomlinson, 1979). Both books are written from a particular sociological perspective. In order to clarify the distinctiveness of this perspective, we shall therefore briefly contrast it with two others.

Perspectives on the urban social structure

The three sociological perspectives, which we distinguished in chapter 4, have been applied to the urban social structure. Let us take an example of each in turn, beginning with functionalism. This tradition is exemplified in the work of Park and his colleagues at the University of Chicago, who, between the wars, put forward 'the first comprehensive urban social theory' (Saunders, 1981). The 'ecological approach', which Park et al. applied to the city, was based on an elaborate analogy with biology. Similar processes which had brought about the orderly distribution and adaptation of plants and animals operated in the case of human beings. Thus, competition between individuals led to a division of labour between them and their distribution to environments to which they were best suited. The tendency for human communities to remain in such a state of balance is disturbed, however, by new competitors who invade particular areas and, if better adapted to their environment, succeed the present incumbants as the dominant group. With the completion of this process, a new state of balance is reached and social order is strengthened by the development of a distinctively human phenomenon, a shared culture.

How then is the ecological approach applied specifically to the city? For Burgess, the city can be pictured as comprising five concentric zones, with the central business district surrounded by four further zones. Moving outwards, these comprise a zone in transition, a zone of working men's houses, a residential zone and a commuters' zone. The city expanded as a result of the invasion by each zone of the adjacent outer zone. The result of this is that different groups are located in different parts of the city according to their suitability. Although there is a tendency for the city to move towards a state of balance, Burgess recognizes that the inner city area around the central business district is characterised by extensive mobility as existing inhabitants seek to leave and are replaced by new migrants (Park et al., 1925).

This picture of the city as comprising a number of zones, each characterised by different kinds of housing and different kinds of life style, has, as we shall see later, been applied to Birmingham. Two criticisms have, however, been made of the ecological approach. Firstly, the explanation put forward for the emergence of these zones is too mechanical with the result that human beings are seen as determined by forces outside their control rather than as active agents. Secondly, the notion that human communities tend to move towards a state of balance underestimates the way inequalities continue to generate conflict. In view of these criticisms, let us therefore turn to the Marxist tradition and the work of a writer who has recently been extremely influential, Castells.

For Castells, the urban system can only be understood in the context of the capitalist system as a whole. The specific function it performs is 'the reproduction of labour power'. The maintenance of a capable and healthy work force demands, however, the 'consumption' of services such as housing and education which individual firms find increasingly unprofitable to provide. The local state, which is under pressure from the working class, steps in therefore to provide these services. Although this promotes the long term interests of the dominant class, it is an extremely expensive undertaking. The gap between its expenditure and revenues widens until the local state is forced to cut back its expenditure. The basic problems which led to state intervention in the first place emerge again but this time the state itself is seen as responsible. In this situation, it is possible that 'urban social movements' will develop. Here urban struggles against the state are brought together under the wing of a radical political movement. The significance of such a development is that it unites manual workers with other classes, extends the class struggle into the sphere of consumption and thus brings closer the transformation of society (Castells, 1977).

Although Castells' work has generated a great deal of interest, it has also been subject to severe criticism. Two will be mentioned. The first concerns Castells' picture of human beings. Like other 'structuralist' Marxists he does not examine the way actors define their situation and thus tends to portray their actions as determined by their position in the wider system. Thus the state is conceptualised as necessarily promoting the long term interests of the dominant class so that the possibility of other classes' interests being served at the expense of those of the dominant class is discounted. The second concerns the paucity of evidence supporting Castells' theory of, for example, urban movements. Thus, in Britain the empirical evidence indicates that urban struggles have remained 'fragmented, isolated, localised and limited' (Saunders, 1981).

Let us finally turn to the tradition which has been the most prevalent sociological perspective on the city in Britain, conflict theory (Elliott and McCrone, 1982). According to this tradition, urban resources and facilities are distributed unequally with the result that conflict is a normal feature of the city. In order to understand how resources are allocated, we are urged to focus our attention on the actions of estate agents, local government officers and others who manage urban resources. Although it is recognised that such 'urban managers' do operate under organisational and other constraints, those who work for the state are not pictured as necessarily promoting the interests of the dominant class. Conflicts which arise over the distribution of urban resources do not therefore invariably coincide with class conflicts generated at work (Pahl, 1975).

Of the three sociological perspectives on the city which we have briefly outlined – functionalism, Marxism and conflict theory – it is the latter which underlies the two studies on Birmingham. The main author has in fact been a major exponent of conflict theory, emphasising in particular the central importance of the distribution of housing for an understanding of conflicts in the city. According to

Rex, people's life chances are affected not only by their position in the labour market but also by their access to scarce and desirable housing. Since the opportunity to acquire such housing does not depend purely on occupation, conflicts which arise over the distribution of housing do not therefore necessarily coincide with class conflicts generated at work. To highlight the centrality of struggles over housing, Rex draws on the work of Weber to argue that people who have access to different kinds of housing belong to distinct 'housing classes' which often come into conflict with each other. This 'theory of housing classes' (Rex, 1968) underlies Rex and Moore's study of Birmingham in which it is argued that 'there is a class struggle over the use of houses and that this class struggle is the central process of the city as a social unit' (Rex and Moore, 1967). Let us then turn to this study.

The case of Birmingham

For Rex and Moore, the picture of the city put forward by Burgess is broadly applicable to Birmingham. Thus it is that the housing map of the city indicates the existence of an inner ring, comprising the central business district and a zone of transition, surrounded by three further rings. Each ring is characterised by different kinds of housing and the pursuit by its residents of different life styles. The inner ring developed during the nineteenth century and comprised a mixture of the old town houses of the upper class, the red bricked terraced cottages of the working class and the larger terraced properties of the middle class. With the move of the upper and upper middle classes in the early part of the twentieth century into the inner suburbs, the 'great urban game of leapfrog' began. The lower middle and upper working classes, aided by mortgages, leapt beyond them to the second ring to live in semi-detached houses and the established working class, with the accession to power in the city of the Labour party, later moved to the third ring to rent houses on the newly built council estates. And this isn't the end of the game. For since then, many of the wealthy have jumped beyond this to move into the green belt outside the city limits.

What about those who are left in the inner ring? For Rex and Moore, these groups are the ones who have failed in the competition for the more desirable kind of housing. It is here in the 'zone of transition' or 'twilight zone' that black immigrants are to be found. Their income is not considered to be large enough or secure enough to warrant a mortgage so that one route to suburbia is cut off. In addition, they find themselves, because of a five year residence qualification, not entitled to council housing so that the other route to suburbia is also cut off. Constrained to live in the inner ring and confronted by racial discrimination, the immigrants, whom Rex and Moore studied in Sparkbrook, find that in order to house themselves they have to buy the houses once occupied by the middle class. Since this involves borrowing money from diverse sources at high rates of interest, as many tenants as possible are needed to finance the venture. The spread of such multi-occupation means that the most important conflicts in the twilight zone are between the landlords and tenants of the lodging houses on the one hand and the two other major housing classes in the zone on the other hand: the owners and tenants of the remaining non slum houses still in single family occupation and the tenants of the slum houses awaiting demolition. The former see the spread of multi-occupation as still further lowering the status of the area and the latter see the lodging house population as misusing high standard housing which they have unfairly acquired. The hostility of these two groups is in turn reinforced by the actions of the local authority which, while unwilling to provide alternative housing for those who live in lodgings, acts against the landlords of these houses because the facilities are frequently below accepted standards. As Rex and Moore put it, 'The city, having failed to deal with its own housing problems turns on those upon whom it relies to make alternative provision, and punishes them for its own failure'. The result is that those who live in the lodging houses become scapegoats for the inadequacies of the housing system.

Although the conflict between different housing classes is considered to be the 'central process of the city', Rex and Moore recognise that the organisations to be found in Sparkbrook are not purely based on housing classes. While the immigrants often live in a lodging house with other ethnic minorities and are therefore united by a common housing situation in conflict with other housing classes, they also belong to distinct 'immigrant colonies'. These colonies and the organisations to which they give rise perform three major and closely related functions for people who are trying to adjust to a new society. 'The first of these is the overcoming of social isolation. The second is the affirmation of values and beliefs. The third is the performance of some kind of pastoral and social work function' (Rex, 1973). As such the colony constitutues a necessary 'springboard' for the immigrants' participation in the wider society. Whether the colony will in fact act as a springboard to full participation depends to a large extent on the reception people meet when they leave the colony. If, for example, they are confronted by discrimination, there is a tendency for them to withdraw into the colony. Rex and Moore are not very optimistic. Although they note the emergence of some community wide organisations which transcend the limits of colonies and housing classes, they believe that on the whole the effect of the urban encounter has been to exacerbate whatever tendencies to conflict were present between ethnic groups.

How has the housing situation of the racial minorities changed since Rex and Moore's study of Sparkbrook in 1964? On the basis of a study conducted twelve years later, Rex points out that 'Sparkbrook, was not – as we later found – the real typical inner city phenomenon. It represented one phase of the inner city's development which was particularly important as single men flooded in to beat the ban on immigration which was imposed in 1962. It still exists and it still has that lodging house complex. The more typical phenomenon is that which exists in the four wards which are collectively known as Handsworth' (Rex, 1978). What then is the situation there?

'The settlement of New Commonwealth immigrants has largely taken the form of a horseshoe-shaped belt around the city centre' (Ratcliffe, 1981). Along this belt, Handsworth constitutes one of the main areas of immigrant settlement. While the four wards were a largely white working-class area in 1951, 'by 1961 two of them were marked by the presence of a significant West Indian minority, while by 1971 West Indians and Asians were present in almost equal numbers' (Rex and Tomlinson, 1979). Numerically, this has meant a significant amount of concentration, so that, while the racial minorities comprised 9.1% of the city population in 1971, they constituted much higher proportions of the population of the four wards known as Handsworth: 32.5% of Handsworth ward, 16.6% of Newtown ward, 20% of Sandwell ward and 48% of Soho ward. These figures clearly show that it is inappropriate to talk of Handsworth as a 'black ghetto'. Nevertheless, they indicate that the area now 'has not one population but three' (Rex and Tomlinson, 1979). The three populations are the white, frequently elderly residents, the West Indians and Asians.

What is most noticeable when one examines the different forms of housing tenure of these populations, is the extent of owner occupation among the racial minorities. Rex and Moore's earlier claim that 'the number of immigrants who succeed in entering the class of owner-occupiers is small' (Rex and Moore, 1967) is no longer true. The continuing expansion of owner occupation, not least in an area of high owner occupation like Handsworth, coupled with the contraction of the private rented sector only go part of the way towards accounting for the differences in the housing situation of minorities between Sparkbrook in 1964 and Handsworth in 1976. For 'estimates show that only half of the British sample own their property as against two-thirds of the West Indians and four out of every five Asians' (Ratcliffe, 1981). What is more, a much higher proportion of the lower social classes among the minorities are owner occupiers than among whites and, in the case of the Asians, a very high propor-tion own their properties outright. For Rex and Tomlinson, the major reason for these differences is that the racial minorities 'are forced to buy'. Confronted by racial discrimination, they have re-course to 'unorthodox forms of finance (e.g. council mortgages and bank loans) to obtain inferior inner-city property for purchase' (Rex and Tomlinson, 1979).

In the late 1960s the post war policy of slum demolition and redevelopment was replaced by a policy in which people were encour-aged 'to improve their houses up to a certain standard. Large parts of the city became, first, General Improvement Areas and then Hous-ing Action Areas' (Rex, 1981b). This policy meant that local authorities could set up schemes to improve certain areas and within these areas decide which houses needed to be demolished and which improved. According to Rex, local authorities, through council mortgage schemes for example, pursued policies 'which *directed* immigrant families' into improvement areas. Thus it is that in Handsworth so many are located 'in the least desirable sections of an area which is itself regarded as a "problem" in the eyes of policymakers' (Ratcliffe, 1981). In view of this, it comes as no sur-prise to learn that the racial minorities tend to live at higher densities per room than the whites and that, in the case of the Asians, there is a much greater chance that household amenities will be deficient. Owner occupation is clearly not the privileged form of tenure here that we usually assume it to be. Ratcliffe sums up the position which faces the more deprived racial minority in the following terms: 'although owner-occupation is extremely high among the Asians, the property which they acquire appears, often, to lack the basic amenities, and families are frequently living in over-crowded conditions . . . [in addition] . . . much of this property is of the short-lease variety, thus undermining the individual's security of tenure' (Ratcliffe, 1981).

What about the housing situation of the racial minorities in other forms of tenure? Within the private rented sector, a high proportion of West Indians are renting from housing associations while a high proportion of Asians are renting from a relative. In both cases, however, they tend to live at higher densities per room than the whites and, in the case of Asians, often have to share basic amenities. For Rex, there is little to choose between owner occupiers and tenants. 'The West Indian or Asian descended occupant of a house in the improvement area is trapped there. Once he gets a house of his own or a housing association tenancy, he comes off the Council's list' (Rex, 1981b). It is true that the owner occupier can sell his property but this becomes increasingly less easy as the area becomes unpopular with whites. In view of the similarities between owner occupiers and tenants in the improvement areas, Rex argues that 'a new housing class' (Rex, 1981b) has emerged, which, while clearly better off than the inhabitants of lodging houses, is none the less 'distinctly underprivileged'.

The minority population don't all belong to this distinctly under-privileged class. Despite the fact that Handsworth is an area of low council housing and preference has been given to whites, the West Indians in particular have made inroads into council tenancy. Again, however, there is evidence that the racial minorities do not receive equal treatment. 'There is an increasing amount of evidence to suggest that few blacks are found on the more popular (and higher-quality) estates' (Ratcliffe, 1981). It is also apparent that the racial minorities have to wait longer to be allocated council property and that such property often does not prevent overcrowding.

Although Rex and Tomlinson recognise tenure divisions among the racial minorities, their primary emphasis is on the common situation of disadvantage that blacks face in Handsworth. The latter, they argue, have either bought/rented 'inner-city property' or 'finished up in inner-city [council] estates'. 'Very few have made the suburban migration' with the result that there are 'very little differences in the observed attributes of those housed in the public and private sectors' (Rex and Tomlinson, 1979).

Since our primary concern in this chapter is with housing, we have focused on what Rex and Tomlinson and, in a companion volume, Ratcliffe highlight is happening here. Rex and Tomlinson do point out, however, that their study 'seeks to correct' an 'overemphasis' apparent in the earlier study of Sparkbrook on housing. Thus it is that they emphasise how people's life chances are determined by their position in employment and education as well as housing. In the case of the racial minorities, it is argued that 'there are clear differences of life chances between them and the white British' such that the former have 'a different kind of position in the labour market, a different housing situation, and a different form of schooling'. Subject to racism and distinctly dis-advantaged in these three sectors, the minorities constitute an underclass in British society, increasingly conscious of their sub-ordinate position. The significance of discrimination in housing in this context is that it 'has given rise to partially segregated areas' and provided an opportunity for neighbourhood based ethnic organisations to develop. The latter have become increasingly militant and in the process have reinforced the cultural distinctiveness of the West Indian and Asian minorities. Given the increasing racism among the whites, who see the newcomers as responsible for the deterioration of the inner city, and the absence of any community wide organisations, the authors pessimistically conclude that 'the greatest likelihood is that conflict in this community will grow'.

The two studies on Birmingham, which we have spent some time examining, have of course been subject to criticism. In order to assess the validity of the picture which these studies depict of the changing housing situation of racial minorities, we shall discuss four criticisms.

The first, which is now accepted by Rex, was put forward by Karn (Karn, 1967), who drew attention to the fact that, due to a statistical error, the proportion of immigrants in lodging houses in Sparkbrook had been exaggerated. She also pointed out that the Census figures indicated that the number of owner occupiers among West Indians and Asians in Britain as a whole was much greater than Rex and Moore's study suggested. Karn's criticism does not mean that there wasn't a 'lodging house era'. A number of studies, one of which we mentioned earlier in this chapter (Ballard and Ballard, 1977), point in particular to South Asians going through this phase. What the criticism does mean is that the change in the housing situation of racial minorities was not as dramatic for many immigrants as Rex's work suggests.

The second criticism, which is now partially accepted by Rex, was put forward by Dahya, who argued that at least in the case of Pakistanis, 'the immigrants' choice of poorer housing in the inner city wards of industrial cities and their preference for living there is related to their motives and orientations, and is not the outcome of racial discrimination' (Dahya, 1974). Oriented primarily to their village of origin, the early immigrants were concerned primarily with saving as much money as possible to send back home. Living with their fellow countrymen, who could provide mutual aid in austere conditions, fitted this objective well, it is argued. Even Rex accepts that, in explaining the housing situation of the minorities, account has to be taken of their preferences. The much smaller proportion of Asians than West Indians in council housing must 'be seen against the background of . . . cultural . . . considerations' (Ratcliffe, 1981) and the predominance of West Indians on inner city estates partly arises from the fact that most 'preferred central areas . . . where they could maintain communal links with their property owning kinsmen' (Rex and Tomlinson, 1979). The significance of choice in the housing situation of minorities is particularly well brought out in a study of a South Asian settlement in Blackburn (Robinson, 1981). Here the author discovered that Asians were not only highly segregated from the white British but that within the Asian community segregation had developed along national, religious and linguistic lines. With the transition from the lodging house era to that of family reunion in the 1960s, Asians moved into single-family dwellings, which enabled them 'to recreate the spatial distance which had been missing in the lodging houses' (Robinson, 1981). To point to the need to take account of ethnic preferences does not mean of course that racial discrimination should be discounted. Although 'it is hard to disentangle the fact of discrimination', as Rex and Tomlinson point out, 'from that of ethnic choice', both are clearly important. What this stress on ethnicity does mean, however, is that within the limits set by racial discrimination, choices are made over where to live.

The third criticism, which Rex does not accept, has been very well summarised by Saunders, who points to three problems with Rex's 'theory of housing classes' (Saunders, 1979). The first involves the identification of housing classes. Rex points in his work to a multitude of housing classes but does not give us any criteria by which to delimit a specific number of classes. The second problem involves the assumption that people share a belief in the desirability of suburbia. Although Rex now recognises that the racial minorities in Birmingham do not share this belief, he does not acknowledge the import of this admission. If the minorities do not aspire to suburbia, the housing classes which are identified are not in conflict with each other. This in fact was the situation earlier depicted by Lawrence in Nottingham. Immigrants had generally been able to buy houses there from the plentiful supply of cheap properties available. Not only were they satisfied with this housing but its purchase was considered perfectly legitimate by white people. The consequence of such a lack of competition, Lawrence argued, had been to diminish the possibility of conflict between white and black people (Lawrence, 1973). The third problem involves the applicability of the concept 'class' to people's housing situation. Although Rex purports to follow Weber in defining a housing class as a set of people who share a common situation in the housing market and therefore similar life chances, the housing classes he delineates in practise are not invariably distinguished in this way. Both the owner occupiers and tenants of houses in the improvement areas and council tenants in inner city estates, for example, despite being pictured as distinct classes, are seen by Rex as having similar life chances. The major differences between them revolves instead around the different prestige different forms of tenure receive. In Weber's terms, the housing groups which Rex distinguishes here are really housing status groups. To point to three problems with Rex's theory of housing classes 'does not mean that a Weberian analysis of housing classes is not possible'. Saunders, for example, suggests that the ownership and non-ownership of housing which can generate an economic return constitutes the basis of distinct housing classes in conflict with each other, 'namely those who live off the economic returns from house ownership (such as landlords and private developers), those who use housing purely as a means of consumption (tenants in the private and public sectors), and those who, in the process of consuming housing, typically enjoy a return on capital (most owner-occupiers, who achieve considerable capital gains from their ownership of housing)' (Saunders, 1981). Such an analysis has not yet been applied to race relations. It is nevertheless interesting to note, however, that in a recent article, Ward suggests that while in some urban areas like London, Asians have an opportunity of enjoying economic returns through the ownership of good quality domestic property which is not dissimilar to that of whites, in other areas like Birmingham and Bradford the Asians are in a markedly less favourable position (Ward, 1982).

The fourth criticism concerns the appropriateness of conceptualising the situation of black people as that of an underclass. In the previous chapter, it will be remembered, we questioned whether the evidence, which Rex and Tomlinson produced about the disadvantaged situation of racial minorities at work, was sufficient to warrant labelling them an underclass. What about their housing situation now? This is, as we have seen, a relatively disadvantaged one. Whether it is so distinctive as to justify talking of black people forming a housing underclass is doubtful, however. Although black people are still concentrated in the inner city, the increasing 'spatial polarisation' some commentators anticipated between the indigenous population and the immigrants has not been 'borne out by the data' and instead there has been 'the gradual spread of the ethnic minority groups into other neighbouring middle-ring areas' (Ratcliffe, 1981). The housing they occupy is on the whole disadvantaged relative to that of whites. Nevertheless it is generally an improvement on the earlier form of lodging housing and, in the case of the West Indians, is no worse in terms of amenities than that of inner city whites. In view of this, it is perhaps not surprising that, in contrast to the views of white residents, the minorities express satisfaction with where they live. The situation may of course deteriorate but at the moment there is little evidence that the minorities living in different forms of tenure are being mobilised as a housing underclass.

Despite the four criticisms of Rex's work which have been made, it should be stressed that an emphasis on the significance of housing for people's life chances and an awareness that housing constitutes an important issue of urban conflict have proved extremely valuable. What is more, the broad picture of the changing housing situation of racial minorities in Birmingham has been confirmed by other writers. Ward and Sims, for example, point out 'how the housing market in the post-war period was tight, and many of those arriving to take up employment were obliged to find housing by sharing with other new arrivals in lodging-houses in inner areas'. Although, as they go on to argue, 'the overwhelming trend is still to concentration in areas of decaying housing in inner areas which they share with elderly white people who for economic or sentimental reasons have not joined the flight to the suburbs' (Ward and Sims, 1981), now 'for the most part, their housing in these areas is owner occupied' (Karn, 1977), while, in the case of West Indians, a significant minority are council tenants (Flett, 1982).

The extent of racial disadvantage in housing in Britain

The account of the housing situation of Birmingham, which Rex and Tomlinson outline, is not atypical in its essentials of the housing situation nationally. Let us then briefly summarise the findings of the PEP survey of racial minorities on this issue, beginning with a comparison of the pattern of tenure of Asians and West Indians with the general population:

Table 13   Tenure – racial minorities and the general population

Heads of household	Asians	West Indians	General population (from the 1971 Census)
	%	%	%
Owner-occupied	76	50	50
Rented from council	4	26	28
Privately rented	19	24	22
Not stated	1	1	

Source: Smith, 1977

What emerges most clearly from such a comparison is the unusual housing situation of the Asians, who are much more likely to be owner occupiers and much less likely to be council tenants. Its unusual nature is even clearer, however, when account is taken of the fact that they are overrepresented in lower level occupations. In the following table therefore we compare the pattern of tenure among the different groups at different job levels.

The pattern of tenure of the Asians is most unusual. While among the general population, it is more likely for those in higher level occupations to be owner occupiers, among the Asians the reverse is true. Whereas council housing is far more common among the general population especially at the lower occupational levels, among the Asians it is uniformly low. Finally in contrast to the tendency for

Table 14 Tenure analysed by job level of head of household – racial minorities and the general population

Heads of household	Professional/ Management %	Non-manual %	White collar %	Skilled manual %	Semi-skilled manual %	Unskilled manual %
Owner occupied						
Asians	58		59	81	82	85
West Indians		35		59	53	39
General population (from the 1972 General Household Survey)	77		58	45	33	20
Rented from council						
Asians	4		7	4	4	2
West Indians		27		21	24	31
General population	9		23	39	46	56
Privately rented						
Asians	35		33	15	13	11
West Indians		35		20	23	29
General population	14		19	16	21	24

Source: Smith, 1976

private renting to be lower for those at higher job levels among the general population, for Asians the opposite applies.

How do we account for the unusual pattern of tenure of Asians? If we put council housing to one side since it is a form of tenure which Asians have not tended to favour, there are three possible kinds of housing: 'privately rented accommodation', 'poor quality owner-occupied housing' and 'good quality owner-occupied housing'.

Smith argues that Asians at lower job levels opt for the second as soon as they can. 'Asians from the lower socio-economic groups, because they tend to have little English and for other reasons, need to live within an Asian community; because they tend to have particularly large families, they will find privately rented accommodation inadequate'. As a result they try to 'get out of privately rented accommodation as quickly as possible; since the only alternative is owner-occupation, they are bound to buy relatively cheap and poor accommodation in central areas, within the communities whose support they need'. It is interesting, in this context, to note that owner occupation is most common in areas with high concentrations of immigrants. While a remarkably high number of Asians, and in particular those at lower job levels, are outright owners, having been constrained to buy extremely cheap properties for cash, the majority are reliant on mortgages. The latter, however, come more often from local authorities and banks and less often from building societies than is the case with the general population. What is more, a relatively high level of these properties are held leasehold rather than freehold. Asians at higher job levels on the other hand often plan to buy much more expensive and better quality suburban property. They 'tend to have considerably smaller families; most of them speak English well; they are generally sophisticated and westernised, have comparatively little need of the support of an Asian community, and might, on the contrary, prefer to go to live in predominantly white suburbs. As a short-term solution to the housing problem, they go into privately rented accommodation, which they can probably endure for longer because their families are smaller' (Smith, 1977).

The pattern of tenure of the West Indians is not as unusual as the Asians. Neverthless the level of owner occupation is higher among West Indian manual workers than among manual workers generally. Much the same reasons account for this as for the high level of owner occupation among Asians. 'The main differences are, first, that council housing is a serious possibility for substantial numbers of West Indians'; (although it should be noted here that among manual workers a much smaller proportion of West Indians are in council housing than the general population) 'and secondly, that private renting is more often used as an alternative to owner occupation by the poorest West Indians than by the poorest Asians, probably because their familes tend to be smaller, and because they are more likely to live in areas where suitable cheap houses have not been so readily available' (Smith, 1977).

When we move from a comparison of different patterns of tenure to an examination of the quality of housing, we find that the housing which the racial minorities occupy is 'markedly inferior' on average to that occupied by the general population. After measuring the quality of housing enjoyed by the minorities and the indigenous population on a number of indicators, Smith lists the differences between them as follows: 'Two-thirds of the minorities compared with one-third of whites live in terraced houses: 88% of the minorities compared with 48% of whites live in properties built before 1940; 72% of the minorities compared with 46% of whites live in properties which are externally in poor or only average condition; over one-quarter of the minorities compared with 4% of the general population live in shared swellings; 37% of the minorities compared with 18% of the general population are without exclusive use of bath, hot water and inside WC; on average the minorities are living at a density of 1.75 persons per bedroom compared with 1.25 among whites' (Smith, 1976).

Although the housing conditions of the racial minorities in privately rented accommodation are appreciably worse than the conditions of those in owner occupation and council tenancy, they are at a relative disadvantage compared with whites in each form of tenure. This is partly attributable to the fact that the minorities are over-represented at the lower job levels but it is primarily a consequence of racial discrimination, if by the latter we include not only direct discrimination but the way institutions devise procedures, which, while not intentionally discriminatory, work to the disadvantage of black people.

The results of the PEP survey of racial minorities tend to confirm the broad picture of the housing situation of black people outlined by Rex and Tomlinson. The survey did exclude, however, 24% of the minority population who lived in districts where they formed a very small proportion of the population. Since these people tend to have a more favourable housing situation than those in inner cities, the PEP survey tends to exaggerate the differences between the housing situation of the minorities and the population as a whole. Let us therefore turn to the Census and National Dwelling and Household Survey to see what changes have taken place over time.

If we examine changes in the pattern of tenure of different groups, we find that since 1961 the proportion of Asians, West Indians and the general population in owner occupation and council housing has risen and the proportion in the private rented sector has fallen. Owner occupation remains more common among Asians while council housing remains very low. In contrast, owner occupation among the West Indians, which was not very different from white levels in the 1960s, has fallen since 1971, while council housing has increased so that now the proportion of West Indians in council housing exceeds the proportion of the general population in such housing. Field et al. after looking at the changing pattern of tenure of different groups, conclude that 'all in all, these results suggest that Asians and West Indians are somewhat freer than when they first arrived to move between sectors of the housing market' (Field et al., 1981).

When we turn to housing quality we find that the housing of Asians and West Indians 'has improved substantially according to those measures which have regularly been made'. Thus, household density, as measured by the proportion of households living at more than 1.5 persons per room, has been 'converging quite strikingly' and the proportion of minority households in shared dwellings has 'decreased sharply'. Differences do remain between the minorities and the general population, but they are less marked than the PEP survey suggests and have become smaller over time so that since 1961 there have not only been 'important absolute advances' in the housing conditions of West Indians and Asians but 'some important progress relative to the rest of the population in housing' (Field et al., 1981).

Whether the minorities have become more evenly dispersed throughout the country is more debatable. Smith concludes somewhat hesitantly that 'from all the available evidence, the answer to the question "Is dispersal happening?" seems to be no'. Certainly the degree of segregation in housing remains higher than that in employment. A common indicator of the relative level of concentration of a group in a particular area is the segregation index, which shows the percentage of members of a group who would have to move to be distributed in the same way as the population as a whole. The index varies from 0, where members of a group are distributed in an identical fashion to that of the general population to 100, where there is total segregation. Calculations in the United States of black concentration in particular urban areas, known as census tracts, indicate an average index of 'about 75' (Farley, 1982). This tends to be higher than that normally found in Britain but it is matched in some cities when small areas are taken (Jones and McEvoy, 1978).

Residential segregation in Britain clearly remains significant then. Some of the segregation is a result of the jobs people do. A study which examined the segregation of black people in London, however, showed that most of this segregation 'cannot be explained by their jobs' (Runnymede Trust, 1980). In order to understand why such segregation persists, therefore, account needs to be taken not only of ethnic preferences but also of racial discrimination. This is not to say that there are no changes. 'Evidence from local studies suggests that Asians are becoming more concentrated, West Indians less' (Field et al., 1981), with Asians buying houses left by whites in areas where they already live and West Indians moving into council housing in different parts of the city.

Summary

Having examined the employment situation of racial minorities in the previous chapter, we have concentrated in this chapter on a second major determinant of their life chances. Both at the local level of Birmingham and at the national level of Britain as a whole, we have seen how the minorities are concentrated in the inner cities. While their housing at first often took the form of private renting from a member of their own ethnic group, increasingly they have turned to owner occupation supplemented in the case of West Indians by council housing. This change in the pattern of tenure has not, however, meant the elimination of racial disadvantage in housing. Although significant absolute and relative improvements have been made, such disadvantage still persists.

Guide to reading

It is J. Rex, above all, who has stressed the significance of housing for the life chances of racial minorities. For a clear and brief summary of the changing housing situation of the minorities in Birmingham, see J. Rex, *Race in the inner city*. The two studies of Sparkbrook in 1964 and Handsworth in 1976 are to be found in, respectively, J. Rex and R. Moore, *Race, Community and Conflict* and J. Rex and S. Tomlinson, *Colonial Immigrants in a British City*, although a useful complement to the latter is the companion volume, P. Ratcliffe, *Racism and Reaction*. Of the local studies conducted outside Birmingham, D. Lawrence, *Black Migrants: White Natives*, a study of the situation in Nottingham, is particularly interesting. Systematic evidence on the housing situation of racial minorities nationally can be found in D. Smith, *Racial Disadvantage in Britain*, Part 3 and S. Field et al., *Ethnic Minorities in Britain: a Study of Trends in Their Position Since 1961*, chapter 3.

Discussion points

1. How significant do you consider housing to be as a determinant of people's life chances? How does its influence compare with that of employment? How independent are the housing and labour markets?
2. How valuable do you find the theory of housing classes? How would advocates of a different sociological perspective, say Marxism, criticise it? How damaging are the criticisms of the two studies of Birmingham mentioned in this chapter for the theory? How useful is the theory for understanding the situation of racial minorities?
3. What do you understand by the term, 'ghetto'? Is there any evidence that ghettos are being formed in Britain? What arguments are there for and against the maintenance of ethnic concentrations? How significant do you consider racial discrimination as opposed to ethnic preferences to be in the formation of ethnic concentrations in Britain?
4. What do you consider to be the main priorities in the field of housing policy? How can racial disadvantages here best be eliminated?

7

Race and education

If employment and housing are critical to people's life chances, so is education. Indeed so far as the future of race relations in Britain is concerned, it may well be that 'of the three institutional sectors of employment, housing and education . . . education is the most important' (Rex and Tomlinson, 1979). For it is the education system which prepares pupils for their future occupational roles.

Perspectives on the education system

Both the major sociological perspectives on the relation between education and the economy recognize the crucial contribution the education system plays in preparing children for their roles in the economy. They differ, however, over how this is done. Before we examine how the racial minorities are faring in British schools, let us briefly outline then the way the functionalist and Marxist perspectives picture the education system (Karabel and Halsey, 1977).

According to the functionalist perspective, the education system performs three crucial functions on behalf of society as a whole. We shall take each in turn.

The first function the education system performs is to enable people to acquire the skills which are needed in an industrial society. For the economy to function effectively, all children must be taught basic skills and those talented enough taught the more specialised skills needed in certain key occupations. From this point of view, the expansion of the education system, which industrial societies have witnessed, stems from the need for an increasingly skilled labour force.

The second function the education system performs is to allocate individuals to jobs for which their talents most suit them (Parsons, 1961). In order to ensure that the key occupations are filled by those who are most able, children are continually assessed in schools and their educational attainments used by employers in order to select the most suitable candidates for any job vacancies which arise. In this way, the education system provides an opportunity for those with talent to be upwardly mobile and enter the more highly rewarded occupations. Indeed, with the development of equality of opportunity in education, we can speak of the emergence of 'meritocracy', a society in which one's occupational position is achieved on the basis of merit and where 'being born into a humble home . . . [is] . . . no barrier to success, and being born into a wealthy or powerful family no cushion against failure' (Bilton et al., 1981).

The third function the education system performs is to pass on to a new generation the basic values of society, in particular, the values of achievement and equality of opportunity. It is acknowledged that children from some social groups (for example, the working class) achieve results which are on average lower than those of children from other social groups (for example, the middle class). But, because the educational system already provides equality for all members of society, explanations for such differences in educational attainment are sought elsewhere. For some, the differential is explained by the fact that children from some groups tend to have lower levels of inherited intelligence than children from other groups. For others, the differential is explained by the fact that children from some groups tend to acquire in the course of socialisation in the home beliefs, ideas and values which are less conducive to educational attainment than those picked up by children from other groups. In both cases, the source of the problem is not seen to lie in the way the education system is organised.

In moving from the functionalist perspective to the Marxist perspective, we find a similar stress on the importance of the education system in preparing children for their roles in the economy. The emphasis here, however, is on the fact that the economy is a capitalist one and that, for such an economy to function effectively, what is required are workers with the personality characteristics which will suit them for their position in the economy. From this point of view, the expansion of the education system, which capitalist societies have witnessed, stems not so much from the need for an increasingly skilled labour force so much as from the need for a passive and disciplined labour force.

For the most well known exponents of a Marxist perspective to education (Bowles and Gintis, 1976), there is a 'correspondence' between the way work is organised and schooling, with the latter mirroring the former. Thus schools are bureaucracies, governed by a system of rules and organised hierarchically. The children are told what to do and are motivated to learn discrete bits of knowledge by external incentives such as grades. As such, schools help to prepare children to fill their allotted places in the workforce. Given the way work is organised hierarchically, they will experience little autonomy at work and given the way work is fragmented into a number of discrete tasks, they will experience little intrinsic meaning in their work. It is therefore important that students learn to be obedient and to be motivated by external incentives such as pay. This is not to say that all children are similarly socialised in schools. What is noticeable is that children from different social origins are often placed in different schools or streams and treated differently. Those from more privileged backgrounds tend to achieve better results and accordingly end up in more advantaged destinations. From this point of view, the education system does not provide a possible avenue of social mobility so much as channels children into occupational roles similar to those of their parents and thus 'reproduces' a labour force.

While the education system prepares children for their future roles in the economy and in the process helps to maintain a system of inequality, at the same time it puts forward an ideology which legitimates that inequality. Children are taught that they have the same chances of advancement, so that if they are able and work hard, they will do well. In suggesting that those who are successful in school and later at work thus deserve the rewards they acquire, the education system not only persuades people that the system of inequality is just but also presents a distorted picture of the system. Our society is not in fact a meritocratic one and class differences in educational achievement persist, it is argued, because the education system in a capitalist society is suffused with middle class values which disadvantage the working class child.

In the light of the two perspectives on education, which we have briefly outlined, we shall be concerned in this chapter with two major questions. Firstly, does the education system provide racial minorities with a possible avenue of social mobility, as the functionalist perspective suggests, or does it channel them into occupational roles similar to those of their parents, as the Marxist perspective suggests? Secondly, if the racial minorities are achieving on average lower results than the indigenous population, is this a consequence of what they bring with them to school – their innate ability or their culture – or a result of the way the educational system operates?

The education performance of minority children in Britain

Let us begin then by exploring how the racial minorities are faring in British schools. Although little systematic research has yet been done in this area, two recent overviews of the studies, which have been undertaken, agree that 'the performance of "immigrant" children tends to be lower than indigenous' (Tomlinson, 1981a) on the main criteria of achievement utilised by educationalists – 'children from immigrant families' tend to be underrepresented in selective schools and more likely to be placed in lower streams; they tend to be overrepresented in ESN schools, and in both individual and group tests they tend to score lower than their indigenous counterparts (Rutter and Madge, 1976). While the performance of 'immigrant' children generally has been a cause of concern, it is children from West Indian families whose educational performance has given most cause for concern.

Let us take each of the indicators of educational performance in turn. Because the Department of Education and Science stopped collecting statistics on 'immigrant' children in schools in 1972, the information on the school placement of minority children, which we have on a national scale, is somewhat dated. Nevertheless, the national survey of local education authorities in the late '60s (Townsend, 1971) and the subsequent more intensive survey of schools with higher numbers of immigrant pupils in 1970 (Townsend and Brittan, 1972) clearly indicates that minority children were finding difficulty gaining admission to grammar schools and that they tended to be clustered in the lower streams of schools, where the pupils were grouped by ability. What was true of minority children generally was found to be even more pronounced among West Indian children. Although we cannot be completely sure what the national picture is now, 'the more recent information, albeit limited, which is available . . . confirms the disadvantaged position of pupils of West Indian origin' (Taylor M., 1981).

The issue which has served to symbolise for West Indian parents the general underperformance of their children is the fact that West Indians have been much more likely than other children to be taken out of the normal education system and placed in special schools for the educationally subnormal. Coard, a West Indian teacher in ESN schools, alerted people to the issue in a widely read polemic, appropriately entitled *How the West Indian child is made educationally subnormal in the British School system* (Coard, 1971) and the statistics produced by the Department of Education and Science for 1970 confirmed that West Indian children were indeed overrepresented in ESN schools. While as many as 2.33% of West Indian children were placed in such schools, only 0.68% of non immigrant children were so located, with Indian and Pakistani pupils being in fact underrepresented at 0.32 and 0.44% respectively (Townsend and Brittan, 1972). Although we do not have any up to date figures, a recent study suggests that West indian children are still overrepresented in ESN schools, so that while the percentage of children in the school population in ESN schools is 0.5, the percentage of West Indian children is 2.5 (Tomlinson, 1981b).

As yet no large scale national survey comparing the test scores of indigenous and minority children has been undertaken. We are therefore reliant on more localised studies for our information in this area. In view of the fact that most of these studies contain small numbers of minority children and cover specific localities, we cannot be confident that they are representative of the national situation. Indeed, in the case of many of the early studies, the research is vitiated by a failure to distinguish minority children born in this country and those who are immigrants.

'The most significant large scale investigation' (Taylor M., 1981) and the one which has had most impact has been that undertaken by the Inner London Education Authority between 1966 and 1975. Here the performance of a large number of children (4269 immigrant and 22023 non immigrant pupils) in English, Mathematics and Verbal reasoning, on transfer to secondary school in 1968, was compared. As with the rather smaller 1966 Survey (Little, Mabey and Whitaker, 1976), the performance of pupils in English and Mathematics was based on the primary school teachers' assessments, while that in Verbal reasoning was based mainly on test results. The 1968 survey replicated many of the findings of the earlier study – 'immigrant' pupils were performing at lower levels, with the West Indians doing worse than Asians, but those who had been fully educated in Britain were performing better than those who had only been partially educated here (Little, 1975). The following table compares the position of pupils, fully educated in this country, from three ethnic groups in English, Mathematics and Verbal reasoning. For each ethnic group, the proportion of pupils in the top quarter is as follows:

Table 15   Percentage of pupils fully educated in the UK placed in upper quartile on transfer to secondary school in 1968 – by ethnic group

	English	Mathematics	Verbal reasoning
West Indian origin	9.2	7.4	7.2
Asian origin	19.3	20.2	21.1
Indigenous	25	22.9	19.8

Source: Little, 1975

What this table indicates is that while Asians, who are fully educated in this country, are performing at a level comparable with the indigenous population, West Indians, who are fully educated in this country, are performing at a lower level compared with the indigenous population. Particularly disturbing, in this context, is evidence which indicates that West Indian children are performing at a level below disadvantaged members of the indigenous population. In an area considered to be suffering from such severe disadvantage that it has been designated an Educational Priority Area in which the children need extra help, differences in the level of attainment are apparent on, for example, a standard reading test and a vocabulary test conducted in the primary school (Little, 1975).

What is more, the gap in performance does not seem to be closing, over time. Indeed the ILEA Literacy Survey, which tested the same children aged 8+, 10+ and 15+ between 1968 and 1975, found a deterioration over time in the reading attainment of West Indian pupils relative to their indigenous counterparts. This is borne out in the following table, which indicates the reading test scores of different groups:

Table 16   Mean scores on a standard reading test at 8, 11 and 15 (National mean = 100) – different groups

	All children of West Indian origin	Indigenous children	West Indian children fully educated in UK	White children from unskilled backgrounds
1968 (aged 8)	87.9	98.4	89.9	93.7
1971 (aged 11)	87.4	98.6	88.7	93.5
1975 (aged 15)	85.9	98.2	87.1	92.1

Source: Little, 1978

A comparison of columns 1 and 2 confirms that the gap in mean reading scores between West Indian and indigenous pupils is growing, while, even more disturbingly, a comparison of columns 3 and 4 indicates that white unskilled working class children continue to perform on average at a higher level than children of West Indian origin. Such a gap in performance between black pupils and socially disadvantaged white pupils is corroborated not only by a further analysis of the ILEA Literary Survey (Mabey, 1981) but also by the results of a national survey (Essen and Ghodsian, 1979).

The National Child Development Study, an investigation of children born in one week of March 1958, included an assessment of the children at 16 on tests of reading and mathematics. For the purposes of the study, a first generation immigrant was defined as 'a child born abroad with at least one parent born abroad' and a second generation immigrant as 'a child born in Britain with at least one parent born abroad'. Although all the first generation groups distinguished – the West Indians, Asians, Irish and Europeans – had lower scores on both tests, 'among the second generation groups, however, it is only the West Indians who have clearly lower mean scores than indigenous children.' What is more, 'when children of similar financial and housing circumstances are compared' a clear difference between the West Indian pupils and their indigenous counterparts still persists.

The most important indicator of educational attainment for the future occupational roles of minority children is their performance in public examinations. Here the most wide ranging recent data derive from a survey of school leavers in six local education authorities during 1978/9. The results of the survey, which includes about half of the school leavers from ethnic minorities in England, are briefly set out below:

- In CSE English and GCE 'O' level English Language, only 9% of West Indians obtained higher grades (i.e. Grades A–C at 'O' level and Grade 1 at CSE), compared with 21% of Asians and 29% of all other leavers in these LEAs;
- In CSE and GCE 'O' level Mathematics, only 5% of West Indians obtained higher grades compared with 20% of Asians and 19% of all other leavers in these LEAs;
- In all CSE and GCE 'O' level examinations, only 3% of West Indians obtained 5 or more higher grades compared with 18% of Asians and 16% of all other leavers in these LEAs;
- In GCE 'A' level examinations, only 2% of West Indians gained one or more passes compared with 13% of Asians and 12% of all other leavers in these LEAs;
- Only 1% of West Indians went on to University compared with 3% of Asians and 3% of all other leavers in these LEAs; and
- Only 1% of West Indians went on to full time degree courses in further education compared with 5% of Asians and 4% of all other leavers in these LEAs (Rampton Report, 1981).

These results seem to indicate that while Asian children as a group are performing at a comparable level with the indigenous population, 'West Indian children as a group are underachieving in our education system' (Rampton Report, 1981). Such a conclusion, however, has not gone unchallenged and it has been pointed out, in particular, that the school leavers survey takes no account of class and gender (Reeves and Chevannes, 1981). We can only hypothesise about what difference taking these factors into account would make.

In the case of gender, there does seem to be evidence that West Indian girls tend to do better than West Indian boys so that a recent review of research into the education of West Indian pupils is able to conclude that 'there is a fairly strong tendency for West Indian girls in general to perform better on all measures, but especially on reading, than West Indian boys' (Taylor M., 1981). If this is indeed the case, the major cause of concern is the underachievement of West Indian boys. It has been suggested, however, that such 'underachievement' is primarily attributable to their disadvantaged class position. Since class differences in educational achievement have been remarkably persistent in Britain (Halsey, 1978) and since West Indians are much more likely to come from working class backgrounds than Asians and other school leavers, one would expect, it is argued, West Indian pupils to perform at a lower level. The limited evidence we have does lend some support to this suggestion. Thus both Mabey (Mabey, 1981) and Essen and Ghodsian (Essen and Ghodsian, 1979), on the basis of their respective studies, claim that about half the difference in the test scores of indigenous and West Indian pupils is explained when account is taken of social disadvantage. This still leaves, however, a significant part of the difference unexplained in class terms.

What is the upshot of our examination of the educational performance of minority children then? On all the indicators, which we have investigated, West Indian pupils come out worst. When only pupils born and fully educated in this country are studied, the evidence indicates that, while Asians as a group are performing at a comparable level with the indigenous population, West Indians as a group are underperforming. The Rampton committee of enquiry, which was set up in 1979 to examine the education of minority children, produced its interim report on West Indian children in schools in 1981. Its conclusion, 'that West Indian children as a group are underachieving' in relation to their peers (Rampton Report, 1981), seems then to be well founded.

To point to West Indian underachievement does not mean that black children generally constitute an 'underclass' in the education system (Rex and Tomlinson, 1979), with the latter '"reproducing" the young black worker as labour at the lower end of employment, production and skill' (Hall et al., 1978). While the performance of West Indian pupils in British schools does indeed lend support to the Marxist claim that the primary function of the education system is to 'reproduce labour power', the performance of Asian pupils corroborates the functionalist claim that the education system provides a possible avenue of social mobility.

Before we move on to explore different explanations of the underachievement of West Indian pupils, two caveats need to be borne in mind. Firstly, to say that West Indian children are performing at a lower level than their indigenous counterparts is to say that they are performing *on average* at a lower level. It is not to say that many children from West Indian backgrounds are not performing at a level equal to and indeed above many children of the indigenous population

(Driver, 1980). Secondly, given the paucity of systematic research in this area, explanations proffered for the lower performance of West Indian children on average are inevitably speculative. Although informed by the extensive research which has been conducted to explain the underachievement of black Americans and the white working class, the speculative nature of the explanations put forward for West Indian underachievement must not be forgotten.

Explanations of differences in educational performance

Three different kinds of explanation will be examined: those which claim that racial differences in intelligence are inherited; those which point to the culture of the home and those which focus on the education system.

The fact 'that West Indian children tend to score lower than white children on tests of intelligence' (Taylor M., 1981) has suggested to some writers that the differences in educational attainment are primarily attributable to differences in intelligence and that these differences are in turn genetically determined. Although the notion that racial differences in ability are inherited was thoroughly rejected by the scientific community after the Second World War, it was given renewed respectability by Jensen in an article entitled *'How much can we boost IQ and scholastic achievement?'* (Jensen, 1969) and has been popularised in this country by Eysenck (Eysenck, 1971).

The essence of this argument is as follows. A person's intelligence, or 'abstract reasoning ability' can be measured by means of an intelligence test. This gives an individual's intelligence quotient or IQ. An individual's IQ, along with his other characteristics, is the product of an interaction between the genetic information received from his parents and the environment in which he develops. Just as it does not make sense to claim that the area of a rectangle is the result primarily of its length or breadth, so it is impossible to see an individual's IQ as the result primarily of genetic or environmental factors. However, just as one can show that the differences in the areas of two rectangles stem from a difference in their length and breadth or both, so, it is argued, one can provide an estimate (the heritability estimate) of the extent to which differences between the IQs of individuals are attributable to genetic factors.

The best way of estimating the contribution of heredity is to compare the IQs of identical twins who have been reared apart in different environments from an early age. Since these twins have the same genetic endowment, similarities in their scores are attributable to genetic factors. Studies of this sort which have been conducted among whites in the United States and Europe and, to a lesser extent, among blacks in the United States, show a high correlation in IQ scores between the twins reared apart. Coupled with other evidence to the same effect, it is concluded that as much as 80 per cent of the variation between individuals in IQ is in fact genetically determined.

The significance of this 'finding' for race and education is apparent when we compare the IQ scores in the United States of whites and blacks. In most studies, whites score on average fifteen points higher than blacks. This is an appreciable difference and of such a magnitude that no environmental factors have yet been proposed which can explain it. Since IQ is largely genetically determined among whites and blacks, it is therefore extremely likely that the difference between the IQ scores of white and black children is primarily attributable to genetic factors. If this is the case, the implication is that little can be done to reduce the gap. Moreover, in view of the fact that intelligence test scores provide a reasonably accurate predictor of scholastic achievement, it follows that one should not be very surprised at the lower educational attainment of black children.

Jensen's argument has received extensive criticism since the publication of his article in 1969. Among the more pertinent criticisms are the following four which, taken together, are very damaging to the 'genetic' argument. Firstly, estimates of the heritability of IQ are more variable than Jensen implies, with many authorities putting it lower than 80% and one well known one putting it at 45% (Jencks, 1972). Secondly, the estimates of heritability are based on tests administered to particular populations and cannot properly be generalised to other populations. Thus, while within the white population and within the black population the differences in IQ scores may be largely attributable to genetic factors, it does not follow that the same phenomenon accounts for differences in IQ scores between the two populations. Although it is theoretically possible to envisage the gap as primarily attributable to genetic differences between the two populations, it is difficult to see how an estimate could possibly be reached in practise, when a critical difference in the environments between blacks and whites in the United States depends on whether individuals are classified as black or white (Green, 1981). Thirdly, even if one were to accept that the differences in IQ between the two populations are mainly a result of genetic differences between them, it does not follow that the IQ of black children in the United States cannot be significantly boosted by environmental factors. A heritability estimate is only valid for the population and environment for which it is calculated so that changes in the environment may well alter the estimate (Bodmer, 1977). Fourthly, IQ scores are only partially correlated with measures of educational attainment, so that even if the three objections to the genetic argument, which we have outlined above, are discounted, it still does not follow that the lower educational attainment of black children is similarly attributable to genetic factors (Tyler, 1977). Indeed Jensen himself admits that most of the gap in educational achievement is a result of environmental factors.

Although further criticisms of the genetic explanation could be made, enough has been written to indicate just how speculative it is and to show, at the very least, that it is environmental differences between the West Indian and indigenous population which mainly account for the relative educational achievements of the two populations. More interesting perhaps than the question of its truth or falsity is why the genetic explanation was rediscovered at the end of the 1960s and since taken up.

The 1950s and 1960s constituted a period of relative affluence, in which it was widely believed that the expansion of the education system would bring about greater social justice and economic efficiency. The subsequent slowing down of economic growth made it difficult, however, to maintain educational expansion. Coupled with evidence of continuing group inequalities in educational attainment despite all the measures which had been taken to eradicate them, the liberal consensus broke up. One response was to resurrect the genetic explanation (Bernbaum, 1973). Inequalities in educational attainment between black and white children stubbornly persist, it has consequently been argued, mainly because of genetic differences. We should not be surprised by this and should not therefore waste valuable resources in seeking to change an immutable fact. In view of our earlier arguments, which indicate that this view is false, let us turn to the other two explanations for the underperformance of West Indian children.

Both those who point to the importance of the home and those who highlight the significance of the school agree that it is environmental factors which are responsible for the lower educational attainment on average of West Indian children. As such, they believe that these children are underachieving not only in relation to their peers but also in relation to their potential. Although aware that many of the factors which they point to often disadvantage Asian children and indeed white working class children, it is contended that cumulatively these factors particularly disadvantage West Indian children.

For many writers, a major reason for the lower performance of West Indians compared with Asians concerns the children's cultural background (Little, 1978).

Asians, it is argued, belong to cultures which predate British imperialism. Although some Asians in the towns took up the cultural values of their British rulers, most villagers retained their traditional languages, religions and family systems. Migration to Britain did not result in the erosion of these cultures with the result that the children are taught clearly distinct beliefs and values. Brought up in tightly knit communities to recognize obligations to their fellow kin and sustained by communal associations, the children therefore go to school with a clear sense of their own ethnic identity and personal worth.

For West Indians, British imperialism was culturally more devastating. The experience of being transported from one society to another and being sold into slavery to work on the plantations meant that they were 'deprived of their ancestral culture' (Rex, 1982), losing in the process not only their 'language' and the 'essence' of their 'religion' but also their 'entire family system'. The loss of the latter has had, it is argued, particularly far reaching consequences and is at the root of the continuing 'deficiencies of the family system' (Pryce, 1979).

A number of different family forms continue to coexist in the West Indies. Since a degree of economic security is normally seen as a prerequisite for legal marriage, such an institution remains for many an ideal to which they aspire but rarely achieve. A more common family form, especially among the working class and peasantry, is a common law association. If the union is stable, it may constitute a prelude to legal marriage later but, if it breaks up, as it often does under the strain of poverty, the children normally remain with the mother and a 'matrifocal' family is formed. Since other relations, especially on the mother's side, are expected to help bring up children, the latter often enjoy more stability than appears to be the case at first sight. Nevertheless, there seems little doubt that kinship relations are less clearly defined among the West Indians than the Asians and that as a result 'the West Indian family organisation lacks the system of mutual obligations which typifies the family in South Asian minorities' (Pearson 1981). While this does not warrant talk of 'the shambles of family life in the West Indies' (Pryce 1979), it does suggest that the children might acquire a less secure sense of their own identity. Such an eventuality is thought even more probable when it is recognized that the beliefs and values which the children acquire are not clearly distinct from those which characterise the dominant culture. Since the latter exhibits a 'white bias', valuing the European features of the society while derogating its African features, it is not surprising that some black people internalise these values and develop a negative image of themselves and their ethnic identity (Fanon, 1967).

Even if it is granted that West Indian culture is less cohesive than Asian culture and thus provides a less grounded sense of identity for children, the question still remains as to how its effects manifest themselves in Britain.

West Indian parents generally have a high regard for education and are keen for their children to do well in school. Nevertheless there is some evidence that they do not translate these high aspirations into positive help. After reviewing the evidence, Taylor sums up the situation in this way, 'Although West Indian parents are evidently concerned about their children's development they often do seem to lack understanding of the developmental importance of play, toys, communication and parent-child interaction in the early years' (Taylor M., 1981). Indeed there are some grounds for believing that the parents are more 'likely to be strict and authoritarian with regard to their children' (Bagley , Bart and Wong, 1979). If this is the case, it is perhaps not so surprising that the children tend to enter school not only developmentally disadvantaged compared to their peers but also less well prepared for the more liberal atmosphere of British schools.

In order to understand why particular child rearing practises are adopted, we need to examine the educational experience and economic situation of the parents. Educationally, West Indian parents are likely to have been schooled in a very traditional way, with the teachers being highly authoritarian, the classes formal and the stress placed on rote learning. Since their picture of education tends to be derived from their own experience, they are not in a strong position to prepare their children for the very different schooling system in Britain. Economically, West Indians tend to be relatively disadvantaged. Indeed, according to the National Child Development Study, the parents of the second generation 16 year olds had 'strikingly bad housing, employment and financial conditions,' worse in fact than those of other immigrant groups with a 16 year old born in this country (Ghodsian and Essen, 1980). Such material deprivation does not provide the ideal context for rearing children, so that it is scarcely surprising that the children's pre-school years tend not to be conducive to educational success.

In this context, what is noteworthy is the high proportion of pre-school children who are looked after in the day by child-minders. There are two reasons why West Indian parents are more likely to rely on such care for their children. The first is the higher proportion of West Indian one parent families. Although West Indians seem to conform to the typical family form in Britain and they get married at an earlier age (Foner, 1979), the stresses of life in Britain do result in break ups and the setting up of one parent families. Such a situation is likely to be more disturbing for children in this country than in the West Indies since the family here tends to be shorn of the connections and support of extended kin who have remained behind. The second reason for the greater resort to childminders among West Indians is that a higher proportion of mothers with young children work in order to provide their families with a satisfactory standard of living. As with one parent families, reliance has to be placed on childminders whose care is often inadequate and not conducive to the child's development. Although childminding does not by any means always have deleterious consequences, Taylor concludes, after surveying the evidence, that frequently children 'are by being placed with childminders receiving a low quality of care' (Taylor M., 1981).

If there is evidence that West Indian children tend to enter school developmentally disadvantaged in relation to their peers, there is also some evidence that they go to school with a negative image of themselves. Thus in a small scale study of 42 West Indian children, aged 5–10, in two London schools, 24% expressed a wish to change their skin colour and another 19% were equivocal (Bagley and Coard, 1975). The most influential study in this area, however, is that of Milner, who investigated the attitudes of 100 English, 100 Asian and 100 West Indian children, aged 5–8, towards different racial groups. Each child was asked a series of questions, being requested in each case to choose between two dolls or two pictures, one representing the child's own racial group, the other representing the main racial group in the child's locality. The most dramatic evidence of low self esteem emerged in response to the question, 'Which doll looks most like you?' The following table sums up the situation:

Table 17   Children's responses to the tests of 'actual' identity

	% choosing own-group figure	% choosiung other-group figure
English	100	0
Asian	76	24
West Indian	52	48

Source: Milner, 1975

When the same children were asked 'If you could be one of these two dolls, which one would you rather be?', evidence that minority children apparently would prefer to be white emerged even more strongly. While 100% of the British children again chose the white doll, as many as 65% of the Asians and 82% of the West Indians also made that choice. Disturbingly such preferences were accompanied by unfavourable stereotypes from many of the minority children towards the doll which represented their own racial group. While their doll was the 'bad' and 'ugly' one of the pair, the white one was the 'nicest'.

The responses of the children to the doll and picture tests suggest to Milner that, between the ages of 5 and 8, children internalise the negative image of black people prevalent in our society. Where West Indian and Asian children differ is over the extent to which they believe this negative image has implications for themselves. West Indian children find it more difficult to distance themselves from the derogatory picture of black people, which they have picked up, because their culture does not insulate them as much as that of Asian children's from the dominant culture.

Research, which has subsequently been conducted on children's self images, has produced contradictory findings. Nevertheless, most of it has questioned the notion that negative self images are prevalent among West Indian children. Let us briefly take two examples. The first comprises a study of 512 children – 256 white, 128 West Indian and 128 Asian – aged 7–10 from 16 primary schools, with varying degrees of minority concentration, in London and Yorkshire (Davey and Norburn, 1980). The second comprises a study of 375 adolescents – 108 English, 140 West Indian and 127 Asian – in the middle stream of the fifth year of four secondary schools in the Midlands (Louden, 1978).

In the first study, 'the children were presented with three photographs of children of the same sex as themselves, one for each ethnic group, and asked: "Which one looks most like you?"' A few weeks later, they were shown the same photographs, but this time they were asked: 'If you could choose, which one would you most like to be?' Responses to the second question indicated a significant difference between black and white children, with 86.2% of white children expressing a preference for their own group but less than half the West Indian and Asian children doing so. But if the preference, especially marked among the younger children, for the picture of the white child leant some support to Milner's suggestion that black children internalise the image of black people in our society, the responses to the first question made it clear that 'there has been a shift away from the pattern of self-rejection amongst minority group children since the late 1960s when David Milner carried out his tri-racial study' (Davey and Norburn, 1980). For the likelihood of a black child saying that he or she looked like a white child was no greater than a white child saying that he or she looked like a black child. An important reason for the fact 'that most West indian children *now* have a clear sense of identity and average self-esteem' (Milner, 1981; my emphasis), is that they have been encouraged to develop a pride in their own culture and their own ethnicity' (Davey and Norburn, 1980).

In the second study, the self-esteem of the adolescents was assessed, using a ten item scale. After analysing the results, Louden concluded that 'the overall finding of this study is that there is no significant differences in self-esteem between Asian, West Indian and English adolescents' (Louden, 1978). For the low status of a group to generate low self-esteem in its members, at least three conditions have to be satisfied. Individuals have to be aware of how their group is seen in the wider society, have to agree with its negative evaluation and have to accept the applicability of such a disparaging picture to themselves. These conditions tend not to be fulfilled because people selectively perceive their situation and in the process fend off threats to their self-esteem. Individuals who live in areas where there are a large number of people from the same ethnic group are in a particularly favourable position, according to Louden, to protect themselves 'from the full force of hostile stereotypes and racial denigration.' Mixing mainly with others from the same ethnic group, black adolescents are thus able to sustain positive feelings about themselves.

To argue that most black children have a clear sense of who they are and positive self-esteem 'is not meant to suggest that . . . [they] . . . do not internalise society's general system of prejudice' (Louden, 1978). According to Louden, minority children 'accept the broad ranking system' with the result that they tend to be disparaging towards other minority groups, 'but they pull their own group out of its place in the order.' In some cases, however, it is difficult for people to exempt their group in this way. Thus in a study of 1900 pupils, including 141 West Indians and 137 Asians, age 14–16 in 39 schools in London, the Midlands and the North of England, the authors confirmed that black children who were in schools in which ethnic concentration was low were 'more likely to internalise the negative view of blacks which are transmitted by the socialisation agencies of the wider society' (Bagley, Mallick and Verma, 1979). In this particular study in fact, the authors concluded, contrary to Louden, that while the self-esteem of Asians does not differ from that of their English counterparts, 'the level of self-esteem in male West Indians is below that of both female West Indians, and of male whites.' This suggests that the underachievement of West Indian boys may still be partially explicable in terms of a negative image of themselves which some of them have picked up (Bagley, Bart and Wong, 1979).

In suggesting that West Indian children are, compared to their white counterparts, less likely to be prepared for school, being developmentally relatively disadvantaged and perhaps having low self-esteem, we have been putting forward an explanation of underachievement which centres on the culture of the home. This kind of explanation has been very popular and was adopted by the Coleman report of 1966 to account for black underachievement in the United States and by the Plowden report of 1967 to account for working class underachievement in Britain.

These reports pointed out that what children brought with them to school from their home was more significant than the kind of school they went to in explaining group differences in achievement. Such a finding prompted some writers to argue that those who were under-achieving were 'culturally deprived' and therefore needed a pre-school enrichment programme if they were to get ahead. Projects, like Head Start in the United States and the Educational Priority Area programme in Britain were thus designed in order to give disadvantaged children extra help and thus compensate them for their deprived backgrounds.

The contention that children from particular minority and class groups fail in school because they are 'culturally deprived' has been severely criticised both in the United States (Baratz and Baratz, 1972) and Britain (Keddie, 1973). To argue that these groups are culturally deprived is to accept three claims: firstly that their children are deficient in some way; secondly that such a deficiency stems from the failure of these groups to develop an adequate culture; and thirdly that in order to rectify this deficiency, early childhood intervention is needed. All three claims, it is argued, are unfounded.

Take the issue of language, for example, where evidence from tests has suggested to some commentators that children from particular groups are linguistically deprived. Labov has shown how misleading such an interpretation is, on the basis of an analysis of the speech of some black children in the United States. Asked to repeat the sentence 'I asked Alvin whether he knows how to play basketball,' one of the boys said 'I axt Alvin does he know how to play basketball' (Labov, 1973). At first glance, the boy's failure to reproduce the sentence might suggest a deficiency. What must be recognised, however, is that the boy understood the sentence and that he translated it into a dialect he was more familiar with. This dialect is different from standard English but works according to perfectly logical and regular rules so that, in the case of the sentence which the boy uttered, 'the order of the direct question' rather than the word 'whether' was employed to express the underlying meaning. To argue that the boy is linguistically deprived constitutes, from this point of view, an extreme form of cultural bias, involving as it does an unjustified claim that standard English is not just one form of English but the only proper one.

The contention that it is the culture of the home which is primarily responsible for the underachievement of West Indian children has recently been criticised on similar lines by the Race and Politics group of the Centre for Contemporary Cultural Studies. Slavery, it is argued, was not as culturally devastating as is often supposed. 'The extent of escapes from the slave plantations, and the frequency with which maroon communities were established ... indicated a continuing resistance to slavery' (Lawrence, 1982). Far from being '"zombies" ... waiting conveniently to be filled with European culture' the West Indians 'developed distinctive cultures' retaining in their languages, religions and family systems African elements. While different, such cultures cannot legitimately be considered 'pathological'. To suggest that the failure of West Indian children stems mainly from the culture of their home is therefore a form of racism, which, in the course of laying the blame at the door of the West Indian community, absolves the education system of any responsibility (Carby, 1982).

There is clearly a great deal of truth in the criticisms levelled at the notion of cultural deprivation. Many commentators have indeed failed to appreciate that other cultures may be different but not pathological and that individuals who belong to these cultures may consequently be competent participants in distinct ways of life and not deficient. As a result, it has not been unusual for commentators to imply that parents are somehow to blame for the underachievement of their children, thus letting the education system off the hook.

Many of those who point to the culture of the home as a key factor in underachievement are unsympathetic however to the notion of 'cultural deprivation' and thus reject the view that other cultures are pathological. What they recognize is that cultures are not equally 'cohesive and supportive'. Take the case of the West Indians. There is little doubt that historically they suffered 'a more severe process of cultural fragmentation' than Asians and that, despite the efforts since then to fashion a distinctive culture, their culture remains less 'cohesive and supportive' (Hall et al., 1978). In suggesting that this culture is less conducive to educational success than that of Asians, it is not implied that the parents are to blame for the failure of their children. The socialisation, which West Indian children tend to receive, may not be the most helpful for their development and may not always generate positive self-esteem, but it must be seen in the context of the material disadvantage and racism West Indians face – and West Indians can hardly be blamed for these phenomena. Given the pressures, which West Indian parents face in bringing up their children, many of the commentators, who believe that the culture of the home is a significant factor in underachievement, argue that it is incumbent upon the education system to be more active. There are therefore calls for the expansion and improvement of facilities for children under five in order to promote the children's development (HMSO, 1981) and there are cries for a 'multicultural curriculum' in order (on one argument) to help all children develop a 'positive image' of themselves (Jeffcoate, 1979).

Before we move on to examine the view that it is the education system which is responsible for the underachievement of West Indian children, reference needs to be made to what is often seen as a crucial factor intervening between the general socialisation process of the home and educational achievement, notably language.

What is important in this context is that West Indians tend to speak a dialect of English at home, known as Creole. This developed during the period of slavery to facilitate communication between the planters and slaves, and indeed among the slaves themselves, who often came from different language communities. The vocabulary is mainly English, but the sound system and grammar are very different, exhibiting to some extent the influence of West African languages. Despite these differences between Creole and standard English, it should not be thought that they are completely distinct, with West Indians only familiar with the first. Rather, there is a continuum, with Broad Creole at one end and standard English at the other. Whether speakers operate towards one end of the continuum or the other depends on a variety of factors, including their class position and the context. The working class are more likely to be nearer the Broad Creole end of the continuum, but so are many others when the conversation is an informal one.

Although it is often suggested that anything which departs from standard English is deficient in some way, Creole 'works according to perfectly logical and regular rules and can express anything which standard English can. In other words it is different, not deficient' (Edwards, 1976a). Nevertheless, the distance between Broad Creole and standard English is so much greater than any other dialect range in Britain (Sutcliffe, 1982), that some writers have suggested that West Indian children may face particular difficulties in learning standard English.

There are two potential kinds of difficulty which can be distinguished. The first concerns the understanding of standard English and the second concerns the production of standard English. Let us take each in turn.

In relation to the question of whether Creole interferes with comprehension, there is some dispute. Despite the fact that Creole and standard English are mutually unintelligible language varieties, research undertaken at Birmingham University (Wight and Norris, 1970) found that most of the West Indian children were able, in the infant school, to modify their dialect quickly and without systematic teaching to the point where they achieved a classroom dialect intelligible to their English peers and teachers. Such a facility suggests that Creole may not act as a significant break on understanding. Moreover, tests conducted in eight junior school classes with children, aged 7–9, indicated that where West Indian children did have difficulty in oral comprehension, Creole was not the main cause. On the basis of this research, Wight accordingly concluded that the West Indian child 'will, provided he has reasonable exposure to the dialect of the teacher and the school, develop skills of language reception to cope with the contrasts between Creole and standard English' (Wight, 1971).

This conclusion has subsequently been questioned, however, by Edwards whose own research led her to the view 'that the language problem of West Indian children has been greatly underestimated' (Edwards, 1976b). Using the Neale analysis of reading ability, two groups of children, 40 English and 40 West Indian, aged 11–12, from three secondary schools in Reading were tested firstly on their reading and secondly on their comprehension of increasingly difficult passages. The children in each group were subdivided on the basis of their reading performance into poor, average and good readers and then their comprehension scores were compared. Although no significant differences were found between the average comprehension scores of the two groups of poor readers, West Indian average and good readers had markedly lower scores than their English counterparts. Some supplementary tests indicated that those who scored poorly on the comprehension tasks were strongly influenced by Creole. Edwards concluded that there were good grounds for supposing 'there was a relationship between dialect interference and underperformance on comprehension tasks' (Edwards, 1976b). In view of the fact that such interference has not been discovered among younger children who are learning to read and among the poorer readers in her own study, Edwards has subsequently suggested that 'although dialect does not seem to interfere with the acquisition of reading skills . . . it may become an important factor in the later stages of reading' (Edwards, 1979). This is conceivable, but at the moment the supporting evidence is very limited, being based on a small sample and the supposition that the correlation between being strongly influenced by Creole and scoring poorly on comprehension tasks is a causal one, when other factors than dialect interference might be responsible for inhibiting understanding.

If there is some doubt about whether Creole significantly interferes with oral comprehension or reading comprehension, there is agreement that the dialect affects the production of standard English. Particularly important, in this context, is the children's writing, where both the spelling and the grammar can exhibit the influence of Creole. The recurrence, for example, of certain non standard grammatical features, such as the omission of both the plural and possessive 's', often indicates dialect interference (Wight, 1971). Here the children are writing perfectly in line with the rules of Creole but are making mistakes in terms of standard English. Since they need to develop the capacity to write standard English if they are not to be disadvantaged in examinations, West Indian children, whose writing manifests persistent interference, may therefore require some special help. To this end, 'teachers in schools with children of West Indian origin should have an understanding of Creole dialect and a positive and sympathetic attitude towards it' (Bullock Report, 1975). Without some knowledge and respect for the children's dialect, there is the danger that the dialect features in the children's work will be constantly 'corrected' and the children given the impression that their dialect is unacceptable. If this happens, there is every likelihood that the children's self confidence will be affected and their capacity to master standard English and develop language skills more generally, impaired (Edwards, 1979).

Unfortunately, the limited evidence, which we have, on teachers' knowledge of and attitudes towards West Indian speech is not very comforting. Whereas the problems facing Asians in learning a second language have been recognised and special arrangements (however inadequate) have been made to accommodate their needs, the problems facing West Indians have gone largely unrecognized (Little, 1978) and little special help has been provided at the local level (Pilkington, 1976b). Indeed, 'the teacher's ignorance of Creole, and perhaps his traditional attitudes to non standard forms of English' have encouraged the dismissal of 'Creole features in the West Indian child's speech as incorrect or "sloppy" English' (Bullock Report, 1975). One study has gone even further to suggest that teachers view West Indian speech very negatively. 20 student teachers were asked to listen to a sample of children's speech, which had been recorded, and then to judge each speaker on a series of scales. The fact that the West Indian speakers were viewed least favourably and that one of the speakers was judged more favourably when speaking with a working class English accent than a West indian accent, suggests that West Indian speech evokes a negative stereotype (Edwards, 1978). Although the findings of such a small study can only be suggestive, they do alert us to the crucial issue of the school's attitudes towards the children's language.

In the view of a number of writers, it is the school's attitudes towards the children's language rather than the language itself which has a greater influence on educational achievement (Stubbs, 1976). Certainly this is the judgement, which the Rampton report came to, in concluding that 'we do not believe that for the majority of West Indian children in our schools . . . linguistic factors play a part in underachievement . . . but . . . it is important that a West Indian child's language is looked at in a positive light in the classroom since a rejection by the teacher of the home language may be a serious obstacle to motivation and subsequent achievement' (Rampton Report, 1981). In view of the extremely limited evidence, which points to the deleterious effects of Creole on comprehension, and the fact that children, whose first language is Creole, can with sympathetic help master standard English, this judgement seems a reasonable one.

Let us move on then to examine the view that it is the education system which is responsible for the underachievement of West Indian children. This kind of explanation takes a number of forms. A common one points to features which schools share, claiming that what matters is not so much which school West Indians go to as the fact that schools in Britain share certain values. Schools are, it is argued, suffused with white middle class values so that what 'knowledge' teachers choose to convey, what teaching methods they decide to employ and what forms of assessment they select, exemplify these values. The curriculum is in short an ethnocentric one, reflecting the outlook of one culture. As such it is biased against children from minority groups, who find that their own cultures are either ignored or belittled.

In the view of some commentators, the bias against West Indians is particularly severe and takes a racist form. Although much of the evidence in this area is somewhat anecdotal (Giles, 1977), one major piece of research in 1972, which involved 510 teachers from 25 schools around the country, revealed 'a high degree of consensus of opinion concerning the academic and social behaviour' of West Indian pupils, with more than two thirds of teachers agreeing in effect that such pupils are less able and give rise to more disciplinary problems. Since the teachers exhibited a much greater willingness to accept unfavourable generalisations about pupils of West Indian origin than those of Asian or European origin, it does indeed seem 'that there is large scale stereotyping of 'West Indian' pupils.' Interestingly, many of the comments made on the questionnaire pointed to the self contradictory nature of the stereotypes 'in that black pupils were descibed as lazy/passive/withdrawn and also boisterous/aggressive/disruptive' (Brittan, 1976).

The willingness of so many teachers to accept negative stereotypes about West Indian pupils is very disturbing. It is likely to lead to the dismissal of West Indian speech as 'bad English' and to low expectations of the children's academic potential (Edwards, 1979). In the process, a 'self fulfilling prophecy' can be set in motion, whereby those who are expected to perform at a low level do so. One way in which this can happen is as follows.

Children who are labelled as 'less able' are normally not given the same encouragement as others and therefore are often not as stretched. Aware of how they are seen by their teachers, they may respond by losing confidence in their own ability and become less motivated to succeed academically. In view of the evidence, which suggests that West Indian children tend to have lower self-esteem than children from other groups, the teacher's expectations are likely to meet with little resistance (Milner 1975). The pupils accept their teachers' judgement, make fewer efforts and thus confirm the apparent correctness of the original label.

Discouraged, some of the children may indeed become rebellious at school. In this context, it is interesting to note that in a study of over 2000 10 year old children in London, 41% of the West Indians compared with 19% of the whites were judged deviant by their teachers (Rutter et al., 1974). Although subsequent interviews with the teachers indicated that the extent of deviant behaviour in black children had been exaggerated, it was agreed that 'nevertheless, a significant excess of black children are deviant and rebellious in the school situation' (Bagley, 1975). Since the same children appeared on their parents' evidence, to be 'as well adjusted as their white peers,' it seems plausible to attribute their greater likelihood of behaving in a deviant way in school 'to difficulties in the school situation' (Rutter and Madge, 1976). In responding in this manner to the way they have been labelled, however, these children help to reinforce the negative stereotypes of West Indians held by teachers and contribute to their own eventual failure in school.

Although few studies have yet directly examined relations between teachers and pupils in a multiracial classroom, one, which investigated the fourth year of a secondary modern school in the West Midlands, came to the conclusion that teachers inadvertently contributed to the underachievement of West Indian boys. Unfamiliar with West Indian culture, the teachers frequently mis-interpreted the behaviour of their West Indian pupils and conse-quently responded to them in an inappropriate manner. 'Faced with the limitation of their own cultural competence in such interactions, such teachers often felt that their only way forward was a power-based insistence that these pupils act according to the standards which they (the teachers) stipulated for them. This tended to in-tensify an already conflictual situation and to heighten the ethnic awareness of those involved' (Driver, 1977). While the teachers became more critical of West Indian pupils, feeling that the boys in particular were frequently not only uncooperative but less able, the pupils 'turned to ethnic sources of support.' In the case of the girls, this usually meant the family. Encouraged by their mother and other members of the family, the girls in fact achieved better examination results than their English counterparts and surpassed their teachers' expectations. The boys, on the other hand, became increasingly frustrated at school and therefore turned to their peers for support. This was not conducive to educational success and served to 'discredit them' even further 'socially and academically in the eyes of their teachers' (Driver, 1981). This tendency of West Indian boys, who are 'failing' in school, to turn to their peers for support is also apparent in a study of a rigidly streamed boys' school (Troyna, 1978a). Here the West Indian boys in the lower streams dissociated themselves from the school by withdrawing into 'racially exclusive peer groups.' Their preference for reggae music signified their adherence to a distinct subculture and confirmed their belief that black people have 'a common identity and shared destiny.' While this subculture emerged, in part, in response to 'the youths' failure to cope in school' (Troyna, 1979), it also ensured further failure as the boys increasingly became disenchanted with the school.

What then are we to make of the suggestion that it is the teachers' negative stereotypes and low expectations which are responsible for the underachievement of West Indian children? We must recognize immediately that, in view of the paucity of evidence, this explanation remains a speculative one. Without further research, we cannot be sure that low expectations tend to lead to poor performances rather than the other way round. As it is, teachers do not invariably have low expectations of West Indian pupils and the latter do not respond in the same way to these expectations. Indeed, in a study of a small group of West Indian girls in a London comprehensive school, the author concluded 'that the black girls' achievement was not related to whether teachers saw them as good or bad pupils' (Fuller, 1981). Aware of their double disadvantage, being both black and female, they were determined to achieve academic qualifications. Although they 'worked conscientiously at the school work or homework set,' they did not seek their teachers' approval and in fact thought 'that other highly aspiring pupils placed too great an emphasis on teachers' opinions in relation to pupils' success.'

Even if too much emphasis can be placed on teachers' attitudes in accounting for patterns of achievement, the judgement of the Rampton report that they have 'a direct and important bearing on the performance of West Indian children in our schools' seems a reasonable one. In view of the extensiveness of racial prejudice in Britain, it is scarcely surprising to learn that many teachers hold 'negative, patronising or stereotyped views about ethnic minority groups.' Since such views tend to affect their behaviour towards members of these groups, teachers must therefore be held to be partially responsible for the underachievement of West Indian children. In recognizing this, we must be careful, however, not to place too much blame on individual teachers. The latter, often hard pressed in disadvantaged inner city schools, have been left to a large extent to fend for themselves, with little institutional support.

Unfavourable attitudes towards racial minorities are not only apparent in the attitudes of individual teachers but also percolate the school curriculum. An awareness of this has prompted some people, including the authors of the Rampton report, to argue that teachers should not only critically examine their own attitudes and behaviour but also adopt a 'multicultural approach' to the curriculum. Let us therefore briefly turn to this issue.

Multicultural education

Although multicultural education still remains more of an ideal than an actuality, some initiatives have nevertheless been made. In the case of the early attempts to devise such a curriculum, 'overriding importance' was attached 'to the affective objectives of respect for self and respect for others' (Jeffcoate, 1981). Aware that the traditional curriculum either ignored or belittled racial minorities, efforts were made to develop a curriculum which would portray racial minorities in a positive nonstereotyped way, and thus boost the self-esteem of minority children. Despite the laudible intentions behind this venture, both its underlying rationale and its products have been criticised. One West Indian writer, for example, has argued that, since there is no evidence that black children have negative images of themselves, there is no justification for these curricula innovations. Moreover, in the course of setting up activities which purportedly boost the self-esteem of black children, teachers have dabbled in matters which do not concern them. Their proper job is to teach children 'skills and knowledge and encourage the development of general abilities' (Stone, 1981). By tempting teachers to forget this and to focus on affective rather than cognitive objectives with West Indian children, 'multiracial education' may therefore have inadvertently 'contributed towards the low attainment of such children.'

Although Stone's work does raise some doubts about the likely effectiveness of multicultural education in combating West Indian underachievement, it should be said that not all forms of it are subject to her strictures. Other arguments than the promotion of black pupils' self images have been put forward in favour of a multicultural curriculum, for example, the claim that children have a right to have their culture reflected in the school curriculum. In addition, the adoption of a multicultural approach has not meant that cognitive objectives have invariably been sacrificed in favour of affective objectives, so that minority pupils find themselves with fewer opportunities to acquire basic skills. Indeed one form of multicultural education has not been aimed at black children so much as white children. This form of education seeks to reduce prejudice.

In view of its intrinsic importance, mention must be made of the one systematic attempt in Britain to evaluate the effectiveness of this form of multicultural education, namely the research project on *The problems and effects of teaching about Race Relations*. The teaching, which was undertaken with fourth year secondary school students, took place in the Spring term of 1974. The teacher adopted one of three teaching strategies in teaching about race relations: strategy A, in which the teacher took on the role of neutral chairman of a discussion group, strategy B in which the teacher, whilst acknowledging he was not wholly free from prejudice, given his socialisation, was committed to combating racism, strategy C, in which the teacher used improvised drama. The main finding of the research project is quite encouraging. In contrast to some limited research in the 1960s, it suggested that 'direct teaching about race relations in the age range 14–16', whether through strategy A or B, 'will tend to have positive rather than negative effects upon inter-racial tolerance as compared with not teaching about race relations' (Stenhouse, 1979).

Summary

To sum up. Having examined the employment and housing situation of racial minorities in the previous two chapters, we have concentrated in this chapter on a third major determinant of their life chances. Attention has accordingly been given to the performance of minority children in the education system. We have seen that while Asians as a group are performing at a comparable level with the indigenous population, West Indians as a group are underperforming. In accounting for this, emphasis has been placed both on what the children bring to school from their home and what the school provides the children.

Guide to reading

T. Bilton et al., *Introductory Sociology*, chapter 7 constitutes an excellent introduction to the sociology of education, but unfortunately neglects 'race'. Two clear and forthright overviews of race and education in Britain, which emphasise in particular the effects on children's racial attitudes of growing up in a society where racial prejudice is widespread, are D. Milner, *Children and Race* and two units written for the Open University by R. Street-Porter, *Education and the Urban Environment*, E361, Block 5. A more recent discussion of the main issues confronting schools in a multiracial society can be found in another Open University publication, written by R. Jeffcoate, *Ethnic Minorities and Community Relations*, E354, Block 4. A useful and complementary set of readings is A. James and R. Jeffcoate (eds.) *The School in the Multicultural Society*. For further discussion of the educational underachievement of West Indian children, the two most useful sources are M. Taylor, *Caught Between* and Rampton report, *West Indian Children in our Schools*. Of the journals in this area, *Multiracial Education*, which is produced by the National Association of Multiracial education, is the most helpful in keeping one up to date.

Discussion points

1. How important is education for the future of race relations? Is it more significant than employment or housing? How do the latter affect the schooling of minority children?
2. Which explanation of West Indian underachievement in schools do you find the most persuasive? Why do you think there is persistent disagreement between those who highlight the significance of the home and those who highlight the significance of the school? What changes are needed to enable West Indian children to perform at a comparable level with white children?
3. Take any aspect of the school curriculum with which you are familiar – say, a history syllabus. Is it ethnocentric? Do the teaching materials (books, pictures, etc.) reflect the fact that we live in a multiracial society? Do they present black people in a positive or negative light? What do you understand by the phrase, 'multicultural education'? Are there different forms of it? What are the arguments for and against its inclusion in the school curriculum? Should multicultural education percolate the curriculum or be additional to it? Should it be aimed at all pupils or only those from minority groups?
4. What minority needs are not being met at present by the education system? Are these needs unique to minorities? Why isn't the education system meeting these needs? What changes are needed for them to be met?
5. Is the evidence examined in this chapter more consonant with one sociological perspective rather than another?

8

Responses – The state, the mass media and racial minorities

A race relations situation was defined in the first chapter as one in which two features are present: racialism and racism. Racialism refers to practices which disadvantage people on the basis of their supposed membership of a particular race; racism refers to beliefs which consider that the disadvantaged group in question is inherently inferior. In the course of this book, we have amassed a great deal of evidence to show that racial minorities in Britain have met extensive racialism and racism with the result that their life chances have been impaired. To the question posed earlier, as to whether the entry of West Indians and Asians has given rise to a race relations situation in Britain, our answer must therefore be an emphatic yes.

Once it is recognised that Britain has a race relations situation, the question arises as to how people have responded to this situation. In this chapter, attention will be focused on the responses of three key agencies/groups: the state, the mass media and the minorities themselves.

The role of the state

In beginning our examination with the state, we are turning to a sector which is generally recognised to be an important determinant of people's life chances. Needless to say there are different conceptions of the state. But whether we go along with the claim of some Marxists, that the state primarily serves the long term interests of capital, or with the claim of some conflict theorists, that the state responds to the demands of a plurality of groups, we need to acknowledge the 'autonomy' of the state. Its actions are not at the beck and call of any one social group and make a significant contribution to the pattern of race relations.

The state did not anticipate the scale of immigration from the New Commonwealth and Pakistan and made no plans to help the newcomers settle in Britain. The measures taken by governments have therefore tended to be responses to immediate problems. In the process, however, a policy accepted by both the main political parties emerged. This policy has two aspects: controls over immigration on the one hand and measures designed to combat racial disadvantage on the other hand. While the Conservative party was the first to advocate immigration control which the Labour party later came to support, the latter was the first to put forward measures to redress racial disadvantage which the Conservatives then came to accept. Let us deal with each aspect in turn.

The opportunity, which the British Nationality Act of 1948 offered citizens of the British Commonwealth to enter Britain, seek work and settle here with their families, lasted throughout the fifties. The right of West Indians and Asians to migrate to Britain was indeed defended by politicians in both the main political parties. While Conservative spokesmen pointed out that citizens of the Commonwealth were 'British subjects', Labour spokesmen emphasised that they were 'our comrades' (Rex and Tomlinson, 1979). It is true that a vociferous minority on the back-benches objected to the arrival of black immigrants but such views did not gain much support in Parliament. The anti-immigration lobby gained a more responsive audience at the local level, however, where the white residents often felt resentment towards their new neighbours. Such feelings came to a head in the race riots in Nottingham and Notting Hill in 1958 when some white youths openly attacked blacks.

The riots shook many politicians out of their complacency and prompted them to take one of two positions. According to the first view, the riots exemplified racism. Disadvantaged whites had vented their frustrations on a group of people whom they considered inferior. For there to be racial harmony, governments needed to devise policies to combat racism and to eradicate the disadvantages faced by both whites and blacks. According to the second view, the riots indicated that traditional British tolerance towards immigrants had been stretched beyond reasonable limits. The presence of a large number of black and culturally distinct immigrants had provoked resentment. To allay people's anxieties and thus promote racial harmony, governments needed to restrict the number of black immigrants and encourage those already here to assimilate.

Although the subject of race relations rarely arose during the 1959 election, the re-elected Conservative government faced mounting demands for immigration control as immigration rose. Eventually the government succumbed to the pressure and passed the Commonwealth Immigrants Act of 1962. Under the Act, citizens of the British Commonwealth had to acquire an employment voucher to come to Britain unless they held passports issued in Britain or through a British High Commission abroad. Although the Act was vigorously opposed by the Labour party, the election of the Conservative candidate Peter Griffiths at Smethwick in the 1964 general election, prompted the party to change its mind. The Conservative candidate's victory on what most commentators consider to have been an extremely racist platform had been gained against the national trend. The lessons were not lost on the Labour government. Far from repealing the 1962 Act, it tightened it up and reduced the number of work vouchers for Commonwealth immigrants in 1965.

Two events in 1968 confirmed that the second view depicted above had won the day. They were the passing of legislation apparently designed to reduce the number of East African Asians entering Britain and what one writer has called 'the rise of Enoch Powell' (Foot, 1969). Let us take each in turn.

The 1962 Act did not cover East African Asians who had opted, on the independence of Kenya and other African countries, to hold British passports. When, however, many of them took up their right to migrate to Britain during 1967, as a result of the Kenyan government's 'Africanisation' policy, panic set in. The Commonwealth Immigrants Act of 1968 was rushed through Parliament and became law within a week. Under the Act, people who held British passports did not have the right to enter and settle in Britain unless they had a 'close connection' with the country, for example a parent or grandparent born here. The Act proved to be racially discriminatory in nature. For its effects were to allow Kenyan whites to enter Britain but to prevent Kenyan Asians from doing so until they were lucky enough to be granted one of the limited number of vouchers issued each year.

If 1968 witnessed a piece of legislation which was effectively racialist, it also saw a leading politician apparently lend respectability to racism. In graphic language, Powell advocated halting black immigration and indeed exploring ways of repatriating black people already here. Unless such measures were taken, he argued, the future was fearful. In his most famous speech, he concluded: 'As I look ahead I am filled with foreboding. Like the Roman I seem to see "the River Tiber foaming with much blood".' Although this speech was denounced by many politicians and caused him to be sacked from the Shadow Cabinet, Powell received phenomenal support from the public. In the light of this, few politicians were tempted any longer to take a more liberal line on immigration. Indeed, with the election of a Conservative government in 1970, a new Immigration Act was passed, which codified the previous legislation and tightened the controls on black immigration even further.

Under the 1971 Immigration Act, Commonwealth citizens needed permission to enter Britain unless they fell into one of three categories: they were 'patrials' and thus had a 'close connection' with the country; they were close relations of those who had emigrated to Britain under previous legislation; or they were part of the quota of East African Asians accepted each year. If they did not fit into one of these categories, they needed to be in possession of a work permit which henceforth had to be renewed annually. In effect the Act reinforced the racially discriminatory nature of the previous immigration legislation. In view of the paucity of 'patrials' in the New as opposed to the Old and predominantly white Commonwealth, virtually the only black immigrants allowed in since the Act have been close dependents of those already here and East African Asians who had been granted British passports.

The only occasion in which a significant liberal gesture has been made since then was in 1972 when President Amin expelled all British Asians from Uganda. Aware that these British passport holders would otherwise be stateless the British government reluctantly admitted 27000 refugees. This manifestation of liberalism did not last long, however. Indeed the emergence of a 'new political phenomenon' in the shape of a political movement, for whom racism was a central plank, probably helped to persuade most politicians against any further liberalisation (Taylor, 1979).

The new political phenomenon was the growth in support for an extreme right wing movement, the National Front. The movement had been formed in 1967 from other extreme right wing movements and inherited from its predecessors both its personnel and ideology (Taylor, 1978). Indeed continuities have been detected between the National Front and two previous fascist movements, Mosley's British Union of Fascists and Leese's Imperial Fascist League. Not only were leading members of the National Front connected with these movements, but they also retained, as a central element in their ideology, the belief that Jews were conspiring to overthrow the natural order, in which the white race was dominant, so that they could rule the world themselves (Billig, 1978). In seeking popular support, leaders of the National Front played down this ideological strand and emphasised instead the need for black immigrants to be repatriated. Such scapegoating of blacks (Nugent and King, 1979) brought the party little success until the government decided to admit the Ugandan Asians in 1972. Capitalising on the issue, National Front candidates in the local elections in 1973 gained some electoral support with over 10% of the vote in a number of cities. More important, however, than its electoral support – which only remained at this kind of level in 1976–7, when a panic had arisen about the numbers of East African Asians being admitted to the country – was the publicity which the party received through its demonstrations and election campaigns.

The visibility and apparent popularity of a party, which openly expressed racist views, may have encouraged the main political parties to maintain a very restrictive immigration policy. In this context, it is interesting to note than in an interview in 1978 before she became Prime Minister, Mrs. Thatcher made reference to the National Front. After pointing out that some white people felt 'swamped by people with a different culture', she spoke of the fears 'driving some people to the National Front', a party considered to be at least 'talking about some of the problems'. In the light of this the decision of the Conservative party to advocate further immigration restriction becomes understandable and may have contributed to the debacle of the National Front in the general election in 1979. Certainly there have been few signs of any relaxation in the way immigration legislation has been administered since then. Indeed the passing of a new Nationality Act in 1981, to bring citizenship law in line with the changes effected by the immigration legislation of 1962, 1968 and 1971, has been seen by some commentators as yet further evidence of racial discrimination.

Two kinds of Commonwealth citizens had been created under the 1948 Act, citizens of the Independent Commonwealth countries on the one hand, and citizens of the United Kingdom and the Colonies on the other hand. The 1981 Act replaced the latter form of citizenship with three new ones: British citizenship, British Dependent Territories citizenship and British Overseas citizenship. Only those who are British citizens, mainly 'patrials' have the right to settle in this country. Those who hold British Dependent Territories citizenship, mainly people in Britain's remaining colonies, have the right to settle in the dependency in question while those who hold British Overseas citizenship, the remainder, do not have the right to settle in any country at all. Much of the criticism of the Act has centred on the last form of citizenship. For some of the people in this category – mainly Asians – do not have any other nationality. The unwillingness of the government to give British citizenship to those without any other 'contrasts markedly with the solicitude shown to certain people – mainly white' (Bonner, 1983) and suggests racial discrimination.

What conclusions can we draw then from our review of the measures adopted by governments in the field of immigration? The evidence indicates that the controls have not only got tighter but have also in their operation proved more racially discriminatory. The success of the anti-immigration lobby in winning local support for its measures before 1962, Griffiths' victory at Smethwick in 1964, the popularity of Powell's speeches from 1968 and the visibility of the National Front during the 1970s meant that politicians were frequently reminded of the existence of strong opposition to black immigration and were therefore persuaded to adopt increasingly restrictive controls. Fearful of the electoral consequences of appearing too liberal, a leading member of the Labour cabinet, Richard Crossman, explained that after Smethwick the party 'felt [it] had to out-trump the Tories by doing what they would have done and so transforming their policy into a bipartisan policy' (Crossman, 1975). Euphemistically, the cry was for 'immigration' control, but it became increasingly clear that the parties' main concern was to 'out-trump' each other in their control of *black* immigration. In view of the importance attached to this, it is perhaps not surprising to learn of the extraordinary and sometimes inhuman lengths government officials concerned with immigration have gone to in order to ensure that only those who are entitled to come enter the country.

If immigration legislation and administration have tended to be racialist, being apparently presaged on the assumption that an increase in the number of black immigrants is inherently undesirable, the same is not true of the other aspect of government policy in the field of race relations. Measures designed to combat racial disadvantage reflect the adherence of governments to liberal principles. Such measures have taken two forms, being concerned either with disadvantage which stems from racial discrimination, or with disadvantage which has other sources. Let us deal with each form in turn.

The government has attempted to combat racial discrimination through a series of Race Relations Acts. The first in 1965 outlawed racial discrimination in certain places of public resort and set up a Race Relations Board to receive complaints of discrimination and, if necessary, act as a conciliator. In view, however, of evidence of substantial racial discrimination in other fields, a second Act was passed in 1968 outlawing racial discrimination in employment, housing and commercial services. If the Race Relations Board was unable to conciliate the two sides in a dispute, it was empowered to take the case to court. The Act also set up a new body, the Community Relations Commission to promote 'harmonious community relations'. Although overt racial discrimination declined considerably following the Act, evidence that considerable covert discrimination still persisted prompted the government to pass a third Act in 1976.

The most recent Race Relations Act was strongly influenced by anti-discrimination law in the United States. As such, it diverges from the previous Acts in three main ways. Firstly, the definition of racial discrimination is extended to include indirect forms, where practices have a disproportionately adverse effect on a particular racial group, even when there is no intention to discriminate. Secondly, the Commission for Racial Equality, which replaces both the Race Relations Board and the Community Relations Commission, is empowered to carry out its own investigations of organisations to find out whether they were discriminating. If discrimination is discovered it can require the organisation to change its practices and check that this has been done. Thirdly, individuals who believe that they have been discriminated against can take their complaints directly to the courts or industrial tribunals.

Although writers from different theoretical positions believed that the Act might significantly reduce the level of racial discrimination (for example, Sivanandan, 1982 on the one hand, and Smith, 1977 on the other hand), the signs so far are not promising. Take the case of employment, where, following the American experience, the CRE has urged employers to adopt formal equal opportunity policies in the hope that they will check their existing practices for possible discrimination and take appropriate action. Initial evidence suggests that this policy is proving less effective than in the United States in providing 'a steady improvement in the opportunities for some blacks' (Braham et al., 1981). Three broad reasons have been put forward for this.

The first concerns the law itself. 'The prospect of successful litigation against those who discriminate is much greater and the economic consequences for those successfully sued are vastly greater' in the United States (Bindman, 1981). While the courts in the United States have tended to be sympathetic towards legislation where the objective is to end the 'social wrong' of racial discrimination, British courts have often been keener to protect 'the private rights of the individual, including the right to discriminate on the grounds of the colour of a man's skin' (Griffith, 1977). As a result the latter have been 'much less willing to accept that discrimination has been proved' (Bindman, 1981) so that in the period 1978–1980, only 97 complaints of discrimination in employment (18% of those taken to tribunals) were upheld and in the majority of these cases no compensation was given. The derisory amounts of compensation which have tended to be awarded in Britain again provides a contrast with the situation in the United States. In Britain, damages cannot be awarded where indirect discrimination which is unintentional occurs, and there is no possibility of a 'class action', where claims can be put forward in court simultaneously on behalf of a large number of complainants, each of whom may receive damages. The consequence is that, by comparison with the United States, employers do not face the possibility of huge fines.

The second reason for the relative ineffectiveness of anti-discrimination legislation concerns the state. The state is in a powerful position, both as an employer and through its contracts with firms in the private sector, to promote an effective equal opportunities policy. In contrast to the United States, a low priority, however, has tended to be given to this.

The third reason why the Race Relations Act has not been as successful as had been hoped concerns the CRE. The body has been severely criticised by the Home Affairs Select Committee for overstretching itself and thus failing to fulfil its law enforcement duties satisfactorily (Home Affairs Committee, 1981). Certainly the results of its investigations into organisations suspected of discrimination have so far proved disappointing, with too many being directed at small organisations and with only one having been translated into a published report by 1982. The problem does not, however, lie purely with the CRE. It has not been given the resources and the government support necessary for it both to enforce the law and undertake promotional work.

Racial disadvantage does not stem purely from racial discrimination but arises also, for example, from the fact that black people tend to live in inner cities. Aware of this, governments have devised a number of 'colour blind' measures which it is hoped will prove beneficial to the disadvantaged generally. In view of the fact that black people tend to be disproportionately disadvantaged, it is expected that they will particularly benefit from these measures. As yet, however, there are few signs that these attempts to deal with the problems of racial minorities by stealth have proved any more successful than the antidiscrimination legislation (Runnymede Trust, 1980). Commenting on government policy in the field of housing, Rex has argued that there has not been 'any clear policy towards immigrant minorities. At best the policies which have been evolved have been piecemeal compromises to deal with contingencies as they arise' (Rex, 1981b). And in similar fashion, with reference to government policy in the field of education, Little has concluded that 'no national policy on ethnic minority education has emerged' (Little, 1978).

To conclude that the measures governments have devised to combat racial disadvantage have so far proved relatively ineffective is not to claim that they were 'conceived in terms of giving the impression [of] something . . . being done' (Ben-Tovim and Gabriel, 1982). The organisations, such as the Campaign Against Racial Discrimination, which first put forward these proposals, genuinely wished to end racial discrimination and the government, in making a positive response to this demand, acted in line with liberal principles.

Having examined both aspects of government policy in the field of race relations, what conclusions can we come to? Government policy has exhibited the influence of two contradictory traditions, racism and liberalism. While immigration policy and administration have tended to exemplify the first tradition, the measures designed to combat racial disadvantage have tended to exemplify the second tradition. In view, however, of the fact that both main political parties reached a consensus during the 1960s that tight control on *black* immigration was a necessary prerequisite for racial harmony, it is the first tradition which has been the more dominant one (Parekh, 1978). In seeking to appease public opinion, by imposing steadily tighter controls on black immigration, governments appear to have not only acted in a racially discriminatory way but also to have reinforced racist attitudes in the electorate (Dummett and Dummett, 1982). Although it is true 'that neither party has sought to exploit the race issue to anything like its full extent' (Lawrence, 1978), it is also true that neither party has stood steadfastly by liberal principles and thus opened up the possibility of liberal attitudes in the electorate being reinforced.

Government policy in this field does not have to take the form which it has done. It is not determined in some mechanistic way by public opinion any more than it is by the needs of capital. Rather it is the product of human decisions. If racial disadvantage is to be combatted and race relations to be improved, the major political parties must stop trying to out-trump each other in seeking to appease 'racist sections of public opinion' and instead take decisive action to fight racism and eradicate the deprivations faced by both whites and blacks.

The mass media

While the state is in probably the most powerful institutional position to influence race relations, it is the mass media which constitute for most people the major source for their picture of what is going on. Indeed it is primarily through the mass media that the messages of the politicians are transmitted and the latter learn about the state of public opinion. Before, however, we examine the news media, reference needs to be made to the entertainment media.

Although we do not turn to the entertainment media to find out what is going on in the field of race relations, such media do nevertheless provide us with images of people and countries and in this way lead us to hold certain expectations about relations between people with different skin colours. In view of the evidence which indicates that racial attitudes are picked up at an early age, much of the research here has been conducted on the media aimed primarily at children. The conclusions of the research are uniformly bleak, as three reviews have pointed out. 'In their comics children are provided with a world in which blacks hardly figure; but where they are present in the action it is as superstitious natives, docile, humble servants, or brute savages' (Husband, 1974). An image of the world is conveyed which derives from colonialism and visualises both black people and the countries they come from as 'primitive'. Such assumptions are also apparent in children's popular fiction. Again, if blacks do figure, they are allotted limited roles, tending to oscillate between 'naughty, evil and menacing roles', such as the golliwogs in the Noddy stories, on the one hand, and being 'merry, simple, childlike people', such as Little Black Sambo, on the other hand (Dixon, 1977). A similarly one sided treatment is even apparent in school textbooks where 'one finds again the same unfavourable images of black people and the same pictures of white-dominated black countries' (Laishley, 1975). What tends to be true of the media aimed primarily at children seems to apply generally to the entertainment media. These 'reflect on the whole a white man's world in which coloured people, if they are visible at all, tend to have a marginal or subordinate position or to strike a discordant note in an otherwise harmonious world' (Hartmann and Husband, 1974).

In moving from the entertainment media to the news media, the question arises as to whether the latter also present a picture of the world in which black people only tend to figure as problems. The most systematic evidence pertinent to this question comes from a study which analysed the treatment of race in the British national press between 1963 and 1970 (Hartmann, Husband and Clark, 1974). Every thirteenth issue of the Times, Guardian, Daily Express and Daily Mirror was examined over the seven year period to discover what the race related material was about. The content analysis revealed that 'Race in Britain was portrayed as being concerned mainly with immigration and the control of entry of coloured people to the country, with relations between white and coloured groups, discrimination and hostility between groups, with legislation, and with the politician, Enoch Powell' (Hartmann and Husband, 1974). The fact that these increasingly became the main terms in which race was presented suggests that a framework for the presentation of race news developed over this period, whereby black immigration was seen as a threat and black people as a problem. Thus despite the fact that the newspapers held different attitudes towards Enoch Powell and the accurcay of his statistics on immigrant numbers, there was agreement on the fact that immigration was a critical issue because of the undisputed assertion that a large black population needed to be avoided. Items which did not fit this framework tended to be seen as increasingly peripheral so that the positive contribution of black people to our society was discounted and the underlying sources of racial tension in the unequal way resources are distributed in our society was ignored.

Confirmation of the existence of a framework, which depicted black immigration as a threat and black people as a problem, across the news media can be found in two further studies of race relations reporting, the first a study of the coverage of the local press between 1963 and 1970 (Critcher et al., 1977) and the second of television in 1970 (Downing, 1975). On the basis of a content analysis of five West Midlands newspapers, Critcher et al. noted that immigration constituted a significant element in race reporting and that the issue was 'defined almost exclusively as a problem of control'. A similar conclusion was reached by Downing, who pointed out that the media 'have used whites in overwhelming preference to blacks to define the issues; and the whites they have used have often been those determined to expel the black minority from Britain' (Downing, 1980). In view of this, it is not surprising to learn that a content analysis of three quarters of news bulletins, current affairs programmes and documentaries during 1970 revealed that the vast bulk of time devoted to race in Britain concerned black immigration, or Enoch Powell and that 'the taken-for-granted framework' of the coverage rested on 'the fundamentally racist view that "immigration *creates* problems"' (Downing, 1975).

Although the news media's coverage of race related material since 1970 has not received the same systematic analysis, the studies which have been done agree that the media continue to present black people in a negative light. In 1976, for example, over a period of six weeks a 'combination of stories' appeared which 'left the strong impression that Britain was being taken over by swarms of Asians, who were not only "conning" their way into Britain illegally, but once they got here were "conning" a "lush living off the state"' (Evans, 1976). As time has passed, however, the notion of swarms of black people entering the country has become less central and the issue of immigration has been replaced by others. One such issue is 'mugging'.

'Mugging' was first used by the press to describe a specific crime in England in 1972. According to Hall et al., the term had served to symbolise the crisis of law and order in American cities so that when it was transferred to Britain it meant much more than a particular kind of street robbery. It evoked images of black youth mindlessly creating havoc in the inner city. Since 1972 such images have solidified so that mugging has now become unambiguously associated with West Indian youth in certain areas such as Brixton (Hall et al., 1978). The prominence given to such a crime is illuminating when put alongside the media's neglect of racial attacks.

In November 1981, a Home Office study revealed that Asians were 50 times and West Indians 36 times more likely to be victims of racially motivated attacks than whites. The survey was in Smith's words 'curiously underplayed by the mass media' (Smith, 1982). Four months later, the Metropolitan police issued its annual crime figures which purportedly showed that blacks were more likely that whites to be involved in 'robbery and other violent theft', i.e. the category of crime which incorporates mugging. Despite the fact that 'robbery and other violent theft' comprised the smallest category of crime in London, involving only 3% of recorded offences, the media latched on to the figures and in the process conveyed the totally unwarranted impression that black people were disproportionately criminal (Pierce, 1982).

The relative weight given to the Home Office study on racial attacks and the Metropolitan police's racial breakdown of one category of crime, is not so curious when it is recognised that the news media tend to adopt a framework for race related news which assumes that black people constitute a problem. As one assistant editor of a major national newspaper has put it, 'everything to do with coloured people takes place against an underlying premise, that they are the symbols or the embodiments of a problem' (Young, 1971). Items which fit this framework are given prominence, while contrary items are played down.

To argue that the news media tend to present black people in a negative light does not imply that there is some kind of media conspiracy against black people. In many newspapers, there is a marked contrast between the news headlines and the editorials, with the latter qualifying the sensationalism of the former and emphasising the need for racial tolerance. This indicates that the news media do not consciously set out to convey a negative image of black people. That such a picture is unwittingly conveyed is a result of newsmen following their normal practices.

To illustrate what these practises involve – and therefore why some items become news rather than others and why they are presented in one way rather than another – let us take the case of a daily newspaper. The latter faces at least three demands: a need to ensure that news is regularly produced every 24 hours, a need to ensure that the news is interesting and a need to ensure that the news is intelligible. Let us take each demand in turn.

To enable it to produce news regularly, a newspaper relies on certain routines. One routine is to allocate specific proportions of a paper to different types of news (e.g. home, foreign, sport, etc.). In the process of maintaining a particular balance between these different types of news, irrespective of what happens in the real world, the organisation of the newspaper clearly affects what items become defined as news. Of more importance, however, to race news is the routine whereby preference is given to events which occur within a period of a day. Such a routine tends to mean that the media focus on the manifestations of racial conflict and not their underlying causes. A demonstration, especially when accompanied by violence, therefore becomes news while the factors which lead up to it and make it explicable are ignored.

Although the adoption of various routines enables newspapers to produce news regularly, it does not ensure that the news is interesting. This is where 'news values' comes in. These comprise a set of assumptions, generally shared by journalists across the news media, about the kinds of events which are newsworthy and how they should be presented. The employment of such values involves a stress on the unusual, on the dramatic, on conflicts and on personalities, especially well known personalities. 'Two things follow from this: the first is that journalists will tend to play up the extraordinary, dramatic, tragic etc. elements in a story in order to enhance its newsworthiness; the second is that events which score high on a number of these news values will have greater news potential than ones that do not' (Hall et al., 1978).

In the light of our discussion of news values, the form which race relations reporting has taken becomes more explicable. While the positive contribution of black people to our society scores low on all news values, Enoch Powell's famous speech in 1968 almost perfectly meets the requirements of a good news story. After all, the speech – expressed in dramatic language and rife with personal anecdotes – was by a leading politician apparently in conflict with his party on a matter of public concern (Seymour-Ure, 1974).

In addition to the need to produce news regularly and in an interesting way, newspapers must also ensure that the news is intelligible. To this end, journalists tend to present news within frameworks which are already familiar to the audience. In chapter 3, we argued that 'our whole way of thinking about coloured people, constitutes a built-in predisposition to accept unfavourable beliefs about them' (Hartmann and Husband, 1971). In view of this, it is perhaps not surprising that the media imported from America a framework for race reporting which visualises black people as a problem.

This framework depends upon a particular image of society – a consensus image – according to which people in Britain are assumed to share the same fundamental values. One such value which the British are deemed to hold is that of tolerance. In view of this, responsibility for any problems which arise between white and black people is laid at the door of those who are not 'truly' British – perhaps a few 'sick' or 'corrupt' whites, but more often blacks. In scapegoating black people in this way, the media not only confirm Britain's image of itself as an essentially tolerant society, but also convey a sense of its people as united against an alien threat. Such a picture inevitably gives the impression that Britain is fundamentally a white society. Take, for example, the media's coverage of the National Front. Despite the fact that the NF's explicit racism was condemned, their right to propagate such a belief system was defended. In the process, 'the "freedom" of black people to be protected from the NF's racial insults [was] constantly overlooked' and the impression underlined 'that blacks exist outside the mainstream of British society' (Troyna, 1982).

Even if it is granted that frameworks, which presume that people in Britain share fundamental values in common, are frequently used by the news media to interpret events (Cohen and Young, 1981), the question still arises as to the origins of such frameworks. Of crucial importance here are those in powerful institutional positions. They are frequently consulted by the mass media and given preferential access to it, for two main reasons. The first stems from the fact that the media need to ensure that news is produced regularly. Faced with the problem of constantly working against the clock, journalists find it helpful to turn to institutional spokesmen who can be relied upon to provide a story. The second stems from the professional values of journalists. Obliged to be as objective as possible, journalists constantly turn to 'accredited sources', notably representatives of the major institutions. The result of giving such preferential access to those in powerful positions is that these '"spokesmen" become . . . the primary definers of topics' (Hall et al., 1978). As such, they provide the initial framework for understanding these topics and are the first to outline what the main issues are. Alternative frameworks and alternative interpretations of the main issues do of course get a hearing, but once a topic has been defined in a particular way, it is extremely difficult to change the terms of the debate. 'Once race relations in Britain [had] been defined as a 'problem of numbers', for example, most of the discussions of the issue centered on the question of numbers. Those who suggested that the primary problem should instead be British racism were seen as 'not addressing the problem' (Hall et al., 1978).

In the light of our discussion of the significance of those in powerful institutional positions for the production of news, the congruence between the issues defined by both the state and the media as central becomes more explicable. Given the institutional links between the Metropolitan police and crime correspondents, it is understandable that the media have given more prominence to 'mugging' than racial attacks.

To argue that the news media tend to present black people in a negative light, through following their normal practices, is not to claim that the coverage inevitably has to take a particular form. Newspapers do differ in the topics they highlight, in the tone they adopt and in the depth of their coverage (Braham, 1982). Take, for example, the coverage given to the Metropolitan police's disclosure in 1983 that blacks were still more likely than whites to be involved in 'robbery and other violent theft'. For the *Sun*, this was a major story. Blazoned over its front page were the headlines *BLACK CRIME SHOCK* and two subsidiary headlines *Twice as many muggings as by white thugs* and *82% of all attacks in one London area*. So important was the story considered to be that it continued on page two (although not on page three) with a new headline *BLACK MUGGINGS SHOCKER* and warranted a leader the following day. For the *Guardian*, by contrast, this was not a major story. It made no reference to the topic on the day it broke in the *Sun* and even on the following day did not consider it worthy of front page coverage. The topic appeared on the back page under the headline *Garbage crime figures come under attack* and was taken up in a leader, in which the statistics were criticised for being misleading. If the priority given to the topic was different, so was the tone adopted. While the *Sun* conveyed the impression that black people were disproportionately involved in crime, the *Guardian* was at great pains to avoid giving this impression. As to the depth of coverage, while the *Sun* took the figures at face value, the *Guardian* critically examined them and presented them in context.

Even if the news media do not necessarily present black people in a negative light, there is nonetheless a tendency for them to do so. In view of this, the question arises as to the effects of such a presentation on people's attitudes and perceptions.

Research on the effects of the mass media on people's attitudes has tended to show that the media reinforce already existing attitudes rather than bring about significant changes. To give one example, a study of viewers' responses to the television series, *'The nature of prejudice'* indicated that on the whole the programmes served to confirm previous views (Elliott, 1972). Such a conclusion is not surprising in view of what we know about selective perception. People do not passively respond to media material but actively use it. Content, which contradicts existing attitudes, tends therefore to be ignored or forgotten, while content, which backs them up, is more likely to be sought out and remembered. The result of this is that the media are normally unable to override the effects of other socialising agencies such as the family and the influence of the groups to which individuals belong.

To argue that short term exposure to media material does not have a marked impact on people's attitudes is not to suggest that the media have no important effects. In particular there is some evidence that 'the media provide people with a picture of the world which makes the development of one kind of attitude more likely than another' (Hartmann and Husband, 1974).

The most systematic attempt to show that the mass media's race relations coverage influences people's perceptions of what is going on comes from a survey by Hartmann and Husband. In this study, white school children, aged 11–15 and their parents were interviewed and asked a series of questions about race. Despite the fact that the respondents came from different parts of Britain and lived in areas with different levels of black settlement, there was a remarkably similar perception of the major issue in race relations. Too many black immigrants were thought to be entering the country.

Although it is likely that some of the respondents came to the belief that 'immigrant numbers are too great' through first hand contact with black people, it is difficult to see how those living in areas with few black people could have acquired their belief other than through the mass media. Confirmation that the media were indeed a crucial source for this belief emerged from the content analysis of the press and during the survey itself. The content analysis of the press revealed, as we have already seen, the same preoccupation with the question of numbers and in the course of the survey many of the respondents indicated that they had derived their information about race relations from the mass media (Hartmann and Husband, 1974).

Further evidence of the media's influence on people's perceptions of race relations comes from a study by Little and Kohler. According to their survey, 58% of the respondents felt that race relations had deteriorated nationally between 1970 and 1976, while only 17% of them felt that they had deteriorated locally. As the authors point out, 'views about change in ones own locality are largely based upon direct experience of relations and feelings in that locality. A national or general view, however, can be based only upon secondary sources, in particular, the media' (Little and Kohler, 1977).

All in all, there do seem good grounds for believing that the news media do play a major part in defining for people what the major issues are in race relations. In focusing on issues like immigration and crime among black people, however, the media may well have amplified white people's anxieties about black people – anxieties which the government then feel they need to respond to. This is not inevitable, however, and, as we saw earlier in our discussion of press coverage of the 'mugging' statistics, newspapers can – if they are extremely careful (Critcher, 1979) – avoid presenting black people in a negative light.

The reaction of racial minorities

Finally, we come to the racial minorities themselves, and to the question of how they have reacted to a race relations situation in Britain. According to Phizacklea and Miles, there are three possible strategies open to them. They can organise around colour, class or ethnicity (Phizacklea and Miles, 1980). Let us examine each strategy in turn and see what has so far been the most common basis for organisation.

In view of the fact that the racial minorities have been subject both to racialism and racism, one might have expected a consciousness of colour to emerge and become a significant basis for organisation. In practice, however, the minorities have tended to be more aware of their cultural differences so that it has been rare for them to organise together on the basis of colour. Occasionally they have come together for a specific campaign, but such 'black unity' has so far proved extremely fragile. As Moore has pointed out, we still 'seem to be a long way from the day when all non-white immigrants and their descendents in the UK refer to themselves as "blacks"' (Moore, 1982).

If 'black unity' has not constituted a very feasible strategy for the minorities, what of 'class unity'? In view of the fact that black people are predominantly working class, one might have anticipated that their response to disadvantage would take a similar form to that of their white comrades. And there indeed do seem to be signs of similarities. Thus evidence indicates that 'black workers are just as likely as white workers, or more so, to vote Labour and to join a trade union' (Phizacklea and Miles, 1980). Electoral support for Labour and union membership do not of course necessarily indicate class consciousness. The former may exhibit a preference for a party which is rather more liberal than its main rival on race relations, while the latter may merely be convenient. Nevertheless, evidence of a willingness on the part of black workers to participate in industrial action, such as strikes, alongside white workers does point to a degree of class unity.

Despite the fact that industrial disputes have often brought black and white workers together in opposition to management, there has been a tendency on the part of some writers to think that disputes which primarily involve black people are 'complicated by a racial element'. We must be wary of making such an assumption (Bentley, 1981). Take, for example, the dispute which arose at Grunwick in 1976. Here the basic demand of the strikers was to gain Union recognition from an employer who had refused to accept one. The fact that the strikers were primarily Asian women was irrelevant. Indeed, in this particular case, the 'solidarity' which was shown towards those fighting for union recognition by other (often white) workers was 'considerable' (Phizacklea and Miles, 1981).

If there have been signs of class unity during industrial disputes, there have also been some indications of it during local campaigns. Thus – to give one example – the decision of the local authority to slum clear Moss Side, Manchester, gave rise to a number of housing protest movements, each 'characterised by a multi-racial membership' (Ward, 1979).

To point to examples of black and white people acting together should not blind us, however, to the occasions when racial divisions have inhibited collective action. Although both the Labour Party and the Trades Union Congress have campaigned against racism, there have been instances in which the Labour movement has failed to support black workers and has indeed been involved in discriminatory practices. The disputes at Mansfield Hosiery Ltd and Imperial Typewriters, for example, stemmed from the fact that the white dominated unions were more anxious to restrict access to promotion opportunities to whites than represent the interests of Asian workers. The latter were therefore 'forced to organise as an Asian workforce, relying on the resources of the Asian community rather than their unions' (Moore, 1982). In other words, they turned to 'ethnic organisation'.

In view of the fact that the racial minorities belong to different groups, with their own distinct cultures, it is not surprising that organisations have frequently formed around ethnicity. Keen to maintain their cultural distinctiveness, the minorities have not only created a plethora of neighbourhood based organisations to enable their community life to function, but have also used these organisations to further their interests in the wider society. Sometimes this has involved waging campaigns to change prevailing practices. Thus – to give one example – the Sikhs have fought to be allowed to wear turbans rather than crash helmets on motorcycles.

To point to the existence of distinct ethnic groups among the racial minorities is not to suggest that the boundaries between such groups are rigid or that the beliefs and values, which they espouse, are static. While the experience of being rebuffed by British society has tended to encourage the minorities to maintain a separate ethnic identity, 'the ethnicity of the second generation is rather different from that of their parents' (Ballard and Ballard, 1977). In particular there is evidence that a wider ethnic identity is developing, with the children becoming aware of themselves as Asians or West Indians and not just Mirpuris or Trinidadians.

Of the three possible bases for organisation we distinguished earlier – colour, class and ethnicity – the latter has proved the most common. The cultural distinctiveness of the minorities has allowed ethnic organisations to emerge and the racism of the wider society has ensured that they maintain their importance. We must be careful, however, not to think that such an ethnic respone precludes a class response. The minorities are not, as we have seen, totally reliant on separate organisations and especially at work are represented by the same organisations as their white colleagues. Whether the reaction of the second generation continues to be mainly on ethnic lines or not will depend to a large extent on the actions of the wider society and not least the Labour movement. If 'class unity' is to develop then the recognition, which the unions now have of racism in their midst, will need to be translated into decisive action to combat it (Miles and Phizacklea, 1981).

In the course of examining whether the minorities have been more likely to organise around colour, class or ethnicity, reference has been made not only to the responses of those who migrated but also to those of their descendents. Given the importance of the latter for the future of race relations, let us explore further the reactions of the second generation. We shall begin by looking at Asian youth and then go on to West Indian youth.

Asian and West Indian youth

According to many commentators, young Asians face a range of distinctive problems. As one writer puts it, 'Asian youth suffer very distinctly from inhabiting a different world at home from that at school' (Brake, 1980). The culture, which is imbibed at home clashes with that picked up at school so that the children invariably experience some stress. Attracted by Western values, they subsequently often come into conflict with their parents during adolescence.

There is obviously some truth in this picture. Thus there are indeed significant differences between British and Asian cultures. Particularly important are their respective conceptions of the relationship of the individual to the community. While the British tend to place paramount importance on the freedom of the individual, Asians tend to believe that 'the interests of the group as a whole always take precedence over those of the individual members' (Ballard, 1979). The British consequently tend to view marriage as a contract between two individuals and Asians to picture it as an arrangement between families. In view of these contrasts between British and Asian cultures, it is not surprising to learn of Asian adolescents expressing a preference for the 'western model of marriage based on individual choice' (Brah, 1978) and of conflicts between them and their parents (Ballard, 1979).

We must be careful, however, not to caricature the situation. Although Brah discovered that his sample of 15–16 year olds in Southall tended to express a preference for own-choice marriages, he also noted that there was 'an acceptance on the part of these teenagers of the prospect of arranged marriages'. Similarly, after acknowledging that many young Asians in Leeds did 'rebel against their parents' social and cultural values during their teens', Ballard pointed out that 'by their late teens and early twenties the majority of them do largely conform to Asian behavioural norms within the sphere of family and community life'. There are a number of reasons for such conformity, of which two in particular stand out: the process of socialisation in the home and the experience of racial discrimination outside. Growing up in an Asian family encourages individuals to feel loyalty to their community and being rejected by British society helps to reinforce this feeling.

To acknowledge the deep loyalty of young Asians to their community does not mean that they completely adhere to their parents' values. They 'are not faced with an either/or situation', whereby they have to choose between two completely distinct cultures but instead 'work towards their own synthesis of Asian and British values' (Ballard C., 1979). In the light of this, it is noteworthy that young Asians do tend to be more individualistic and militant than their parents (Brah, 1978). While a growing individualism indicates some acceptance of British values, an emerging militancy points to a fierce rejection of these values and vehement pride in their separate cultural identity.

If there is some evidence that young Asians are adopting a more militant response to racism that their parents, there are also indications that young West Indians are exhibiting a greater willingness to reject their stigmatised position in society than their parents. Indeed, according to many commentators, what distinguishes the responses of young West Indians to their disadvantaged position is their resistance to white society or, as one writer puts it, their 'rebellion' (Brake, 1980). Three accounts in particular come to this judgement: those by Pryce, Hall et al. and Cashmore and Troyna.

On the basis of fieldwork conducted between 1969 and 1974 in Bristol, Pryce discovered a variety of 'life styles' within the West Indian community. Although he acknowledged that the majority of West Indians were 'ordinary, steady . . . law abiding' people, he paid particular attention to those who rejected 'slave labour' and 'shit work' – the 'hustlers', the 'first generation refusers' and the 'teenyboppers', the 'second generation refusers'. While both the hustlers and the teenyboppers had chosen 'the criminal path of survival as an expression of their contempt for the system that "puts them down"', the latter had in addition developed a consciousness of themselves as black. In view of the attractions of a life style which positively values black people to those subject to 'endless pressure', Pryce anticipated that West Indian youth would increasingly adopt a teenybopper life style and reject white society (Pryce, 1979).

This expectation is echoed by Hall and his colleagues. In their view, the rejection which the first generation of West Indians met ruled out for most of them the possibility of assimilation into British society. They therefore turned to each other and created a space for themselves in particular areas where they could feel at home. In other words, they created a 'colony' within white society. The birth of this colony not only made possible 'an alternative black social life' but also enabled 'a new range of survivial strategies' to emerge. While 'the majority survived by going out from the colony every day to work, . . . others survived by taking up permanent residence inside the ghetto' and in some cases taking up 'that range of informal dealing, semi-legal practices, rackets and small-time crime known . . . as hustling'. Brought up in this colony 'the second generation simply *is* a black generation, knows it is black and is not going to be anything else but black'. Aware of the racism of British society, it is less willing than the first generation to put up with a stigmatised position. This 'refusal' sometimes gives rise to conflict between the generations with the result that the youth leave home, take to the streets and drift into petty crime (Hall et al., 1978).

A similar emphasis on the centrality of blackness for West Indian youth can be found in the account provided by Cashmore and Troyna. According to these writers, young West Indians 'perceive clearly that blackness is a potential obstacle to advancement in society and . . . have now resigned themselves to this perception' (Cashmore and Troyna, 1982a). Despite the fact that they do not 'adopt one cultural life style, but mix many', there is nonetheless a recognition among them that 'they are black and share the experiences of all other blacks in some way'. This realisation emerges during the later stages of their secondary school education and the encounter with the wider society reinforces its salience. Aware that British society is racist and yet believing 'they cannot change things', such youngsters are inclined to give vent to their frustrations through violence. Sometimes this takes a collective form and communities are disrupted for short periods of time. These occasions reveal in an extreme form the 'antagonistic values, and frequently oppositional attitudes' of many young West Indians (Cashmore and Troyna, 1982b).

For all three accounts of West Indian youth, which we have been examining, the major source of the purportedly growing black consciousness and resistance to British society lies in Rastafarianism, a movement which emerged during the 1930s among the black poor in Jamaica. 'The inspirational springboard for Rastafarianism' was provided by Marcus Garvey who, in addition to his advocacy of repatriation to Africa, was credited with having made the following prophecy: 'Look to Africa when a black King shall be crowned for the day of deliverance is near' (Troyna, 1978b). When Ras Tafari was subsequently crowned Emperor of Ethiopia and assumed the title of Haile Selassie 1, many of Garvey's supporters believed the day of deliverance had arrived. A Black Messiah had emerged to lead his people from Babylon to the promised land of Africa. At last the social order, which had resulted from white imperialism and had belittled black people for so long, was to be toppled and replaced by a new one.

The Rastafarian movement has survived in Jamaica but more importantly, for our purposes, began to take root during the 1970s among West Indian youth in Britain. Its adherents are clearly visible – they wear their hair in locks, put on woolly hats decorated in Ethiopian colours and adopt a distinctive style of speech which expresses the sense of unity ('I and I') felt by brothers and sisters who have been touched by God. The distinctive appearance of Rastafarians symbolises their disengagement from Babylon, a society which devalues black people. While most West Indian youngsters are not Rastafarians, the latter are seen as having had a pervasive influence through the medium of Reggae music on the consciousness of West Indian youth (Hebdidge, 1979). In particular they have encouraged West Indians to recognise blackness as a central aspect of their identity, take pride in their colour and feel opposition towards a society which they recognise can meaningfully be described as Babylon.

What are we to make then of the picture of West Indian youth depicted in the three accounts above? There is clearly some truth in it. The Rastafarian movement has gained more support over time and has helped to generate among West Indian youth a positive attitude towards blackness and a critical attitude towards a society which disparages black people. Nevertheless, we must be extremely careful not to assume that what is true of the most visible West Indians is generally true of young West Indians. In focusing on Rastafarianism and in highlighting the likelihood of West Indian youngsters becoming 'teenyboppers' or turning to street crime/violence, these accounts have concentrated on the 'exotic' and 'deviant' and have ignored the activities of the less newsworthy but more numerous ordinary West Indians (Allen, 1982b). In the process they may well have exaggerated the extent of 'alienation' felt by most young West Indians and have unintentionally given the impression that the majority of young West Indians are not law abiding. Such an impression is totally unwarranted (Gaskell and Smith, 1981).

Although the responses of young West Indians and Asians to their situation have generally been as unnewsworthy as those of their parents, there have been occasions when their actions have taken a more dramatic form and have brought them to public attention. The most notable occasion was in 1981, when their involvement in the riots which disturbed a number of British cities was frequently commented upon.

The 1981 riots were not unprecedented in British history. People who have felt that they couldn't gain redress for their grievances from the authorities have often got together in crowds, employed violence and created temporary disruption. Nor were the 1981 riots particularly severe by comparison with others. There was only one death, for example, which resulted from the troubles and that an innocent bystander struck by a police van. Nonetheless, the sight of nightly confrontations during April and July between youth and the police, accompanied by extensive property destruction and some looting, was rare in post war Britain and was generally recognised to be serious.

Although the 1981 riots took most people by surprise, a forerunner of what was to come took place in Bristol in 1980. Here, following a raid on a cafe suspected of selling illegal drugs, clashes took place between the mainly West Indian youngsters who tended to use the cafe as a major meeting place and the police. Others, including some white youngsters joined in and before the police were able to restore control, significant property destruction and looting had taken place. While these events inevitably provoked a great deal of comment, they did not have the impact of the 1981 riots, which began in an area more closely associated in people's minds with West Indians and continued later in cities throughout Britain.

The 1981 riots did not of course take the same form. While the April confrontations between youth and the police involved mainly West Indians, the disturbances in Southall and in Toxteth, which initiated the wave of rioting in July, involved in the one case mainly Asians and in the other case whites as well as blacks. Despite these differences, the major disturbances did tend to share certain common features. They took place in deprived multiracial areas in which unemployment was high and police/community relations were poor. Matters were often sparked off by an apparent instance of 'police injustice' and, with the exception of the incidents at Southall, West Indian youngsters were usually at the fore-front (Kettle and Hodges, 1982).

There are many explanations of the riots on offer, with each one tending to pick out different features to focus on (Taylor S., 1981). Thus some emphasise the youth of the participants, others their disadvantage and yet others their race. Although we clearly do not have time to look at each one, reference does need to be made to the explanation offered by the 'official' report on the Brixton disorders (Scarman, 1981).

For Scarman, the riots 'cannot be fully understood' unless attention is paid to the situation confronting young West Indians. The latter are extremely vulnerable to disadvantage, mainly because they live in declining inner city areas but also partly because of racial discrimination. As a result, they 'feel neither socially nor economically secure'. Such a sense of insecurity is compounded by the fact that they are not well represented in the political system and because organisations hostile to them are free to demonstrate against them. Feeling politically as well as socially and economically insecure, they 'protest on the streets' where some of them 'live off street crime'. This brings them into regular contact with the police, whom they distrust, so that the possibilities of a serious clash are heightened. Such an eventuality is not inevitable, however. What precipitated it, in the case of the Brixton disorders, was the police decision to persist with a stop and search operation, known as 'Operation Swamp', whereby the area was saturated with officers in plain clothes looking out for street criminals. Although there had been previous operations of this kind – which had left behind an increasing distrust of the police and had only reduced the level of street crime temporarily – this time the tension was so high that an apparent instance of police harassment was able to spark off serious disorders. As Scarman puts it, 'the violence erupted from the spontaneous reaction of the crowds to what they believed to be police harassment'. While the publicity given to the disorder on the Friday meant that whites did participate in the rioting on the Saturday and Sunday, 'the riots were essentially an outburst of anger and resentment by young black people against the police'.

The Scarman report was generally well received by people of different political persuasions, with most accepting Scarman's contention that poor police/community relations underpinned the riots. What this apparent unanimity masked, however, were disagreements over the question of who was primarily responsible for the breakdown of police/community relations.

For some commentators, major responsibility lay with the police, whose 'policies' and 'attitudes' exhibited 'racism' (Scraton, 1982). Although systematic evidence is hard to come by in this area, examples of police practices, which have had a racially discriminatory impact, are now well documented. A useful summary of the kinds of practices which have had this impact is provided by Kettle and Hodges. They point to instances where racial attacks have not been given systematic police attention and yet the rights of racist organisations, like the National Front, to march through multiracial areas under police protection have been rigorously upheld. They delineate occasions when black community events, such as the Notting Hill Carnival, have been subject to a particularly massive and visible police presence; when black meeting places, such as the Mangrove Restaurant, have been subject to reported police raids which have failed to result in convictions; and when black people have been subject to identity checks and 'passport raids' because of their colour. Above all else, however, they list examples of where 'the everyday use of police powers of stop, search, arrest and questioning on the street and in the police station' has led to discriminatory treatment. In this context, it is interesting to note that a Home Office study found that in the Metropolitan police district, 'blacks were . . . most heavily arrested in offences where there was particular scope for suspicion to be aroused from preconceived views'. One of these offences was that of being a suspected person. Under the provision of the Vagrancy Act of 1824, police were entitled to arrest someone 'on suspicion of loitering with intent to commit an arrestable offence'. Since blacks were over ten times more likely to be arrested in the Metropolian police district for 'sus', it is not surprising that the issue became 'a symbolic precis' of the criticisms levelled 'against the police by the black community' (Roberts, 1982). Although 'sus' was abolished in 1981, the police have stop and search powers which have had 'effects similar to the use of "sus"' (Harman, 1982). This has been especially true when the police have attempted to combat street crime by saturating an area like Brixton with extra police, such as the Special Patrol Group. On these occasions, Kettle and Hodges point out it is black people who have been most likely to be stopped (Kettle and Hodges, 1982).

While this catalogue of examples of police practices which have had a racially discriminatory impact has convinced some commentators that it is the police who were overwhelmingly responsible for the breakdown in police/community relations, other commentators have been less impressed by the evidence. They admit that there are instances of police injustice but claim that these are rare and that generally blacks and whites are treated equally. The fact that blacks have been more likely to receive police surveillance and to be stopped and arrested for certain offences stems from the fact that they are more likely to be involved in street crime. According to this view, it is not then the police but the black community which was mainly responsible for the breakdown of police/community relations in the main riot areas.

The defenders of the police have a case. While the evidence indicates that examples of discriminatory treatment are far from rare, it is true that no systematic study has been done to gauge just how common police discrimination is. What is more, there are grounds for believing that young West Indians are disproportionately involved in street crime. Thus the Home Office study in the Metropolitan police district, which we mentioned earlier, came to the conclusion that 'victims' reports and arrest rates point to . . . blacks [being] excessively involved in recorded street crime'

(Stevens and Willis quoted in Roberts, 1982). While such figures need to be interpreted with care since they may reflect a racial bias on the part of the police, it seems unlikely that the overrepresentation of young West Indians in this kind of crime can be accounted for wholly in this way (Smith, 1982). As Lea and Young argue, 'it would be implausible to believe that a high recorded rate of street crime for black youths is *merely* a function of police prejudice, although the latter undoubtedly results in an exaggeration of the contribution of black persons to the actual crime rate' (Lea and Young, 1982).

To recognize the limited nature of our evidence on police discrimination and to accept that young West Indians are overrepresented in one kind of crime does not of course mean that we are bound to agree that it is the black community which was mainly responsible for the breakdown of police/community relations. Far from it. The police are in a much more powerful position than the minorities and therefore must take primary responsibility for the breakdown in relations.

While the police must be held primarily responsible for 'the catastrophically bad relationship between the police and young black people' (Kettle and Hodges, 1982), we must remember that the police do operate under certain constraints and in particular have to cope with the problem of an increasing crime rate in the inner city consequent upon the rise in unemployment. The latter sets 'the scene', as Lea and Young point out, 'for the development of a vicious circle whereby relations between police and community deteriorate in such a way that each step in deterioration creates pressure for further deterioration'.

For there to be 'consensus policing', a community must act as a source of information to the police so that the latter can 'catch and/or deter individual law-breakers'. As unemployment generates more crime, however, the police begin to adopt a more aggressive policing policy and turn to operations which involve the 'random stopping of "suspicious" youth'. This inevitably results in large numbers of innocent people being stopped and searched. Once this happens, the community 'begins to become alienated from the police'. It 'comes to see any attempt at an arrest by officers as a symbolic attack on the community' and ceases to provide the police with any information which can help them identify individual offenders. Faced with this situation, the police adopt an even more aggressive policing policy and so the vicious circle continues. In this context, 'whatever racist sentiments exist within the police force are reinforced'. If the drift towards 'military' policing is to be counteracted, the authors argue that the conditions which generate crime need to be attacked and that the police need to be made more accountable to the community (Lea and Young, 1982). As yet neither of these policies has been seriously pursued.

Summary

In the course of this chapter, we have examined the responses of the government, the mass media and the minorities, themselves, to a race relations situation. What has been emphasised throughout is that the responses did not have to take the form they did. The same point applies to the future. Whether race relations in Britain improve or deteriorate will depend on what actions people take and in particular what the dominant institutions in our society choose to do.

Guide to reading

A brief account of both British responses to black immigration and the responses of the racial minorities to their experiences in Britain can be found in a unit written for the Open University by B. Parekh, *Ethnic Minorities and Community Relations*, E354, Unit 10. On British political responses, there are two useful readers: C. Husband (ed), *'Race' in Britain* Part 2 and R. Miles and A. Phizacklea (eds), *Racism and Political Action in Britain*. The first includes an overview of the politics of race and focuses on the government while the latter is rather more wideranging. On the news media, there is an excellent reader by S. Cohen and J. Young (eds), *The Manufacture of News*, which includes articles by P. Hartmann and C. Husband and by S. Hall et al. For a more detailed exploration of the media and race, the best book is still that by P. Hartmann and C. Husband, *Racism and the Mass Media*. As far as the responses of the minorities themselves are concerned, J. Watson (ed) *Between Two Cultures*, chapters 1–5 provides a useful starting point while M. Brake, *The Sociology of Youth Cultures and Youth Subcultures*, chapter 4 examines the responses of the second generation. An extremely readable discussion of the 1981 riots, which includes a discussion of policing and community relations, is M. Kettle and L. Hodges, *Uprising*. To keep up to date on this and other issues The Runneymede Trust Bulletin, *Race and Immigration*, and the journal of the Commission for Racial Equality, *New Community* are extremely useful.

Discussion points

1. How coherent do you consider government policy on race and immigration has been? Why has it taken the form it has? How

desirable has the policy been? What changes in your view are needed? How likely is it that these will come about?

2. Does your reading of the news media suggest that black people are presented in a negative light? What differences are there between what is depicted in one part of the medium and another (e.g. news and current affairs, news reports and editorials, etc.)? Compare the coverage of a particular issue by different newspapers and news media. Are there any significant changes over time? How different is race news from other news? What changes, if any, are needed in race reporting? How possible is it that these will come about? Do the entertainment media in your experience tend to depict black people in a limited range of roles? How significant do you consider the mass media's portrayal of race related matters to be overall?

3. How possible is it to generalise about the responses of racial minorities to their situation? How significant are the differences between different minority groups? And different generations? What kinds of response do you consider are most likely in the future?

4. How significant do you consider police/community relations to be for the future of race relations in Britain? Why have they deteriorated? Compare and contrast different explanations of riots? What changes are needed if such disorders are not to re-occur? How likely is it that these changes will come about?

5. Critically examine any one sociological study discussed in this chapter.

6. Which, if any, of the sociological perspectives, distinguished earlier, have you found most helpful in making sense of the evidence examined in this chapter?

Bibliography

Adorno, T., Frenkel-Brunswick, E., Levinson, D. and Sanford, R. *The Authoritarian Personality* (Harper & Row, 1950)

Ahmed, S. *Is Racial Matching Sufficient?* in Cheetham, James, Loney, Mayor & Prescott, 1981

Allen, S. and Smith, C. 'Race and Ethnicity in Class Formation: a Comparison of Asian and West Indian Workers' in *The Social Analysis of Class Structure* edited by F. Parkin (Tavistock, 1974)

Allen, S. and Smith, C. 'Minority Group Experience of the Transition from Education to Work' in *Entering the World of Work* edited by P. Brannen (HMSO, 1975)

Allen, S., Bentley, S. & Burnat, J. *Work, Race and Immigration* (University of Bradford, 1977)

Allen, S. *Perhaps a Seventh Person?* in Husband, 1982a

Allen, S. *Confusing Categories and Neglecting Contradictions* in Cashmore and Troyna, 1982b

Althusser, L. *Lenin and Philosophy and Other Essays* (New Left Books, 1971)

Amos, V., Gilroy, P. & Lawrence, E. 'White Society, Black Struggle' in *Rethinking Social Inequality* edited by D. Robbins (Gower, 1982)

Association of Directors of Social Services and CRE *Multiracial Britain: The Social Services Response* in Cheetham, James, Loney, Mayor & Prescott, 1981

Avineri, S. (ed) *Karl Marx on Colonialism and Modernisation* (Anchor Books, 1969)

Bagley, C. *Social Structure and Prejudice in 5 English Boroughs* (Institute of Race Relations, 1970)

Bagley, C. & Coard, B. *Cultural Knowledge and Rejection of Ethnic Identity in West Indian Children in London* in Verma and Bagley, 1975

Bagley, C. *The Background of Deviance in Black Children in London* in Verma and Bagley, 1975

Bibliography

Bagley, C. & Verma, G. *Racial Prejudice, the Individual and Society* (Saxon House, 1979)

Bagley, C., Bart, M. & Wong, J. *Antecedents of Scholastic success in West Indian Ten Year Olds in London* in Verma and Bagley, 1979

Bagley, C., Mallick, B. & Verma, G. *Pupil Self Esteem: a Study of Black and White Teenagers in British Schools* in Verma and Bagley, 1979

Bagley, C. & Young, L. *Policy Dilemmas and the Adoption of Black Children* in Cheetham, 1982

Ballard, C. *Conflict, Continuity and Change* in Saifullah Khan, 1979

Ballard, R. & Ballard, C. *The Sikhs: the Development of South Asian Settlements in Britain* in Watson, 1977

Ballard, R. *Ethnic Minorities and the Social Services* in Saifullah Khan, 1979

Ballard, R. & Holden, B. *The Employment of Coloured Graduates in Britain* in Braham, Rhodes & Pearn, 1981

Ballard, R. 'Race and the Census: What an "Ethnic Question" Would Show' *New Society*, 12 May 1983

Banton, M. *Race Relations* (Tavistock Publications Ltd. 1967)

Banton, M. *Racial Minorities* (Fontana, 1972)

Banton, M. *The Idea of Race and Concept of Race* in Verma and Bagley, 1979

Baratz, S. & Baratz, J. 'Early Childhood Intervention: the Social Science Base of Institutional Racism' in *Language in Education* edited by Language and Learning Course Team at the Open University (Routledge & Kegan Paul, 1972)

Barber, A. 'Ethnic Origin and the Labour Force' *Department of Employment Gazette*, August 1980

Barker, D. & Allen, S. (eds) *Dependence and Exploitation in Work and Marriage* (Longman, 1976)

Barratt Brown, M. *After Imperialism* (Heinemann, 1970)

Barron, R. & Norris, G. *Sexual Divisions and the Dual Labour Market* in Barker & Allen, 1976

Bendix, R. *Max Weber* (Methuen, 1966)

Bendix, R. & Lipset, S. (eds) *Class, Status and Power* (Routledge & Kegan Paul, 1967)

Bentley, S. *Industrial Conflict, Strikes and Black Workers: Problems of Research Methodology* in Braham, Rhodes & Pearn, 1981

Ben-Tovim, G. & Gabriel, J. *The Politics of Race in Britain, 1962–79: a Review of the Major Trends and of Recent Debates* in Husband, 1982

Berger, J. & Mohr, J. *A Seventh Man* (Penguin, 1975)

Bernbaum, G. *Knowledge and Ideology in the Sociology of Education* (MacMillan, 1977)

Berry, D. *Central Ideas in Sociology* (Constable, 1974)

Billig, M. *Fascists: A Social Psychological View of the National Front* (Harcourt Brace Jovanovich, 1978)

Bilton, T., Bonnett, K., Jones, P., Stanworth, M., Sheard, K. & Webster, A. *Introductory Sociology* (MacMillan, 1981)

Bindman, G. *Positive Action* in Braham, Rhodes & Pearn, 1981

Blackburn, R. & Mann, M. *The Working Class in the Labour Market* (MacMillan, 1979)

Blalock, H. *Race and Ethnic Relations* (Prentice Hall, 1982)

Blauner, R. 'Colonised and Immigrant Minorities' in *Classes, Power and Conflict* edited by A. Giddens and D. Held (MacMillan, 1982)

Blumer, H. *Industrialisation and Race Relations* in Stone, 1977

Bodmer, W. 'Genetics and Intelligence: The Race Argument' in *Heredity and Environment* edited by A. Halsey (Methuen, 1977)

Bohning, W. *The Self Feeding Process of Economic Migration from Low Wage to Post-Industrial Countries with a Liberal Capitalist Structure* in Braham, Rhodes & Pearn, 1981

Bonner, D. 'Out of the Labyrinth – a Clear and Enduring Scheme of Citizenship?' *Journal of Social Welfare Law*, 1983

Bottomore, T. & Rubel, M. *Karl Marx: Selected Writings* (Penguin, 1961)

Bowker, G. & Carrier, J. (eds) *Race and Ethnic Relations* (Hutchinson, 1976)

Bowles, S. & Gintis, H. *Schooling in Capitalist America* (Routledge & Kegan Paul, 1976)

Brah, A. 'South Asian Teenagers in Southall: Their Perceptions of Marriage, Family and Ethnic Identity' *New Community* Vol VI No 3, Summer 1978

Braham, P. 'Immigrant Labour in Europe' in *People and Work* edited by G. Esland, G. Salaman & M. Speakman (Holmes McDougall, 1975)

Braham, P., Rhodes, E. & Pearn, M. (eds) *Discrimination and Disadvantage in Employment* (Harper & Row, 1981)

Braham, P. 'How the Media Report Race' in *Culture, Society and the Media* edited by M. Gurevitch, T. Bennett, J. Curran & J. Woollacott (Methuen, 1982)

Brake, M. *The Sociology of Youth Culture and Youth Subcultures* (Routledge & Kegan Paul, 1980)

Bibliography

Brent Community Health Council *Black People and the Health Service* (Russell Press, 1981)

Brittan, E. 'Multiracial Education 2 – Teacher Opinion on Aspects of School Life: Pupils and Teachers' *Educational Research* Vol 18 No 3, 1976

Brown, J. *Freud and the Post-Freudians* (Penguin, 1964)

Brown, C. *Understanding Society* (John Murray, 1979)

Bullock Report *A Language for Life* (HMSO, 1975)

Bulmer, M. 'On the Feasibility of Identifying 'Race' and 'Ethnicity' in Censuses and Surveys' *New Community* Vol VIII Nos 1 & 2, 1980

Carby, H. *Schooling in Babylon* in Centre for Contemporary Cultural Studies, 1982

Cashmore, E. *Rastaman* (Allen & Unwin, 1979)

Cashmore, E. & Troyna, B. (eds) *Black Youth in Crisis* (Allen & Unwin, 1982a)

Cashmore, E. & Troyna, B. *Black Youth in Crisis* in Cashmore & Troyna, 1982b

Castells, M. *The Urban Question* (Edward Arnold, 1977)

Castles, S. & Kosack, G. *Immigrant Workers and Class Structure in Western Europe* (Oxford University Press, 1973)

Castles, S. & Kosack, G. *The Function of Labour Immigration in Western European Capitalism* in Braham, Rhodes & Pearn, 1981

Centre for Contemporary Cultural Studies *The Empire Strikes Back* (Hutchinson, 1982)

Cheetham, J., James, W., Loney, M., Mayor, B. & Prescott, W. (eds) *Social and Community Work in a Multi-racial Society* (Harper & Row, 1981)

Cheetham, J. (ed) *Social Work and Ethnicity* (Allen & Unwin, 1982)

Coard, B. *How the West Indian Child Is Made Educationally Subnormal in the British School System* (New Beacon Books Ltd, 1971)

Cohen, P. *Race Relations as a Sociological Issue* in Bowker & Carrier, 1976

Cohen, S. & Young, J. *The Manufacture of News. Deviance, Social Problems and the Mass Media* (Constable, 1981)

Coulson, M. & Riddell, C. *Approaching Sociology* (Routledge & Kegan Paul, 1980)

Cowell, D., Jones, T. & Young, J. (eds) *Policing the Riots* (Junction Books, 1982)

Cox, O. *Caste, Class and Race* (Doubleday, 1948)

Critcher, C., Parker, M. & Sondhi, R. 'Race in the Provincial Press: a Case Study of Five West Midlands Newspapers' in *Ethnicity and the Media* (UNESCO, 1977)

Critcher, C. 'Black and White Rag' *The Social Science Teacher* Vol 8 No 4, April 1979

Crossman, R. *The Diaries of a Cabinet Minister* Vol 1 (Hamish Hamilton & Jonathan Cape, 1975)

Dahya, B. 'The Nature of Pakistani Ethnicity in Industrial Cities in Britain' in *Urban Ethnicity* edited by A. Cohen (Tavistock, 1974)

Daniel, W. *Racial Discrimination in England* (Penguin, 1968)

Davey, A. & Norburn, M. 'Ethnic Awareness and Ethnic Differentiation Amongst Primary School Children' *New Community* Vol VIII Nos 1 & 2, Spring-Summer 1980

Davis, S. & Aslam, M. *Eastern Treatment for Eastern Health?* in Cheetham, James, Loney, Mayor & Prescott, 1981
Deakin, N. *Colour Citizenship and British Society* (Panther, 1970)

Dixon, B. *Catching Them Young: Sex, Race and Class in Children's Literature* (Pluto Press, 1977)

Dollard, J. *Caste and Class in a Southern Town* (Doubleday, 1957)

Downing, J. 'The (Balanced) White View' in *White Media and Black Britain* edited by C. Husband (Arrow, 1975)

Downing, J. *The Media Machine* (Pluto Press, 1980)

Driver, G. 'Cultural Competence, Social Power and School Achievement: West Indian Pupils in the West Midlands' *New Community* Vol V No 4, Spring-Summer 1977

Driver, G. 'How West Indians do Better at School (Especially the Girls)' *New Society*, January 17 1980

Driver, G. *Classroom Stress and School Achievement: West Indian Adolescents and Their Teachers* in James & Jeffcoate, 1981

Dummett, M. & Dummett, A. *The Role of Government in Britain's Racial Crisis* in Husband, 1982

Dumont, L. *Caste, Racism and 'Stratification' Reflections of a Social Anthropologist* in Stone, 1977

Edmonds, J. 'Disadvantage in the Labour Market' *Poverty* No 51, April 1982

Edwards, V. *West Indian Language: Attitudes and the School* (National Association for Multiracial Education, 1976a)

Edwards, V. 'Effects of Dialect on the Comprehension of West Indian Children' *Educational Research* Vol 18 No 2, 1976b

Bibliography

Edwards, V. 'Language Attitudes and Underperformance in West Indian Children' *Educational Review* Vol 30 No 1, 1978

Edwards, V. *The West Indian Language Issue in British Schools* (Routledge & Kegan Paul, 1979)

Eisenstadt, S. *The Absorption of Immigrants* in Bowker & Carrier, 1976

Eldridge, J. *Recent British Sociology* (MacMillan, 1980)

Elliott, B. & McCrone, D. *The City* (MacMillan, 1982)

Elliott, P. *The Making of a Television Series* (Constable, 1972)

Essen, J. & Ghodsian, M. 'The Children of Immigrants: School Performance' *New Community* Vol VII No 3, Winter 1979

Evans, P. *Publish and Be Damned* (Runnymede Trust, 1976)

Eysenck, H. J. *Race, Intelligence and Education* (Temple-Smith, 1971)

Fanon, F. *Black Skin, White Masks* (Penguin, 1967)

Farley, J. *Majority-Minority Relations* (Prentice Hall, 1982)

Field, S., Mair, G., Rees, T. & Stevens, P. *Ethnic Minorities in Britain: a Study of Trends in Their Position Since 1961* Home Office Research Study No 68 (HMSO, 1981)

Flett, H. 'Dimensions of Inequality: Birmingham Council Housing Allocations' *New Community* Vol X No 1, Summer 1982

Foner, N. *The Jamaicans: Cultural and Social Change Among Migrants in Britain* in Watson, 1977

Foner, N. *Jamaica Farewell* (Routledge & Kegan Paul, 1979)

Foot, P. *The Rise of Enoch Powell* (Penguin, 1969)

Fuller, M. *Black Girls in a London Comprehensive* in James and Jeffcoate, 1981

Gaskell, G. & Smith, P. 'Are Young Blacks Really Alienated?' *New Society*, 14 May 1981

Genovese, E. *Materialism and Idealism in the History of Negro Slavery in the Americas* in Bowker & Carrier, 1976

Ghodsian, M. & Essen, J. 'The Children of Immigrants: Social and Home Circumstances' *New Community* Vol VIII No 3, Winter 1980

Giddens, A. *Capitalism and Modern Social Theory* (Cambridge University Press, 1971)

Giddens, A. *The Class Structure of the Advanced Societies* (Hutchinson, 1973)

Giddens, A. *Studies in Social and Political Theory* (Hutchinson, 1979)

Giddens, A. *Sociology: A Short Introduction* (MacMillan, 1982)

Giles, R. *The West Indian Experience in British Schools* (Heinemann, 1977)

Giner, S. & Salcedo, J. 'Migrant Workers in European Social Structures' in *Contemporary Europe* edited by S. Giner & M. Scotford Archer (Routledge & Kegan Paul, 1978)

Glazer, N. & Moynihan, D. *Beyond the Melting Pot* (MIT Press, 1970)

Goldthorpe, J. & Hope, K. 'Occupational Grading and Occupational Prestige' in *The Analysis of Social Mobility* edited by K. Hope (Oxford University Press, 1972)

Goldthorpe, J. & Bevan, P. 'The Study of Social Stratification in Great Britain: 1946–1976' *Social Science Information* 16, 1977

Green, P. *The Pursuit of Inequality* (Martin Robertson, 1981)

Griffin, J. *Black Like Me* (Panther, 1964)

Griffith, J. *The Politics of the Judiciary* (Fontana, 1977)

Hall, S., Critcher, C., Jefferson, T., Clarke, J. & Roberts, B. *Policing the Crisis* (MacMillan, 1978)

Halsey, A. *Change in British Society* (Oxford University Press, 1978)

Haralambos, M. *Sociology, Themes and Perspectives* (University Tutorial Press, 1980)

Harman, H. *Civil Liberties and Civil Disorder* In Cowell, Jones & Young, 1982

Hartmann, P. & Husband, C. 'The Mass Media and Racial Conflict' *Race* Vol XII, January 1971

Hartmann, P., Husband, C. & Clark, J. 'Race as News: a Study in the Handling of Race in the British National Press from 1963 to 1970' in *Race as News* (UNESCO, 1974)

Hartmann, P. & Husband, C. *Racism and the Mass Media* (Davis Poynter, 1974)

Hebdidge, D. *Subculture: The Meaning of Style* (Methuen, 1979)

Henley, A. *Asians in Britain, Introduction* (National Extension College, 1981)

Hiro, D. *Black British, White British* (Pelican, 1973)

Hobsbawn, E. *Industry and Empire* (Pelican, 1969)

Home Affairs Committee *Racial Disadvantage 1980–1981* (HMSO, 1980)

Home Affairs Committee *Commission for Racial Equality 1981–1982* (HMSO, 1981)

Bibliography

Horn, E. *A Survey of Referrals from Asian Families in Four Social Services Area Offices in Bradford* in Cheetham, 1982

Hubbuck, J. & Carter, S. *Half a Chance* (CRE, 1980)

Hurd, G. *Human Society* (Routledge & Kegan Paul, 1973)

Husband, C. 'Education, Race and Society' in *Education or Domination* edited by D. Holly (Arrow, 1974)

Husband, C. 'Culture, Context and Practise: Racism in Social Work' in *Radical Social Work and Practise* edited by M. Brake & R. Bailey (Edward Arnold, 1980)

Husband, C. (ed) *'Race' in Britain: Continuity & Change* (Hutchinson, 1982)

James, A. & Jeffcoate, R. (eds) *The School in the Multicultural Society* (Harper & Row, 1981)

Jeffcoate, R. *Positive Image* (Chameleon Books, 1979)

Jeffcoate, R. *The 'Multicultural' Curriculum* in James & Jeffcoate, 1981

Jencks, C. et al. *Inequality: a Reassessment of the Effect of Family and Schooling in America* (Basic Books, 1972)

Jensen, A. 'How Much Can We Boost IQ and Scholastic Achievement?' *Harvard Education Review* Vol 39 No 1, 1969

Jones, T. & McEvoy, D. 'Race and Space in Cloud-Cuckoo Land' *Area* 10 3, 1978

Jordan, W. *First Impressions: Initial English Confrontations with Africans* in Husband, 1982

Jowell, R. & Prescott-Clarke, P. 'Racial Discrimination and White Collar Workers in Britain' *Race* Vol XI, April 1970

Karabel, J. & Halsey, A. 'Educational Research: a Review and an Interpretation' in *Power and Ideology in Education* edited by J. Karabel & A. Halsey (Oxford University Press, 1977)

Karn, V. 'A Note on Race, Community and Conflict. A Study of Sparkbrook' *Race* Vol 9 No 1, July 1967

Karn, V. 'The Financing of Owneroccupation and its Impact on Ethnic Minorities' *New Community* Vol VI Nos 1 & 2, Winter 1977/78

Keddie, N. (ed) *Tinker, Tailor . . . The Myth of Cultural Deprivation* (Penguin, 1973)

Kettle, M. & Hodges, L. *Uprising! The Police, the People and the Riots in Britain's Cities* (Pan Books, 1982)

Kumar, K. *Prophecy and Progress* (Penguin, 1978)

Labov, W. 'The Logic of Nonstandard English' in Keddie, 1973

Laishley, J. 'The Images of Blacks and Whites in the Children's Media' in *White Media and Black Britain* edited by C. Husband (Arrow, 1975)

Lane, A. (ed) *The Debate Over Slavery* (University of Illinois Press, 1975)

Lawrence, D. *Black Migrants: White Natives: a Study of Race Relations in Nottingham* (Cambridge University Press, 1973)

Lawrence, D. 'Prejudice, Politics and Race' *New Community* Vol VII No 1, Winter 1978/79

Lawrence, E. *In the Abundance of Water the Fool is Thirsty: Sociology and Black 'Pathology'* in Centre for Contemporary Cultural Studies, 1982

Lea, J. & Young, J. *The Riots in Britain 1981: Urban Violence and Political Marginalisation* in Cowell, Jones & Young, 1982

Leach, E. *What Should We Mean by Caste?* in Bowker & Carrier, 1976

Lewis, O. *La Vida* (Random House, 1966)

Liebow, E. *Tally's Corner* in Bowker & Carrier, 1976

Little, A. 'Performance of Children from Ethnic Minority Backgrounds in Primary Schools' *Oxford Review of Education* Vol No 2, 1975

Little, A., Mabey, C. & Whitaker, G. *The Education of Immigrant Pupils in London Primary Schools* in Bowker & Carrier, 1976

Little, A. & Kohler, D. 'Do We hate Blacks?' *New Society*, 27 January 1977

Little, A. *Educational Policies for Multiracial Areas* (Goldsmiths College University of London, 1978)

Lockwood, D. *Race, Conflict and Plural Society* in Zubaida, 1970

Lomas, G. & Monck, E. *The Coloured Population of Great Britain* (Runnymede Trust, 1977)

Louden, D. 'Self-Esteem and Locus of Control in Minority Group Adolescents' *Ethnic and Racial Studies* Vol 1 No 2, April 1978

Mabey, C. 'Black British Literacy: a Study of Reading Attainment of London Black Children From 8 to 15 Years' *Educational Research* 23 2, 1981

Marsh, A. 'Who Hates the Blacks?' *New Society*, 23 September 1976

Merton, R. *Discrimination and the American Creed* in Stone, 1977

Michaelson, M. 'The Relevance of Caste among East African-Asians' *New Community* Vol VII No 3, Winter, 1979

Miles, R. & Phizacklea, A (eds) *Racism and Political Action in Britain* (Routledge & Kegan Paul, 1979)

Miles, R. & Phizacklea, A. *The TUC and Black Workers, 1974–76* in Braham, Rhodes & Pearn, 1981

Bibliography

Miles, R. *Racism and Nationalism in Britain* in Husband, 1982a

Miles, R. *Racism and Migrant Labour* (Routledge & Kegan Paul, 1982b)

Milgram, S. *Obedience to Authority* (Tavistock, 1974)

Milner, D. *Children and Race* (Penguin, 1975)

Milner, D. 'The Education of the Black Child in Britain: a Review and a Response' *New Community* Vol IX No 2, Autumn 1981

Moore, R. 'Migrants and the Class Structure of Western Europe' in *Industrial Society: Class, Cleavage and Control* edited by R. Scase (Allen & Unwin, 1977)

Moore, R. 'Immigration and Racism' in *Exploring Society* edited by R. Burgess (British Sociological Association, 1982)

Morgan, G. & Hooper, D. 'Labour in the Woollen and Worsted Industry: a Critical Analysis of Dual Labour Market Theory' in *Diversity and Decomposition in the Labour Market* edited by G. Day (Gower, 1982)

Nugent, N. & King, R. *Ethnic Minorities and the Extreme Right* in Miles & Phizacklea, 1979

Oakley, A. *Sex, Gender and Society* (Temple Smith, 1972)

O'Callaghan, M. .'Introductory Notes' in *Sociological Theories: Race and Colonialism* (UNESCO, 1980)

O'Donnell, M. *A New Introduction to Sociology* (Harrap, 1981)

O'Muircheartaigh, C. & Rees, T. 'Migrant/Immigrant Labour in Great Britain, France and Germany – 2' *New Community* Vol V No 3, Autumn 1976

Open University *Making Sense of Society* D102 Units 21 & 22 (Open University, 1975)

Open University *Social Work, Community Work and Society* DE 206 Unit 5 (Open University, 1978)

Open University *An Introduction to Sociology* D207 Unit 14 (Open University, 1980)

Open University, *Social Science: a Foundation Course* D102 Unit 28 (Open University, 1982a)

Open University *Ethnic Minorities and Community Relations* E354 (Open University, 1982b)

Pahl, R. *Whose City?* (Penguin, 1975)

Parekh, B. 'Asians in Britain: Problem or Opportunity' in *Five Views of Multiracial Britain* (CRE, 1978)

Park, R., Burgess, E. & Mackenzie, R. *The City* (University of Chicago Press, 1925)

Park, R. *Race & Culture* in Bowker & Carrier, 1976

Parkin, F. *Marxism and Class Theory* (Tavistock, 1979)

Parsons, T. 'The School Class as a Social System' in *Education, Economy and Society* edited by A. Halsey, J. Floud and C. Anderson (Free Press, 1961)

Parsons, T. *Politics and Social Structure* (Free Press, 1969)

Patterson, S. *Dark Strangers* (Penguin, 1965)

Peach, C. *West Indian Migration to Britain: a Social Geography* (Oxford University Press, 1968)

Peach, C. 'British Unemployment Cycles and West Indian Immigrants – 1955–1974' *New Community* Vol VII No 1, Winter 1978/9

Peach, C., Robinson, V. & Smith, S. (eds) *Ethnic Segregation in Cities* (Croom Helm, 1981)

Pearson, D. *Race, Class and Political Activism* (Gower, 1981)

Pierce, G. 'Unleashing an Uncritical Press' *The Guardian*, 15 March 1982

Phizacklea, A. & Miles, R. *Labour & Racism* (Routledge & Kegan Paul, 1980)

Phizacklea, A. & Miles, R. *The Strike at Grunwick* in Braham, Rhodes & Pearn, 1981

Phizacklea, A. 'Migrant Women and Wage Labour: the Case of West Indian Women in Britain' in *Work, Women and the Labour Market* edited by J. West (Routledge & Kegan Paul, 1982)

Pilkington, A. *What is Sociology?* (Thornhill Press, 1976a)

Pilkington, A. *Summer School 1976: a Report* (Northampton Community Relations Council, 1976b)

Pilkington, A. *CHCS: Problems and Possibilities* (Northampton & District Community Health Council, 1980)

Pryce, K. *Endless Pressure* (Penguin, 1979)

Rack, P. *Asians and the Psychiatric Service* in Cheetham, James, Loney, Mayor & Prescott, 1981

Rampton Report *West Indian Children in our Schools, Interim Report of Inquiry into the Education of Children from Ethnic Minority Groups* (HMSO, 1981)

Ratcliffe, P. *Racism and Reaction* (Routledge & Kegan Paul, 1981)

Rees, T. *Immigration Policies in the United Kingdom* in Husband, 1982

Reeves, F. & Chevannes, M. 'The Underachievement of Rampton' *Multi-racial Education* 10 1, 1981

Bibliography

Reid, I. *Social Class Differences in Britain* (Great McIntyre, 1981)

Rex, J. & Moore, R. *Race, Community and Conflict* (Oxford University Press, 1967)

Rex, J. 'The Sociology ofd a Zone of Transition' in *Readings in Urban Sociology* edited by R. Pahl (Pergamon, 1968)

Rex, J. 'The Concept of Race in Sociological Theory' in Zubaida, 1970a

Rex, J. *Race Relations in Sociological Theory* (Weidenfeld & Nicholson, 1970b)

Rex, J. *Race, Colonialism and the City* (Routledge & Kegan Paul, 1973)

Rex, J. 'Race in the Inner City' in *Five Views of Multiracial Britain* (CRE, 1978)

Rex, J. & Tomlinson, S. *Colonial Immigrants in a British City* (Routledge & Kegan Paul, 1979)

Rex, J. *Social Conflict* (Longman, 1981a)

Rex, J. *Urban Segregation and Inner City Policy in Great Britain* in Peach, Robinson & Smith, 1981b

Rex, J. *West Indian and Asian Youth* in Cashmore & Troyna, 1982

Rhodes, E. & Braham, P. *The Implications of Unemployment* in Braham, Rhodes & Pearn, 1981

Richardson, K. & Spears, D. (eds) *Race, Culture and Intelligence* (Penguin, 1973)

Roberts, B. *The Debate on 'Sus'* in Cashmore & Troyna, 1982

Robertson, R. 'Towards the Identification of the Major Axes of Sociological Analysis' in *Approaches to Sociology* edited by J. Rex (Routledge & Kegan Paul, 1974)

Robinson, V. 'Correlates of Asian Immigration: 1959–1974' *New Community* Vol VIII Nos 1 & 2, Spring-Summer 1980

Robinson, V. *The Development of South Asian Settlement in Britain and the Myth of Return* in Peach, Robinson & Smith, 1981

Rose, E. et al. *Colour and Citizenship: a Report on British Race Relations* (Oxford University Press, 1969)

Runcimann, W. (ed) *Weber, Selections in Translation* (Cambridge University Press, 1978)

Runnymede Trust & Radical Statistics Group *Britain's Black Population* (Heinemann, 1980)

Rutter, M., Yule, B., Berger, M., Yule, N., Morton, J. & Bagley, C. 'Children of West Indian Immigrants. Rates of Behavioural Deviance and of Psychiatric Disorder' *Journal of Child Psychology and Psychiatry* Vol 15 No 4, 1974

Rutter, M. & Madge, N. *Cycles of Disadvantage* (Heinmann, 1976)

Saifullah-Khan, V. *Purdah in the British Situation* in Barker & Allen, 1976

Saifullah-Khan, V. *The Pakistanis: Mirpuri Villagers at Home and in Bradford* in Watson, 1977

Saifullah-Khan, V. (ed) *Minority Families in Britain* (MacMillan, 1979)

Saunders, P. *Urban Politics: A Sociological Interpretation* (Hutchinson, 1979)

Saunders, P. *Social Theory and the Urban Question* (Hutchinson, 1981)

Scarman Report *The Brixton Disorders 10–12 April 1981* (HMSO, 1981)

Scraton, P. *Policing and Institutionalised Racism on Merseyside* in Cowell, Jones & Young, 1982

Scrivens, E. & Hillier, S. 'Ethnicity, Health and Health Care' in *Sociology as Applied to Medicine* edited by D. Patrick & G. Scambler (Balliere Tindall, 1982)

Selwyn, T. 'Caste and Class' in *Media Booklet: An Introduction to Sociology* D207 (Open University, 1980)

Seymour-Ure, C. *The Political Impact of Mass Media* (Constable, 1974)

Sherman, H. & Wood, J. *Sociology: Traditional & Radical Perspectives* (Harper & Row, 1982)

Sivanandan, A. *A Different Hunger* (Pluto Press, 1982)

Slack, P. *Some Aspects of Health Service Planning for Children of Cultural Minorities* in Cheetham, James, Loney, Mayor & Prescott, 1981

Smith, D. *The Facts of Racial Disadvantage: a National Survey* (PEP No 560, 1976)

Smith, D. *Racial Disadvantage in Britain* (Penguin, 1977)

Smith, D. *Unemployment and Racial Minorities* (Policy Studies Institute, 1981)

Smith, S. 'Race and Crime Statistics' *Race Relations Fieldwork* Background Paper No 4, August 1982

Speakman, M. 'Occupational Choice and Placement' in *The Politics of Work and Occupations* edited by G. Esland and G. Salaman (Open University Press, 1980)

Stenhouse, L. 'Problems and Effects of Teaching About Race Relations: the Contribution of the SSRC/Gulbenkian Research Project' *The Social Science Teacher* Vol 8 No 4, April 1979

Bibliography

Stone, J. (ed) *Race, Ethnicity and Social Change* (Duxbury Press, 1977)

Stone, J. *Race Relations and the Sociological Tradition* in Stone, 1977

Stone, M. *The Education of the Black Child in Britain* (Fontana, 1981)

Stubbs, M. *Language, Schools and Classrooms* (Methuen, 1976)

Sutcliffe, D. *British Black English* (Blackwell, 1982)

Taylor, M. *Caught Between* (N.F.E.R. Nelson, 1981)

Taylor, S. 'Race, Extremism and Violence in Contemporary British Politics' *New Community* Vol VII No 1, Winter 1978

Taylor, S. *The National Front* in Miles & Phizacklea, 1979

Taylor, S. 'Riots: Some Explanations' *New Community* Vol IX No 2, Autumn 1981

Thompson, E. *The Poverty of Theory and Other Essays* (Merlin Press, 1978)

Tomlinson, S. *The Educational Performance of Ethnic Minority Children* in James & Jeffcoate, 1981a

Tomlinson, S. *Educational Subnormality* (Routledge & Kegan Paul, 1981b)

Townsend, H. *Immigrant Pupils in England: the LEA Response* (N.F.E.R., 1971)

Townsend, H. & Brittan, E. *Organisation in Multiracial Schools* (N.F.E.R., 1972)

Townsend, P. *Poverty in the United Kingdom* (Penguin, 1979)

Troyna, B. 'Race and Streaming: a Case Study' *Educational Review* Vol 30 No 1, 1978a

Troyna, B. *Rastafarianism, Reggae and Racism* (National Association for Multiracial Education, 1978b)

Troyna, B. 'Differential Commitment to Ethnic Identity by Black Youths in Britain' *New Community* Vol VII No 3, Winter 1979

Troyna, B. *Reporting the National Front: British Values Observed* in Husband, 1982

Tyler, W. *The Sociology of Educational Inequality* (Methuen, 1977)

Valentine, C. *Culture and Poverty* (University of Chicago Press, 1968)

Verma, G. & Bagley, C. (eds) *Race and Education Across Cultures* (Heinemann, 1975)

Verma, G. & Bagley, C. *Race, Education and Identity* (MacMillan, 1979)

Walvin, J. *Black Caricature: the Roots of Racialism* in Husband, 1982

Ward, R. 'Race Relations in Britain' *British Journal of Sociology* Vol XXIX No 4, December 1978

Ward, R. *Where Race Didn't Divide: Some Reflections on Slum Clearance in Moss Side* in Miles & Phizacklea, 1979

Ward, R. & Sims, R. *Social Status, The Market and Ethnic Segregation* in Peach, Robinson & Smith, 1981

Ward, R. 'Race, Housing and Wealth' *New Community* Vol X No 1, Summer 1982

Warner, L. *American Caste and Class* in Bowker & Carrier, 1976

Watson, J. (ed) *Between Two Cultures* (Blackwell, 1977)

Webb, M. 'The Labour Market' in *Sex Differences in Britain* edited by I. Reid & E. Wormald (Grant McIntyre, 1982)

Westergaard, J. & Resler, H. *Class in a Capitalist Society* (Heinemann, 1975)

Wight, J. & Norris, R. *Teaching English to West Indian Children* Schools Council Working Paper 29 (Methuen, 1970)

Wight, J. 'Dialect in School' *Educational Review* Vol 24 No 1, 1971

Worsley, P. (ed) *Problems of Modern Society* (Penguin, 1972)

Young, H. 'The Treatment of Race in the British Press' in *Race and the Press* (Runnymede Trust, 1971)

Zubaida, S. (ed) *Race and Racialism* (Tavistock, 1970)

Author index

Abrams, M., 32–33, 35–36, 40–42

Adorno, T., 34–35

Ahmed, S., 62

Allen, J., 74

Allen, S., 90–92, 96–97, 166

Althusser, L., 70

Amos, V., 15

Association of Directors of Social Services and CRE, 66

Avineri, S., 55

Bagley, C., 36, 41–42, 66, 130–131, 133, 140

Ballard, R. or C., 14, 16, 26, 66, 100–101, 109, 162–164

Banton, M., 3, 7, 17, 19, 43, 100

Baratz, S., 134

Barber, A., 94

Barratt Brown, M., 13

Barron, R., 80

Bendix, R., 51, 69

Bentley, S., 161

Ben-Tovim, G., 71, 152

Berger, J., 80

Bernbaum, G., 128

Berry, D., 65–66

Billig, M., 148

Bilton, T., 68, 119, 143

Bindman, G., 151

Blackburn, R., 80, 89–90

Blalock, H., 41

Blauner, R., 22–23, 60

Blumer, H., 55

Bodmer, W., 127–128

Bohning, W., 95, 98

Bonner, D., 149

Bottomore, T., 44–46

Bowker, G., 58, 74

Author index

Bowles, S., 119–120

Brah, A., 163–164

Braham, P., 95, 97–99, 151, 158

Brake, M., 163–164, 171

Brent Community Health Council, 63

Brittan, E., 139

Brown, J., 34

Brown, C., 68, 73

Bullock Report, 138

Bulmer, M., 86

Burgess, E., 102, 104

Carby, H., 135

Cashmore, E., 164–165

Castells, M., 102–103

Castles, S., 81–83, 95–96, 99

Cheetham, J., 62, 66, 74

Coard, B., 121

Cohen, P., 11

Cohen, S., 158, 171

Coleman, J., 134

Coulson, M., 1, 19

Cox, O., 60, 71

Critcher, C., 155, 160

Crossman, R., 150

Dahya, B., 109

Daniel, W., 22–23, 29, 32

Davey, A., 132–133

Davis, S., 62–63

Deakin, N., 15, 19, 42

Dixon, B., 154

Dollard, J., 34–35

Downing, J., 155

Driver, G., 125–126, 140–141

Dummett, M., 153

Dumont, L., 60

Dunning, E., 5, 19

Durkheim, E., 43–44, 47–49, 54–57, 64–65, 67–68, 74

Edmonds, J., 94

Edwards, V., 135–139

Eisenstadt, S., 58

Eldridge, J., 101

Elliott, B., 103

Elliott, P., 159

Essen, J., 123–125

Evans, P., 156

Eysenck, H., 126

Fanon, F., 129

Farley, J., 6, 19, 33, 116

Field, S., 86–88, 94, 99, 115–117

Flett, H., 112

Foner, N., 13, 130

Foot, P., 147

Freud, S., 34–35

Fuller, M., 141

Gaskell, G., 166

Genovese, E., 7

Ghodsian, M., 130

Giddens, A., 50, 53, 55, 78

Giles, R., 139

Giner, S., 96–97

Glazer, N., 22

Goldthorpe, J., 52

Green, P., 127

Griffin, J., 4

Griffith, J., 151

Hall, S., 125, 135, 155, 157–158, 164–165

Halsey, A., 76–77, 125

Haralambos, M., 68, 73

Harman, H., 168

Hartmann, P., 36, 41, 154, 157, 159–160, 171

Hebdidge, D., 166

Henley, A., 16

Hiro, D., 17, 19

Hobsbawn, E., 13

Home Affairs Committee 1980, 76

Home Affairs Committee 1981, 136, 152

Horn, E., 67

Hubbuck, J., 78

Hurd, G., 5, 19

Husband, C., 66, 153, 171

James, A., 144

Jeffcoate, R., 136, 142, 144

Jencks, C., 127

Author index

Jensen, A., 126–128

Jones, T., 116

Jordan, W., 6

Jowell, R., 24–26, 29

Karabel, J., 118

Karn, V., 109, 112

Keddie, N., 144

Kettle, M., 167–171

Kumar, K., 56

Labov, W., 134

Laishley, 154

Lane, A., 10

Lawrence, D., 36, 40–42, 110, 117

Lawrence, E., 135

Lea, J., 170–171

Leach, E., 60

Lewis, O., 61

Liebow, E., 62–63

Little, A., 122–123, 128, 138, 152, 160

Lockwood, D., 43, 55

Lomas, G., 88

Louden, D., 132–133

Mabey, C., 123, 125

Marsh, A., 38

Marx, K., 43–57, 64, 74, 77

Merton, R., 31–32

Michaelson, M., 16

Miles, R., 71–72, 74, 77, 83, 99, 163, 171

Milgram, S., 31

Milner, D., 36–37, 42, 131–132, 140, 144

Moore, R., 83, 161–162

Morgan, G., 79

Moyniham, D., 60–61

Nugent, N., 148

Oakley, A., 3

O'Callaghan, M., 43

O'Donnell, M., 68

O'Muircheartaigh, C., 96–97

Pahl, R., 103

Parekh, B., 153, 171

Park, R., 58, 101–102

Parkin, F., 55, 72, 74

Parsons, T., 68–70, 118

Patterson, S., 21, 29

Peach, C., 18

Pearson, D., 129

Pierce, G., 156

Phizacklea, A., 38, 71, 83, 91, 93, 160–161

Pilkington, A., 19, 29, 41, 57–58, 138

Plowden Report, 134

Pryce, K., 13, 129, 164

Rack, P., 62

Rampton Report, 124–125, 138–139, 141–142, 144

Ratcliffe, P., 106–109, 111, 117

Rees, T., 14

Reeves, F., 124

Reid, I., 76

Rex, J., 8, 11, 12, 19, 22, 29, 59, 80–81, 99, 101, 103–111, 115, 117–118, 125, 129, 146, 152

Richardson, K., 10

Rhodes, E., 93–94, 97

Roberts, B., 169–170

Robertson, R., 67–68

Robinson, V., 18, 109–110

Rose, E., 32–33, 42

Runcimann, W., 51

Runnymede Trust & Radical Statistics Group, 14–15, 76, 100, 116, 152

Rutter, M., 121, 140

Saifullah-Khan, V., 17, 91

Saunders, P., 102–103, 110–111

Scarman Report, 167–168

Scraton, P., 168

Scrivens, E., 63

Selwyn, T., 15

Seymour-Ure, C., 157

Sherman, H., 72

Sivanandan, A., 70, 78, 150

Slack, P., 64

Smith, D., 22–25, 27–29, 38, 84–85, 89, 91–94, 99–100, 112–117, 150

Smith, S., 155, 170

Speakman, M., 4

Stenhouse, L., 143

Author index

Stone, J., 43, 74

Stone, M., 142

Street Porter, R., 144

Stubbs, M., 138

Sutcliffe, D., 136

Taylor, M., 121–122, 125–126, 130–131, 144

Taylor, S., 148, 167

Thompson, E., 70

Tomlinson, S., 121–122

Townsend, H., 121

Townsend, P., 94

Troyna, B., 141, 158, 165

Tyler, W., 128

Valentine, C., 60

Walvin, J., 6

Ward, R., 111–112, 161–162

Warner, L., 59–60

Watson, J., 17, 19, 171

Webb, M., 93

Weber, M., 43–44, 47, 49–56, 64–65, 67, 74, 76, 78, 104, 110

Westergaard, J., 77, 85

Wight, J., 135–137

Worsley, P., 19

Young, H., 156

Subject index

action approach (see systems and
  action approaches)
alienation   44–45
anomie   48–49
antisemitism   4, 12, 34–35
apartheid   8
authoritarian personality   34–35
authority   50–51

Bangladesh   14
biological perspective,   1–4
  on race   40, 55
bureaucracy   51, 53–56

Campaign against Racial   152
  Discrimination
capitalism   44–47, 49–51, 53–56, 70–
       73, 81–83, 102–103,
       119–120, 145
caste   15–16, 52, 59–60
chain migration   100–101
class,   44–49, 51–56, 70, 72–73,
       76–77
    and race in the UK   70–73, 77–98, 161–162
    and race in the USA   59–60
Commission for Racial Equality   150–152
Community Relations Commission   37, 150
competition for scarce resources   6–7, 38, 72–73, 110
conflict and consensus approaches,   56–57, 64
  defined
    to black poverty in the USA   60–62
    to immigrants in the UK   58–59
    to medicine   57–58, 62–64
    to stratification in the USA   59–60

Subject index

conflict theory, defined,   68, 72, 74
    applied to employment   78–81
    applied to race   72–74, 77–81
    applied to the state   145
    applied to the urban social   103–112
      structure
consensus approach (see conflict and
  consensus approaches)
cultural deprivation   134–136
cultural explanation,   7, 47–56, 64
    and black poverty in the USA   60–61
    and medicine in the UK   62–63
    and race and education   128–139
    and race and employment   91
    and race and housing   109–110
culture and racial minorities   15–18, 21, 129, 132, 135,
      162–166

Creole   136–139
crime and racial minorities,   164–171
    and media coverage   155–156, 158–159

deviance and racial minorities (see
  crime and racial minorities)
dialect interference   136–139
dual labour market, defined   78–79
    and race   79–81, 88

East Africa   14, 16
economic explanation,   7, 44–47, 54, 56, 64
    and black poverty in the USA   61–62
    and race and education   135
    and race and employment   78–83
    and race and housing   103–105
education and racial minorities   120–142
employment and racial minorities   77–98
Ethnic group, definition of   11, 53
    and earnings   89–90, 92
    and educational performance   120–126
    and housing position   104–116
    and job level   84–88, 92
ethnicity,   55, 58, 162
    and organization   162–166
    and settlement preferences   109–110
ethnocentrism   139

family and racial minorities   17, 60–62, 129–131
fascism   148–149
frustration-aggression theory   34–35
functionalism, defined   68–69, 74
    applied to education   118–119, 125
    applied to race   69–70, 74
    applied to the urban social   101–102
        structure

government (see the state)

host-immigrant framework   21–22, 58–59, 69
housing and racial minorities   100–101, 104–116
housing class   104–111

ideology,   46, 70
    and race   6–11, 22, 36–37, 70–71,
                                         153–160
immigrants and assimilation   21–22, 58–59, 165
immigration,
    causes of   17–18, 71
    legislation   14–15, 38, 97, 146–150
    to Britain   12–18, 58–59, 100–101
    to Europe   80–81, 95, 97–98
imperialism   5–8, 12–14, 22, 45, 55, 70–
                                         71, 81–83, 129

indentured labour   13
India   13, 15, 60
industrial society   55
integration   59
intelligence and race   10, 126–128

language and race   134, 136–139

marriage and racial minorities   17, 60–62, 129–131, 163–
                                         164
mass media and race   153–160
Marxism defined,   68, 70, 74
    applied to education   119–120, 125
    applied to employment   76, 78, 81–83
    applied to race   70–72, 74, 77–78
    applied to the state   145
    applied to the urban social   102–103
        structure

medicine, different approaches,   57–58
    and race   62–64
middle class (see class)
migrant labour   71, 80–83, 95–98
mugging   155–156, 158–160
multicultural education   136, 142–143

National Front   148–149, 155–156, 168

organization, by class   161–162
    by colour   161
    by ethnicity   162–163

Pakistan   14, 16
patrials   148–149
perspectives in sociology (see conflict
    theory, functionalism, Marxism)
police and racial minorities   155–156, 166–171
politics and race   46–47, 50–52, 70–73, 95,
    97–98, 102–103, 145–
    153

poverty, and race in the UK   94
    and race in the USA   60–62, 64
psychological perspective,   4–5
    on racial prejudice   34–35
purdah   17, 91

race,
    and classical sociology   43, 56
    definition of   3–4, 11
Race Relations Board   26–27, 150
race relations situation, definition of   11–12, 145
race relations legislation   24, 26–27, 33, 38, 150–152
racial disadvantage in education   120–142
    in employment   83–94
    in housing   104–116
racial discrimination, nature of   22–24, 30, 53
    in Britain   23–28, 78, 84, 92–93, 105,
    107, 110, 114–115, 147–
    150, 153, 168–169

racial inequality, in Brazil   7
    in Nazi Germany   4, 31, 35
    in South Africa   8, 27, 31
    in the USA   5–7, 22–23, 33–35, 58–62,
    79, 116, 126, 157

racial minorities, as proportion of population — 14

racial prejudice, nature of — 24, 30, 34–41, 71
   in Britain — 32–41

racialism, definition of — 11–12, 145
   in Britain — 70–71, 147–150

racism, definition of — 12, 145
   in Britain — 38, 40, 59, 70–71, 78, 108, 139, 146–150, 152–155, 165–170

Rastafarianism — 165–166

reggae — 141, 166

religion and racial minorities — 15–16, 165–166

reserve army of labour — 46, 81

residential concentration and racial minorities — 100–101, 115–116

riots — 146, 166–171

scapegoat — 35

schools (see teachers and race)

self esteem and race — 9–10, 15, 129, 131–136, 166

slavery — 5–7, 9–10, 13, 15, 22, 129, 135–136

social services, — 65–66
   and race — 66–67

socialisation and racial attitudes (see ideology)

sociology and values — 8–10
   as science — 28–29, 39–41
   definition of — 1
   different conceptions of human beings — 64–67
   different conceptions of society — 56–64
   distinct perspectives — 68–73
   founding fathers — 43–56

solidarity — 47–49, 54, 56

state, — 46–47, 50–52, 70–73, 95, 97–98, 102–103, 145–153
   policy in the USA — 134, 151

status, social — 51–55, 73, 78

stereotype — 6–7, 11, 37, 131–132, 138–141, 153–155

structuralism — 70, 103

Subject index

systems and action approaches, defined   64–65, 67
     to social services   65–67
     to the meaning of race   66
     within Marxism   70–71, 102–103

teachers and racial minorities   139–142

underclass   77–81, 90, 93, 98, 108, 111, 125
underdevelopment   13, 70–71, 80–81
unemployment and racial minorities   93–94

values in sociology,   8–10
     of different sociological approaches   60–62, 64

West Indies   12–13, 15, 129–131
women and racial minorities   91–93, 124, 140–141
working class, (see class)
     fraction/stratum   81–83, 90, 93–98

youth and racial minorities   163–166

zone of transition   102, 104